International Series on Computer, Entertainment and Media Technology

Series Editor
Newton Lee
Institute for Education, Research, and Scholarships
Los Angeles, CA, USA

The International Series on Computer, Entertainment and Media Technology presents forward-looking ideas, cutting-edge research, and in-depth case studies across a wide spectrum of computer, entertainment and media technology. The series covers a range of content from professional to academic. Computer Technology includes artificial intelligence, databases, computer networks, computer hardware, software engineering, cybersecurity, human computer interaction, programming languages, bioinformatics, telecommunication, mobile apps, and quality assurance. Entertainment Technology includes computer games, electronic toys, scenery fabrication, theatrical property, costume, lighting, sound, video, music, show control, animation, animatronics, interactive environments, computer simulation, visual effects, augmented reality, and virtual reality. Media Technology includes art media, print media, digital media, electronic media, big data, asset management, signal processing, data recording, data storage, data transmission, media psychology, wearable devices, robotics, and physical computing.

Wallace Wang

The Structure of Game Design

 Springer

Wallace Wang
San Diego, CA, USA

ISSN 2364-947X ISSN 2364-9488 (electronic)
International Series on Computer, Entertainment and Media Technology
ISBN 978-3-031-32201-3 ISBN 978-3-031-32202-0 (eBook)
https://doi.org/10.1007/978-3-031-32202-0

This Springer imprint is published by the registered company Springer Nature Switzerland AG
The registered company address is: Gewerbestrasse 11, 6330 Cham, Switzerland

Preface

Everyone has an idea for a game. Coming up with ideas is easy. The hard part is turning that good idea into a working game that other people can actually play.

There are a million different ways to create a game, but some paths are easier than others. Far too many people get an idea and jump right into making their game right away. While this method can work, it's more likely to lead to multiple dead ends and detours that can to frustration. The end result is often an unfinished game regardless of how good the original idea might have been.

Many people abandon their game ideas because of their lack of proper planning and structure. Making a game requires understanding what you can do, how you can do it, and what you want to accomplish. In other words, game design is both an art and a science.

By playing games, you can get an intuitive feel for what you like (and dislike) in games so you can develop your own style for designing them. By studying the components of games and how they work, you can develop the knowledge and skills needed to turn any idea into a working game.

Too many people believe they can't make a game. That's not true. Even if you only possess a fraction of the skills necessary to make a game, you always have a choice. First, you can develop the skills needed to complete your game. This may not always be easy and will likely take more time than you want, but it's always possible.

Second, you can cooperate with others who possess the necessary skills you need to complete your game. A person's technical skills are actually far less important than their ability to get along with others. A handful of less talented and skilled people working together will get farther than a dream team of highly skilled and experienced people who can't cooperate at all.

Whether you plan to develop your own game making skills, cooperate with others, or do a combination of both, you can make a game. The purpose of this book, "The Structure of Game Design," is to help both novice and experienced game designers understand the common components for creating games. By understanding the mechanics behind how games work, you can pick and choose the best options for turning your own idea into a completed game.

There is no right or wrong way to design a game as long as the end result creates a finished product. However, there are faster and slower, more frustrating ways to design a game. This book can provide guidelines to help you create games faster and more consistently by planning and designing ahead of time to maximize your chance of success.

With this book, you'll have the knowledge you need to make a game. You just need to do the hard work of applying your skills and knowledge into making your game idea into reality.

San Diego, CA, USA   Wallace Wang

Acknowledgments

This book would never have been written if it wasn't for Newton Lee at IFERS.org. Newton not only encouraged me to write this book but also proved instrumental in helping me get a book contract through Springer.

Thanks also go to Dane Henderson at www.theredination.com, who has created numerous opportunities for me in the esports and gaming world. Dane's invaluable network has put me in touch with more people than I could ever imagine.

Other people who helped me on my journey through the esports/gaming industry include six-time Grammy-winning audio engineer, James "Bonzai" Caruso; Katherine Amoukhteh; Mark Carvalho; Tellypuu "Blue" Quisquis; Chris Davis; Eboni Harvey; and Sam Diamond.

Final thanks go to my wife, Cassandra, for putting up with so many computers crammed in one room. Thanks also go to my son, Jordan, for providing me with lots of invaluable information about video games, their history, and the latest news and trends about different games and gaming studios.

Lastly, I'd like to thank my cats, Oscar and Mayer, who like walking across my keyboard and standing in front of my monitor so I can't get any work done until I feed them, pet them, or let them outside.

Contents

Part I
Design Elements of a Game

Most everyone has played a game or watched other people play a game. However, not as many people have ever thought of creating their own game. This part of the book examines common elements found in nearly all games. The better you understand what makes a game work, the easier it will be to design and make your own game.

People play games for a variety of reasons, but the essence of any game is posing a challenge to the players. That challenge can be mental (such as chess or poker), physical (such as pole vaulting or skiing), or a combination of both (such as determining how best to kick a ball closer into a goal when three attackers are rushing two defenders).

Games have goals that define the purpose of playing. Games have rules to create artificial restrictions. Games have a playing field where the game takes place, either on a board or a physical plot of land such as in football fields. Most importantly, games have players who follow the rules, on the playing field, to achieve the game's goal. Games are simply a way to compete against ourselves or against others to test our skills and strategies in a regulated environment.

Designing games is a different skill than playing games. To design a game that others will want to play, aspiring game designers must understand not only what a game is, but also the underlying elements that make a game work, and that's what this part of the book is all about.

Chapter 1
Creating a Game Idea

There's no shortage of ideas for games. The real question isn't what game do you want to make but why do you want to make a game in the first place? If you want to make a game just to make money, it's easy to take shortcuts by chasing the latest trend. Unfortunately this often creates a copycat, generic, derivative game. If that's all you want to do, then this book is not for you.

This book is for people who want to understand how games work so they can turn their ideas into an original game that captures their enthusiasm and creative vision. By understanding what game components exist and how they work, you'll have a better idea which features are best for your game idea. Ideally, a game should satisfy you, the market, and the people playing your game.

The best way a game can satisfy you, as the designer, is to complete it. Unfinished game designs help no one. Even poor game designs can teach you mistakes to avoid so you can create a better game next time. Think of every game design as a learning experience that can help you get one step closer to making the best game possible.

Chances are good that no game will be perfect, but you can learn from each one so your next game will likely be better, more ambitious, and closer to the perfection you keep aiming to reach.

Just completing a game can be a success. Learning new technology or game making techniques can be a success. Developing or enhancing your existing skill and knowledge in designing, marketing, and selling games can be a success. The enjoyment that comes from creating a game can be a success.

Making a game will always involve problems and compromises, yet overcoming these obstacles can be part of the fun of making a game. If you aren't happy making a game, why bother doing it? Given a choice between making a game that you don't care about or a game that taught you numerous lessons, challenged you to overcome problems, and made you happy regardless of its ultimate success or failure, which experience would you rather have?

© The Author(s), under exclusive license to Springer Nature
Switzerland AG 2023
W. Wang, *The Structure of Game Design*, International Series on Computer,
Entertainment and Media Technology,
https://doi.org/10.1007/978-3-031-32202-0_1

Thought Exercise

Identify what you want to get out of making a game. It might be the challenge of making your first game, it might be the chance to experiment with specific technology (such as virtual reality), or it might be filling a particular niche in the game market that's currently being overlooked or ignored. Whatever you want to get out of making a game, write it down and keep this statement where you can see it every day.

By identifying your purpose for making a game, your purpose acts as a guideline. Every day while you're working on your game, use this purpose to make sure you don't stray away from the original reason you even wanted to make that particular game.

Here's the wrong way to make your game. Start with a vague idea and rush into creating the artwork and designing the playing pieces. If you're creating a video game, add in the extra steps of putting music and sound effects into your game as well as writing code to make your game actually work.

This approach will get you started right away so you feel like you're making progress, but it too often leads to a dead end. The problem is that you can't rush into making your game before you even know what game you're putting together in the first place.

Inevitably, you'll wind up creating art you don't need or that doesn't match your game anymore or you'll write code for features that technically make your game work but fail to make your game fun and interesting. The end result is that you'll have to rethink and rewrite large portions of your game over and over again. You'll wind up with different games pieces that don't work together and you can look forward to restarting or rewriting the same items until you finally decide to abandon the whole project out of frustration.

The better way to make a game is to start with an idea and realize ideas are nothing more than empty air. The real value of any idea is how you implement it from a vague, abstract thought into a physical (or digital) working product. People don't pay for ideas. People pay for results. As long as you can turn ideas (your own or other people's) into working products, you'll always be in demand.

So the first step to game design is to imagine you've already completed your game. Now how are you going to describe it to potential publishers, studios, and players? If you can't give a clear, precise description to the question, "What is your game about," your idea is likely still in the formative stage. Now is the time to crystallize your thoughts before wasting time trying to create a game with no clear idea of what you're trying to accomplish.

The first step is to give your game a descriptive name. Game titles must do the following:

- Grab attention
- Hint at what the game's action will be
- Suggest the game tone

Even the best game will be useless if you can't get people curious about playing it. So the main purpose of a game title is to grab people's attention. Once a game title grabs someone's attention, the next step is to hint at what the player will do within the game. Finally, the game title should also describe the game world and tone.

Of course, doing all this may seem impossible, especially when you want to be descriptive without being wordy. Ignoring any artwork, the game title may be the first thing people see so if the game title doesn't sound interesting, nobody will bother to find out if your game is fun to play. Game titles give your game the only chance to make a great first impression.

The best game titles are short, descriptive, and intriguing. Study the following game titles:

- SimCity – The apparent combination of the words "Simulation" and "City" suggests a game about controlling a city.
- Assassin's Creed – The word "Assassin's" hints that the player will have to assassinate enemies.
- Grand Theft Auto – Suggests stealing and driving cars to get away.
- Candy Crush – Suggests multiple pieces of candy that fall to crush items.
- Tomb Raider – Suggests sneaking into tombs to steal valuable objects while avoiding traps and enemies.
- StarCraft – Suggests a science fiction setting involving starships.
- The Last of Us – Suggests a survival game in a bleak setting.
- War Thunder – The word "War" in the title clearly implies battles of some kind.
- Angry Birds – The odd combination between "Birds" and "Angry" suggests controlling birds to fight in a battle.

Study your favorite games and ask yourself what about their titles grabbed your attention? Notice the emotional feeling each game title evokes. "Angry Birds" and "Candy Crush" evoke far different emotions than "The Last of Us" or "Assassin's Creed." The best game titles evoke strong, distinct emotions that accurately describe what your game is about so it appeals directly to your target audience.

Choose words that convey strong emotions, visual images, or action. "Red Dead Redemption" doesn't tell you it's a Western, but each word evokes a strong feeling. "Dead" implies death and the rhyme with "Red" makes the entire phrase memorable. In addition, "Red" can also hint of blood. Finally, "Redemption" suggests a complete story arc.

On the other hand, a game title like "Kitten Rampage" suggests humor involving a kitten causing chaos. Anyone interested in "Kitten Rampage" will likely expect a humorous game involving exaggerated actions from a kitten that the player controls.

Thought Exercise

Create 5–10 titles for your game idea. As a shortcut, study existing game titles that you like and try to mimic those game titles for your own idea. Experiment with short game titles of 1–3 words. Then experiment with longer game titles of 4 or more words.

Focus on the action, emotions, or setting of your game idea. Start with clear descriptions of your game idea and then substitute words or phrases that are more suggestive and less precise. For example, a title like "Car Thief" may be descriptive, but it lacks any sense of intrigue like "Grand Theft Auto." Similarly, "Survive a Serial Killer" may accurately describe the game's action but "Dead By Daylight" sounds far more intriguing.

Compare game titles that cover the same topic but in completely different emotions. For example, "Left 4 Dead" suggests zombies in a horror, survival setting while "Plants vs. Zombies" implies a far more whimsical tone.

Coming up with the perfect game title takes time so make up as many names as possible. A good game title acts like a guideline to help you identify the gameplay and tone of your game idea for both you (and your team) and any outsiders (publishers, studios, investors, and players).

Crafting Your Game's Pitch

A great game title is the first step. The second step is to describe, in one or two sentences, what your game is about. Your game pitch expands on the game title and provides more details without giving everything away.

Imagine a major game studio asks about your game. A short, snappy game title can intrigue them. If they want to know more, they'll ask for the pitch to better understand what your game is about. This combination of a catchy game title and an intriguing description of the game action is meant to get publishers, investors, studios, and potential players to say, "Tell me more."

More importantly, a well-crafted game pitch can also guide you in creating and finishing your game idea. As you create your game, make sure it fulfills the promise of your game pitch. If not, then you either need to modify your game or your game pitch.

A game pitch must describe:

• What players do within the game
• What makes your game different

Suppose a game title suggests a game about dragons. However, you can make any type of game involving dragons. Is it a game about dragon racing like horse racing? Is it a game about controlling armies of dragons to conquer a fantasy world? Is it a game about role-playing as a dragon? Is it a game about raising dragons? The game title might describe dragons and hint at the game tone, but the game pitch must let us know exactly what players actually do.

Thought Exercise

Come up with several potential game titles and pick one. In one or two sentences, describe what players do within that game idea. For ideas of game pitches, visit the Wikipedia page of different video games that offer brief descriptions of the gameplay such as the following:

- Elden Ring is an action role-playing game played in a third-person perspective with gameplay focusing on combat and exploration.
- Call of Duty places the player in control of an infantry soldier who makes use of various authentic World War II firearms in combat.
- Portal consists of a series of puzzles that must be solved by teleporting the player's character and simple objects between two flat planes.
- Overwatch is an online team-based game designed around squad-based combat with two opposing teams of six players each.
- Minecraft players explore a blocky, procedurally generated 3D world with virtually infinite terrain to extract raw materials, craft tools and items, and build structures, earthworks and simple machines.
- 80 Days is a branching, narrative storytelling game loosely based on the Jules Verne novel, "Around the World in Eighty Days."
- Fallout: A Post Nuclear Role Playing Game is a role-playing game that takes place in a mid-22nd century post-apocalyptic and retro-futuristic world.

Notice that each of these game pitches expand on the game title. "Portal" and "Overwatch" are just one word titles that could mean anything, so the pitch further explains exactly what each game is about.

Remember, you can never please everybody. Don't create a generic, vague description of your game to appeal to as many people as possible because you'll likely appeal to nobody. Instead, target a specific audience.

For example, the title of "Call of Duty" might grab someone's attention but when they find out it's a game about controlling an individual soldier, they might be more interested in a military game where players control entire armies instead. Your game pitch is meant to both weed out people who won't be interested in your game at the same time it directly appeals to people who will be interested in your game.

If you keep your game pitch too vague to broaden its appeal, people who want one type of game will eventually find out what your game is really about and lose interest anyway. Game pitches that are too broad will risk feeling too generic and appeal to nobody. Only people interested in exactly what your game offers will ever give you money.

Besides describing your game in finer detail, a game pitch must also emphasize what's different. There are plenty of horror games, but "Dead Space" is different because it's a horror game set in a science fiction setting. "Guitar Hero" is a music game where players imitate rock stars playing a guitar. "Dance Dance Revolution" is also a music game but players must coordinate their movements in time with popular songs as they dance.

Some ways to make a game different include:

- Change the topic
- Change the tone
- Change the scale
- Combine game ideas
- Create a unique game setting/world
- Subvert expectations

Changing the topic of a game creates an entirely different challenge. Civilization is a resource management game that puts you in control of running an entire nation. Apply that same idea to another setting and you might get Roller Coaster Tycoon, where you control an amusement park. Pick a more scientific, futuristic setting and you get Planet Crafter, where you terraform a planet. Even though resource management games work alike, each unique topic creates distinctive challenges for players to overcome.

The tone of a game can be serious, terrifying, romantic, dramatic, or even humorous. Street Fighter is a fighting game that emphasizes cartoonish violence. Super Smash Brothers is also a fighting game that emphasizes cartoonish violence, but in a far more playful manner.

The scale of a game determines whether players focus on tactics or strategy. Metal Gear Solid lets players control a special forces soldier while Company of Heroes is a strategy game where players control entire military units on a battlefield.

Few games are one-dimensional. Games often combine different game elements such as Far Cry 3, which lets players choose between attacking enemies directly with rifles, grenades, and rockets, or choose a stealthier option to slip past enemies using silencers and knives. Rocket League combines elements of car racing with sports to create rocket-propelled cars trying to knock a soccer ball into a goal.

Another way to create a distinctive game is to apply a unique setting to your game world. Fallout 3 is about surviving in a post-apocalyptic world following a nuclear holocaust, but this futuristic world is stuck within a whimsical setting of 1950s style technology. This creates a completely different game from Metro 2033, which depicts bleak survival in a Moscow subway station after a nuclear war.

A final way to create a unique game is to subvert expectations. In most shooting games, the object is to hit enemy players. In Splatoon, the object is to miss enemy players and spray paint on the surrounding area.

There's no point in making a game that's an exact copy of an existing game with minor cosmetic differences. By making a unique game, you can fully express your ideas and creativity as a game designer.

Thought Exercise

Take your game idea and play with all the different ways to twist your idea. Change the scale. Change the topic. Go for the bizarre. Instead of having soldiers fighting on a battlefield, what if you had animals or even plants?

Change the setting to serious to humorous. Choose a different target audience such as only women, only people interested in fantasy, or only people who like horror. The goal is to spur your imagination in ways that you wouldn't normally think about.

Once you know your game title and a brief description of what your game is all about, the final step is to write 3-4 additional sentences that more fully conveys what players will do and experience while playing your game.

The purpose of a game description paragraph is to paint a visual picture of how players begin the game, what they'll experience, and the goal they're trying to achieve. This provides a complete picture of what the game will be. The combination of a game title, game pitch, and game description helps clarify your vision for your game idea while also making it easy for anyone to understand what your game is about. Study these examples to help create a description for your own game:

Ticket to Ride is a board game depicting a railway map of the United States and southern Canada. Players claim train routes across the map and earn points based on the length of the claimed routes, whoever completes the longest continuous railway, and whether the player can connect distant cities. The game ends when one player has only two or fewer of their colored train pieces.

Bejeweled is a video game that displays rows of colored gems (Red, Orange, Yellow, Green, Blue, Purple and White). Players attempt to swap two adjacent gems to create a line or row of 3 or more gems, which disappear once lined up. When gems are cleared from the board, gems above the game board fall downwards, potentially causing chain reactions, which award more points to the player.

Set in the fictional Kingdom of Khanduras in the mortal realm, Diablo lets players control a lone hero battling to rid the world of Diablo, the Lord of Terror. Players must journey through sixteen randomly generated dungeon levels until they finally enter Hell to fight a final battle against Diablo himself.

The combination of your game title, game pitch, and game description should excite and intrigue people so they'll want to play (and buy) your game. By first identifying what makes your idea interesting, you can focus on making your game fulfill the promise of its title, pitch, and description.

- The game title grabs attention.
- The game pitch generates interest in the game and what makes it unique.
- The game description explains what players do within the game from start to finish to stimulate the desire to get the game.

This combination of attention, interest, and desire increases the odds that your game will keep attracting new players for years to come.

Thought Exercise

Share your game title, pitch, and description with others to get their reaction. Ideally, share your title, pitch, and description with people you don't know. The more honest reactions you get from as many people as possible, the better you'll be able to sharpen your game title, pitch, and description.

When you have a great game title, pitch, and description, you'll also have a solid guidepost to follow. This can make sure your game idea doesn't stray from what others found most appealing from your game title, pitch, and description.

Summary

Game design is more than just the technical skills of creating artwork and making up rules for how to play your game. Game design starts by identifying what makes your game idea appealing. Once you know what people find appealing about your game, then you can do the technical work of actually making that game achieve your vision.

Notice that defining your game title, pitch, and description gives you an initial direction. It's entirely possible that as you design a game, you'll run across problems or discover fresh ideas that could change the way your game works. However, if you don't choose an initial direction as soon as possible, you'll risk flailing around with no direction or focus at all, which will waste time and increase frustration. Stay flexible enough to change directions at any time while still retaining the basic structure of your idea.

Further Reading

"30 Things I Hate About Your Game Pitch", GDC, https://youtu.be/4LTtr45y7P0.

Chapter 2
Defining a Game Idea

Unless you're making games as a hobby, solely for your own amusement, you'll probably want to release your game on the market. That means you need to define what success in the market means for your game.

For many games, success means making money. However the financial amount that could spell success for an indie game developer might mean disaster for a major game studio. By identifying what success means for your game, you define what you want to achieve. Every time you need to make a major decision about your game, ask yourself which choices give you the best odds for reaching your definition of success.

Of course, not everyone may want to sell a game. Social conscious games might want to raise awareness for a cause while educational games might want to improve teaching a particular skill or topic. Independent game developers might just be happy seeing other people playing their games and giving them feedback. The point is that by defining success in the market for your game, you can design your game from start to finish towards reaching that specific goal.

Thought Exercise

Imagine your game is complete and on the market. How will you measure if it's a success? If you don't know how to measure if your game is a success or not, you'll risk pursuing a vague goal in the distant future. This is often a recipe for disaster as you lose motivation and focus because you don't know what you're trying to accomplish in the end.

First, identify what people will get out of playing your game. Every game should meet a specific need. Games that fail to meet specific needs are games that likely meet no one's needs (and thus fail in the market).

© The Author(s), under exclusive license to Springer Nature
Switzerland AG 2023
W. Wang, *The Structure of Game Design*, International Series on Computer,
Entertainment and Media Technology,
https://doi.org/10.1007/978-3-031-32202-0_2

Board games typically emphasize encouraging social interaction (poker, Monopoly, Pictionary). Mobile games entertain people for short periods of time, often while they're alone. Console and major PC games often strive to immerse players in a completely different world for long periods of time.

By defining what you want players to get out of your game, you can identify the core of your game, which acts as another guidepost for creating your game.

Thought Exercise

Imagine someone sees your game for the first time. Why would they want to play it? Why would they want to play it multiple times? Why would they want to tell their friends about your game?

Every game's success rests on satisfying the game designer, the market, and the players in various degrees. If a game only satisfies the game designer, nobody else might care about it, but that can still be fine if you achieved a specific goal such as learning a certain programming language or using a graphics design program to create your own artwork.

If a game only satisfies the market, it might be a temporary success, but will likely disappear as people forget about it over time. If you're only making a game for money, fame, or market share, none of that matters if you lose your happiness and well-being in the process.

Sometimes a game may satisfy the players, but still fail in the market if it can't attract a large enough audience. Maybe you defined the target audience too narrowly, maybe you didn't promote the game correctly, or maybe outside circumstances worked against you (such as releasing a game too similar to a rival game from a larger publisher).

Every game will succeed at some level and fail on another level. Game success is a combination of planning, skill, talent, luck, and random circumstances that are completely out of your control. All you can do is strive to create the best game possible with the resources you have right now.

There is no right or wrong way to design a game, but by knowing your three goals ahead of time (designer satisfaction, market satisfaction, and player satisfaction), you can maximize your chances of creating a game that will succeed, whatever your definition of success might be.

Remember, a game can be a success even if it never makes any money and hardly anyone plays it. Making yourself happy creating a game is the first step. Making others happy while playing your game is a second, optional step. Achieving financial success is the third and last optional step.

Define what success means to you for each game you create and then aim to achieve that goal, and you'll be a success regardless of whatever else happens.

Once you know what you want to achieve with your game, start shaping the general game design. Don't get bogged down too soon on specific details, such as deciding which game engine to use or which social network to promote your game.

All that can come later. Initially, the goal at this stage is to flesh out a broad view of your game by answering these questions to sharpen your game's focus:

- What will people play?
- What will people do?
- What will people feel?
- What will people remember?
- What will the game experience mean in the end?

What Will People Play?

There is no completely original game idea because if there was, nobody would recognize it. People recognize games because they look and behave similar to other games they've played and enjoyed. People play games because they enjoy three types of challenges:

- Physical challenges
- Intellectual challenges
- Random chance challenges

Physical challenges often test a player's dexterity in how fast they can move or how well they can coordinate multiple actions simultaneously. Some games that challenge physical abilities include sports (boxing, basketball, skiing, karate, etc.) and video games (first-person shooters, vehicle simulations, 2D platformers, etc.). Even the board game tiddlywinks requires coordination as players attempt to flip discs into a pot.

Physical challenges tend to restrict the number of possible players. Sumo wrestling requires a different body size (big and bulky) than a basketball player (tall and fast). Likewise, video games that emphasize speed and dexterity reward dedicated players while frustrating novices from getting started and sticking with the game long enough to increase their own skill to compete against players who learned the game much earlier.

On the other extreme from physical challenges are intellectual challenges that force players to analyze current situations and then plan a strategy to maximize their chance for success. Popular intellectual challenge games are Go, chess, and Xiangqi (also called Chinese chess), but even a simple puzzle game like Hangman challenges players to think.

Like extreme physical challenge games, extreme intellectual challenge games restrict the number of possible players. Players of different intellectual skills might enjoy chess, but finding opponents close to your own skill level can prove difficult at times.

Random chance challenges are often used in children's games because they give everyone a chance to win regardless of their physical skill or intellectual level. Children's board games such as Candy Land or Chutes and Ladders rely completely on random chance where nobody has an advantage. Many casino games rely mostly on random chance. Slot machines give everyone an equal chance of winning (along with an equally larger chance of losing) regardless of what you know or how skilled you might be.

Most games combine physical, intellectual, and random chance challenges in varying degrees. Sports are mostly physical challenges, but include intellectual challenges in matching players up against opposing players or strategizing team actions. Sports also include an element of chance where players risk dropping or missing a ball.

Video games often combine physical challenges with intellectual challenges and random chance. A first-person shooter video game might force players to run, dodge, and shoot enemies (physical challenge) while deciphering puzzles to unlock access to other areas on a map or plan a strategy for attacking an enemy army (intellectual challenge). Like sports, video games often introduce an element of chance when moving, attacking, or defending.

Random elements in a game forces players to deal with uncertainty. Such uncertainty increases suspense in games by giving players a choice between low-risk, low reward options or high-risk, high reward options. Randomness allows lesser skilled players to defeat higher skilled players, which is nearly impossible in pure intellectual skill games like Go or chess.

All games are a combination of physical challenges, intellectual challenges, and random chance challenges. Every game relies on one type of challenge with lesser degrees of the other two types of challenges. The variation of each challenge is what creates a unique game.

Thought Exercise

Come up with an idea for a game. How would your game idea play differently if it emphasized a player's physical dexterity? How would your game play different if it emphasized intellectual knowledge? How would your game play differently if it was guided largely by random chance?

By choosing one challenge to emphasize with lesser degrees of the other two challenges, you can alter the gameplay until it provides the right balance for your game idea.

Once you have a rough idea for how you want players to experience your game (as a physical challenge, as an intellectual challenge, or a random chance challenge), you can then decide how you want to present your game. Three common types of games include:

- Board games
- Card games
- Video games

Board games rely on a single playing field that defines where all the game action occurs. The size of the board defines the boundaries where playing pieces can go and valid places to move playing pieces.

Card games rely on the interaction between different items printed on each card. This interaction, along with the different types of cards and the total number of cards defines how the game works.

One drawback with both board and card games is that they're often best when played with another person. In the absence of a human opponent, most board and card games aren't as much fun to play alone or may be impossible to play alone.

Video games allow individuals to play games alone because the computer either replaces a human opponent or makes it easy to find players all over the world so you'll always have someone to play the game with you.

Two other unique features of video games are the ability to simplify complex rules and the ability to allow real-time, simultaneous movement.

With board games, the more detailed the gameplay, the more complicated the rules. That means players have to read and understand the rules before playing, which severely limits the number of possible players willing to learn the rules ahead of time.

Video games enforce complex rules without the player needing to know them all. Instead of trying to force players to memorize a complex set of rules, video games simply offer players valid choices. Players can't violate any rules because any rule-breaking options aren't available at all.

Not only can video games enforce game rules, making it impossible for players to choose illegal actions, but video games can also allow hidden and simultaneous movement. In the game Battleship, players secretly position their playing pieces on a board and rely on trust to determine hits and misses. A video game can eliminate this need to trust your opponent and ensure that both players follow the rules.

In board games, players must move in turns. This can create an artificial and less realistic gameplay. In a video game, players can move at the same time and the computer tracks their position at every second, which creates a more realistic and dynamic game that can't be duplicated by any board game.

Finally, video games allow for physical interaction between players and the computer. Video games allow different types of input from traditional keyboard/mouse combinations to dedicated game controllers, gesture recognizers, touch screens, touch pads, and voice input. Such varied input options give video games greater versatility in player control and gameplay interaction.

Thought Exercise

Take your game idea and imagine how it would look as a board game? As a card game? As a video game?

Board games restrict gameplay in a specific area with rules for placing and moving game pieces on the board.

Card games focus on interaction between cards.

Video games can replace a human opponent, enforce complex rules, allow hidden or simultaneous movement, and offer a wide range of player control and input.

What's the best way to present your game for people to play?

What can you learn by imagining your game as a board, card, and video game?

What Will People Do?

A game's challenges (physical, intellectual, or random chance) and game type (board, card, or video) defines what game people can play. The next step is to get more detailed and define what players will do within your game. What players do most often must be fun and interesting because they'll be doing it repeatedly.

Four common gameplay actions include:

- Movement
- Combat
- Resource management
- Puzzle solving

Movement is the most common action players can do in a game whether it's physically running around a playing field, moving a game piece on a board or within a 3D imaginary world in a video game, or selecting and arranging items in a card game.

Movement involves choices. Make the wrong move and you risk losing the game. Make the right move and you increase your chances of winning even against tremendous odds. Ultimately the purpose of movement is to attack or score against opponents. Therefore movement is nothing more than a way to increase your chance of winning the game.

The second gameplay action is combat, which can either mean eliminating an enemy or scoring points. In sports, scoring points often means placing an object such as a ball into a specific goal while your opponent tries to stop you. In racing games, the object is to place yourself or the object you're controlling across the finish line before anyone else.

A third gameplay action involves strategy collecting, managing, and expending resources. In many economic simulation games, resource management defines the entire game where players control the growth and management of a city or country. In other games, resource management is just one aspect of the game, such as trading and acquiring players for a sports team or deciding which weapons, tools, and armor to carry in a role-playing game.

In a sports game, resource management can increase your chances of winning the game but isn't usually the primary purpose of the game. Likewise in role-playing games, choosing which items to carry can increase the chance of success but almost nobody will play such a game solely to manage a character's resources.

Puzzle solving can be the whole point of a game, such as escape rooms where players must find clues to figure out how to get out. In many games, puzzle solving forces players to figure out problems so they can continue the game or gain access to resources.

Ultimately, the whole point of a game is to defeat an opponent who is trying to do the same thing to you. Therefore the fun in a game arises from the physical, intellectual, and random chance challenges involving movement, resource management, combat, and puzzle solving.

Thought Exercise

Pick a game and define how players can attack or score against an opponent to achieve victory.

How does movement within the game increase the chance a player can attack and score?

How does resource management within the game increase the chance a player can attack and score?

How does puzzle solving within a game increase the chance a player can attack and score?

Repeat the above process with your own game idea.

Enhancing Challenges with Constraints and Limitations

Games are about constraints and limitations. In every game, there are a fixed set of valid moves so players must choose the best possible moves within those limited options. It's illegal for soccer players (except for the goalie) to hit a ball with their hands just as it's also illegal for soccer players to run outside of the playing field boundaries, put as many players on to the field as they wish, or use bicycles or scooters to make their players move faster.

Similarly, there are limitations on resource management. In many sports, teams have a fixed budget they can spend to acquire players, and there's a limit on the number of players on every team. In many games, similar economics constrain what players can buy since they have a limited amount of money.

Constraints and limitations are what actually defines gameplay. First, limitations challenge players to win despite any restrictions. In war simulations where players control entire countries, the challenge can be juggling factory production between civilian needs and military needs in addition to outwitting and outmaneuvering your opponents on the battlefield.

Second, limitations force players to get creative within the game rules. In basketball, you're not supposed to foul the other team's players. However when the score is close and the game is nearly over, it's common to foul the opposing team's players to keep them from scoring. The long shot hope is that they'll miss their free throws (which score 1 point each) to give the ball back to your team so you can score a basket (and earn 2 points to catch up or surpass the opponent's score).

Another common restriction involves time or quantity boundaries. Time limits force players to reach a goal by a certain time. In sports, the winner is the player or team with the highest score in the end. Having a higher score in the beginning or middle of the game doesn't matter. Time limits increase suspense because as the game nears the end, players often make last second, desperate attempts to emerge victorious.

Quantity boundaries force a game to end when something runs out such as in Monopoly when every player but one runs out of money. Game tournaments often end when one player or team is the last one who remains undefeated.

Limitations identify what you cannot do. Boundaries define how far you can go before you reach an illegal move. In chess, you must trap your opponent's king using the restrictions of both the playing field and the limitations of the way different playing pieces can move. You aren't allowed to punch your opponent in the face nor are you allowed to reach across the chessboard and knock over your opponent's pieces. Games are interesting precisely because of their boundary restrictions, movement limitations, and resource management constraints.

Look at limitations in two ways. First, limitations define what players cannot do. Second, limitations indirectly define what players can do. In soccer, players cannot touch the ball with their hands (except for the goalie). That indirectly allows players to hit the ball with any other part of their body such as their feet, head, or chest.

Defining what players can do specifically limits their choices only to those fixed list of options. Defining what players cannot do allows for more creative freedom since players can choose actions that bend the rules but don't break them. However, this openness also allows players to take advantage of rules, which can appear as cheating.

Thought Exercise

Pick a sport, board game, card game, or video game and define its boundary restrictions, movement limitations, and resource management constraints. How would the gameplay change if you modified or removed any of these restrictions?

What are the boundary restrictions of your game's playing field? What are the movement limitations of your game's players or playing pieces? What are the resource management constraints?

Summary

This chapter asks game designers to define "What will people play?" and "What will people do?" What people play defines the physical, intellectual, and random change challenges the game offers to players. What people do involves moving, attacking/scoring, and resource management along with boundary restrictions.

Defining these broad principles helps shape the overall game design without getting bogged down in specific details too soon. When you can define the challenges of your game ("What will people play?") and the options available to players ("What will players do?"), you'll have a strong foundation to define the game details that support your original idea.

Further Readings

"The Art of Game Design: A Book of Lenses", Jesse Schell, CRC Press, 2008.
"Game Design: Theory and Practice", Richard Rouse III, Jones & Bartlett Learning, 2004.
"Game Design Workshop", Tracy Fullerton, CRC Press, 2018.

Chapter 3
The Appeal of Games

The previous chapter asked you to answer the questions, "What will people play?" and "What will people do?" These questions help you define the types of challenges in your game and the actions players must take to win.

Many games just focus on this basic level of gameplay, but if you want to create a deeper, more emotional experience, you should answer the following three questions about your game idea as well:

- What will people feel?
- What will people remember?
- What will the game experience mean in the end?

What Will People Feel?

In any game, winners always experience triumph while losers experience disappointment. However, games should go beyond these primal emotions and create additional emotional experiences specific to your game regardless of whether they win or lose. The type of emotion you want players to feel defines the game genre.

Horror games convey a sense of dread and fear as a way to entertain players. Action games emphasize overcoming constant threats through fighting in different ways. Puzzle games challenge players to analyze and solve difficult problems. Humorous games often poke fun at popular game cliches such as Goat Simulator, which mocks simulation games by letting you control a goat on a farm. Games evoke strong emotions to enhance gameplay and make a game more memorable as a result.

© The Author(s), under exclusive license to Springer Nature   19
Switzerland AG 2023
W. Wang, *The Structure of Game Design*, International Series on Computer,
Entertainment and Media Technology,
https://doi.org/10.1007/978-3-031-32202-0_3

One way to evoke emotions is to combine gameplay with the setting. Consider a game where players explore different rooms in a dungeon and examine objects in a fantasy setting like Dungeons & Dragons.

However, you can change the emotions of the game by changing the setting. Instead of setting these rooms in a dungeon, change the setting to a mansion where players must search for clues about a murder. The gameplay is the same but the actions in searching a mansion means something completely different from searching a dungeon. A change in setting evokes different emotions in the player beyond the thrill of winning or the disappointment of losing.

To create emotion in any game idea, identify the core emotion you want players to experience. Once you know the core emotion you want your game to offer, use this as a filter to accept or eliminate any ideas that enhance or fail to support your game's core emotional experience.

To identify the core emotion in your game, look at popular game genres that emphasize different emotions:

- Action – Fighting, running, and other actions that require dexterity (Excitement)
- Adventure – Exploring areas without necessarily relying on dexterity (Escapism)
- Horror – Hiding, running, and escaping (Fear)
- Mystery – Solving puzzles (Psychological satisfaction)
- Comedy – Poke fun at a specific target (Laughter)
- Simulation – Control a realistic vehicle or organization (Wish fulfillment)
- Strategy – Control a large organization such as an army or a corporation (Mastery)
- Romance – Explore relationships between people (Love)
- Serious – Examine a dramatic dilemma (Grief)

Thought Exercise

Define the main emotion you want people to feel while playing your game by identifying the genre of your game. Every genre makes a promise to the player so your game must deliver on this promised emotion.

Of course games rarely embrace a single genre. Most games embrace two genres where one genre defines the main gameplay while the second genre defines the game tone. For example, World of Tanks embraces both the Simulation and Action genres. Action involves fighting in a tank while Simulation comes from choosing to fight using a variety of historical tank models from World War II.

This lets players play "What if?" by letting them compare the strengths and weaknesses of different historical tank models in simulated tank battles. The main genre is Action, since players want to shoot enemy tanks, but the tone is based on Simulation.

Switch these genres around and you can create an entirely different game. Football Manager is a video game that focuses on Simulation first where players manage a football team. Then based on their decisions, they watch their team play against other teams. Thus the main genre is Simulation where the tone is defined by the Action genre.

What is the main genre of your game idea?

What is a secondary genre that can shape the tone of the main genre?

Study games that fall under the same genres as your game idea so you can learn what they did right and what they did wrong.

What Will People Remember?

Most people have played plenty of games. The best games stick in your memory while mediocre games quickly fade from memory. Imagining your game idea as complete, what will make it memorable? What's different about your game compared to every other game already out on the market?

Whenever a popular game appears, numerous copycats appear right away. Despite superficial changes, these copycat games are almost never as popular as the original game that they copied. That's because they offer nothing different. All they can hope for is to siphon off players from the original game.

So if you want to make a game that people will remember, don't just clone an existing game (although cloning an existing game can be an excellent way to duplicate the way a game works). To make a unique and memorable game, consider these options:

- Modify existing features
- Add or subtract features
- Change the setting or tone
- Exaggerate a feature
- Combine features
- Subvert expectations

Modifying existing features simply copies a feature from one game but alters it somehow to give players a different, but similar experience. Consider two racing games: Assetto Corsa and Gran Turismo Sport. Both video games simulate racing realistic cars. However, Assetto Corsa only simulates actual race tracks from around the world while Gran Turismo Sport offers both real racetracks and fantasy race tracks that have never existed.

Adding a feature creates different gameplay while still retaining the main features that players enjoy. In Assetto Corsa, players can only rely on realistic driving methods to defeat their opponents. While Mario Kart is also a racing game, it gives players power ups and weapons to block players behind them or shoot objects at players ahead of them. Adding playful weapons creates an entirely different experience even though Mario Kart is just a racing game like Assetto Corsa.

Subtracting features can be another way to change the feel and experience of a game. Many horror games emphasize fear through realistic, colorful graphics but Limbo subtracts both color and realism to display eerie black and white, simplistic graphics that make the game look and feel unnatural. Just this simple change makes Limbo more memorable than rival horror games.

In many games pitting you against numerous enemies, you may have a chance to fight back, even if you're outgunned and outnumbered. Fighting as an underdog creates a greater challenge. However, strip away the ability to fight back and you create a greater sense of helplessness, which is perfect for horror games. Players in a horror game must find other ways to deal with enemies if you take away the option to fight.

Changing the setting or tone is another way to differentiate a game. The game Civilization lets you nurture a tribe from humble origins that gradually masters different levels of technology as they grow and expand. By substituting magic for technology, Warlock: Masters of the Arcane emulates Civilization except this simple change creates a game that appeals to an audience that enjoys fantasy.

Pokemon Go was one of the first popular augmented reality games. The basic gameplay involves roaming around trying to capture different types of Pokemon characters. However what make Pokemon Go memorable was that instead of roaming around a cartoon map, players roam around the real world in search of Pokemon characters.

While many multiplayer games let people chat and play together over the Internet, Pokemon Go let people chat and play together in real life. Thus the game added a social element where you could meet and team up with fellow players who you could see and talk to without the need for cartoon avatars. It's easy to develop friendships by chatting online, but meeting other players in person made Pokemon Go a far more socially engaging game.

Another way to change a game to make it more memorable is to exaggerate a single feature. In most first-person shooter games, players must maneuver wildly around obstacles while trying to shoot enemies charging at them. Superhot changes this dynamic by exaggerating the player's movement.

Instead of moving frantically around obstacles, Superhot lets players speed up or slow down. If the player moves fast, the enemies move just as fast. If the player slows down, the enemies also slow down. If the player stops altogether, all enemies also stop as well, which can give you a chance to analyze a situation before moving once more. This unique game mechanic turns a traditional first-person shooter game into a combination first-person shooter with a strategy game element.

Combining features can create unique experiences. Creature in the Well lets you control a sword-wielding robot knight exploring a dungeon. This might seem like a typical dungeon crawl game, but inside the dungeon are elements from pinball such as bumpers and pins. Fighting your way through dungeon obstacles based on pinball game elements is an odd combination that creates a distinct and memorable gameplay experience.

Another way to create a distinctive game is to subvert expectations. In most games, players learn the rules and once they understand the rules, the rules remain the same. In the game Move Or Die, the rules change with every level, forcing players to respond to completely different rules within a single game. Such rapid rule changes make Move Or Die similar enough to understand, but different enough from practically every other game on the market.

Players should remember your game because it surprises and delights them in an unexpected manner. Ultimately, what players can do is what they'll remember. The best way to make a game memorable is to give players an experience they can't get from another game.

Thought Exercise

Take your game idea and choose one of the following to modify your idea:

- Modify a single feature
- Add a new feature
- Subtract an existing feature
- Change the setting or tone
- Exaggerate a feature
- Combine features between two different types of games
- Subvert a common feature in games

Apply each of these changes to your original idea, one at a time, and then analyze how this would change the gameplay experience. Then revert back to your original game idea and apply another change. By applying each change one at a time, you can better identify how that change might affect your game's experience.

Remember, keep your core game idea intact. So if your core game is about racing, don't eliminate that idea. Consider also reversing expectations. For example, in most sports, the goal is to get the highest score but in golf, the goal is to get the lowest score.

If your game idea is a first-person shooter, the typical goal is to gun down as many enemies as possible, but reverse that idea and examine how your game might drastically change if players had to avoid killing as many enemies as possible? What if players had to help as many enemies as possible?

Playing around with different game features can help you discover a range of possible alternate versions of your game that could be better than your original idea, so don't be afraid to let your imagination go wild.

What Will the Game Experience Mean in the End?

Many games provide pure entertainment to players and that's perfectly fine. However, many other games provide a meaningful experience by the end. This added meaning gives the game a far greater emotional impact than just gameplay and experiences within the game alone.

If you want your game idea to create a meaningful experience for players at the end, it's far better to define this emotional experience as early as possible. That way you can structure your entire game towards supporting this final emotional experience. Trying to tack on an emotional experience in the end likely won't work.

Meaningful game experiences are essentially life lessons that you want players to learn emotionally. In "Journey," the game is about reaching a distant mountain, but that goal teaches players that the real purpose of life is to enjoy the journey and not focus on the destination. To further mimic real life, "Journey" pairs players up with strangers who must cooperate through limited communication to reach your goal. This teaches you the importance of being nice to others on your journey through life.

In most games, the enjoyment comes from the choices you make. However in games that provide meaning, you're often forced to reflect on why you choose certain actions over others and the consequences of your decisions.

While many games start with an action-oriented premise (such as rescuing a princess from a dungeon), meaningful games often start with a philosophical dilemma. In "To the Moon," players live in a future where scientists can manipulate the memories of dying people to give them one last unique experience before they pass away.

"To the Moon" puts players in the role of manipulating the memories of a dying man who wants to experience going to the moon. The game challenges players to learn why this dying man wants the experience of going to the moon and what it means to him. Deciphering this man's reasons helps you understand that life is short so you should pursue your dreams before it's too late.

Meaningful games are meant to make you feel and think. Some games might simply be enjoyable diversions, but meaningful games can be both enjoyable and emotional. By creating a game that's both fun and thoughtful, you can make your game unique and memorable in the market.

Thought Exercise

Pick a philosophical premise whether it's related to your current game idea or not. Meaningful games force players to confront hard decisions. In action-oriented games, you might have a choice between killing an enemy or sneaking past an enemy. In a meaningful game, you might have that same choice, but later the game will force you to confront the consequences of your actions.

If you kill an enemy, you might be faced with the dead enemy's widow and now fatherless child. If you sneak past an enemy, you might be faced with that enemy later killing one of your friends.

Think of a Catch-22 situation where there's no clear cut right or wrong choice and that's the type of philosophical premise that can make your game idea meaningful.

Pick a Catch-22 philosophical premise.

Define major choices in your game that force players to confront the philosophical premise. Ideally, define the gameplay so it constantly forces players to face this philosophical premise. If you want to explore whether it's right to kill or not, the gameplay could constantly force players to choose between killing enemies or letting them live. In either case, players must deal with the consequences afterwards.

Summary

Everyone plays games. However, not everyone plays the same types of games. What one person might find fun, another person might dislike completely. You can never design a game that appeals to everyone. However, by understanding what makes games appealing, you can design a game that reaches the greatest number of people possible within your specific target audience.

Some games target the mass consumer market, such as Trivial Pursuit or Monopoly. Other games target niche markets such as the children's game market (such as Candy Land or Mousetrap). The narrow the niche, the smaller the potential market but the greater the chances of meeting the needs of that particular target audience.

What makes a game appealing can be subjective, but consider the following traits found in popular games that have lasted for generations:

- Simple to learn, yet difficult to master (chess, Go, poker)
- A unique activity that creates a different and memorable experience from existing games (Scrabble, Pictionary, Twister)
- Engaging to play with others (bridge, sports, charades)

If a game is too easy to master, it gets boring. Tic-Tac-Toe is a simple game that children might enjoy but that adults do not since the game lacks challenge once you know the best moves to make. Likewise if a game can't allow people to choose different strategies for playing, it can never become popular among a broad range of potential players.

If a game is too similar to existing games, it's too easy to ignore.

If a game doesn't allow playing with others, it's potential audience will be too limited.

There will always be room for more games. The only question is what will make your game stand out from the crowd today and years into the future?

Further Readings

"Some Games Have Global Appeal on YouTube, and Some Only Regional", Alissa McAloon, https://www.gamedeveloper.com/business/some-games-have-global-appeal-on-youtube-and-some-only-regional.

"What is 'The Game Experience'?", Douglas Lynn, https://www.gamedeveloper.com/disciplines/what-is-the-game-experience-.

Chapter 4
Game Design Elements

Every game begins with a goal. This goal is the objective that players must achieve and is the whole purpose of playing the game. In many games, players (or teams of players) have identical goals. In sports, both teams are trying to throw the ball in a basket, kick it into a goal, or carry it into the opposing team's end zone.

In board games like Monopoly, players are trying to get the most money. In a game like poker, players are trying to get the highest hand and ultimately win the most money. When players strive for the same goal, the winner is the one who gets the best score. This can mean getting the most (such as the highest score in baseball), getting the least (such as the lowest score in golf), or getting to a goal first (such as in a race). Whatever the case, goals give each player a direction to focus their action.

While some games give players identical goals, other games pose different goals for each player. One player might have the goal of getting to a certain location within a specific time limit while the other player might have the goal of stopping this first player from succeeding.

When players have identical or different goals, the game is often a race for each player to achieve their particular goal first, which they can do in two ways. First, they can direct all their efforts to achieving their goal. Two, they can keep the other player from reaching their goal. Often players do both and strive to reach their goal while hindering the other player at the same time.

With some games, the goal may simply to enjoy the activity in playing the game. Many people try to solve a Rubik's cube in the shortest amount of time possible, but others might set their own goal of simply solving it eventually.

In some games, the goal is explicitly defined by the rules. In other games, players can challenge themselves with their own goals. In that way, each player can choose how they want to play that gives them the most enjoyment. Ultimately, the goal of any game is to have fun, whatever definition of fun might mean to you.

© The Author(s), under exclusive license to Springer Nature
Switzerland AG 2023
W. Wang, *The Structure of Game Design*, International Series on Computer,
Entertainment and Media Technology,
https://doi.org/10.1007/978-3-031-32202-0_4

What makes a game challenging is the difficulty in achieving a goal. The fun in games comes from overcoming limitations and restrictions, which can occur through one or more of the following:

- The playing pieces
- The boundaries of the playing field
- The rules
- The actions of others (players and non-player characters)

Game Playing Pieces

Every game manipulates playing pieces such as a ball, cards, or even themselves (or symbols of themselves). In sports, players are literally in the game. In board games, players manipulate pieces that represent themselves within the game. In video games, players manipulate digital people or objects that represent themselves within the game.

Whether they're literally playing themselves in a sport or manipulating an avatar of themselves within a board or video game, players strive to achieve a specific goal. Part of what's stopping them from achieving that goal easily is their own limitations.

In real life, players can only run, jump, throw, dodge, and kick within physical limits. Even if they're in peak health, they must still deal with fatigue over time within a game. On top of physical exertion, players must also engage in mental exertion by making split second decisions at multiple points during the game. One wrong decision and players could lose. No matter what else happens within a game, players must always overcome their own limitations to achieve their goal.

Limitations define player avatars in board and video games as well. In a board game, players cannot move their playing pieces to an advantageous spot if that's against the rules. In a video game, players must learn to control their avatars through controls such as touch gestures, keyboards, mouse, or game controller.

So part of a video game challenge involves learning what an avatar can do and part of the challenge arises from the player's own physical limitations. Players must make split second decisions and then move fast enough to press the right key or move the mouse at precisely the right moment within a video game to achieve the correct movement that will achieve their goal.

In nearly every game, except those relying on pure chance, overcoming mental and physical challenges plays a decisive role in whether players win or lose the game. The more a game forces player's to confront their physical and mental limitations, the more challenging the game. The joy of winning stems directly from the physical and mental exertion needed to achieve victory.

Thought Exercise

Identify several different types of game such as a sport, a board game, and a video game. Identify the greatest physical challenge needed to win in each game. Identify the greatest mental challenge needed to win in each game.

Imagine removing this greatest physical or mental challenge. How would this affect the gameplay?

The Playing Field Boundaries

The players or their avatars are just one factor in determining the winner or loser of any game. A second factor is the playing field itself, which confines the gameplay within a specified area. In sports, that playing field defines the boundaries where the game must be played. In a board game, the board itself is the playing field while in video games, the playing field could be as vast as a digital universe. Yet even video games contain boundaries.

Even the most expansive, open world video game simulating multiple galaxies must still define what players can and cannot do. A game's playing field always contains boundaries that shape where and how the game is played.

Change a game's playing field boundary and you change the way the game works. If basketball hoops were placed ten inches off the ground instead of ten feet, the sport would be entirely different. Lengthen a basketball court from 28.65 m to 28.65 km and you drastically alter the way people play the entire game as well.

A game's playing field defines the boundaries and playing within these boundaries defines the skills needed to excel in the game. Boundaries force players to develop specific skills and tactics for playing within a specified playing field.

A chess board with chess pieces can fit on a table, eliminating any physical exertion needed by players. On the other hand, a football field allows players to run long distances, making physical stamina and endurance a key factor in winning or losing.

Although video games largely take place in a stationary location, video games can still challenge players physically by forcing them to react and make decisions in split seconds while coordinating their actions through a keyboard, mouse, touch screen, or game controller. Even though the playing field of a video game has boundaries, they can seem so vast that they appear unlimited. Many video games can even generate new playing areas as the player explores, essentially making the playing field completely unlimited.

Thus the purpose of a playing field isn't just to define the game, but to define the physical and mental challenges the game will place on the players. By altering the playing field boundaries, designers can define whether a game requires more or less physical or mental effort.

Thought Exercise

Identify several different types of game such as a sport, a board game, and a video game. Identify the greatest physical challenge needed to win in each game. For each type of game, what change in the boundary would increase (or decrease) the physical challenge? What change in the boundary would increase (or decrease) the mental challenge?

The Game Rules

To win, a player must overcome their own physical and/or mental limitations, defined by the game's playing field's boundaries. Another factor that blocks players from achieving a goal are the game rules.

Rules explicitly define what's allowed. However, rules are based on assumptions. Originally, basketball rules did not define how long a team could hold a ball. The assumption was that players would focus on shooting. In reality, teams would score just enough points to get ahead and then spend the remainder of the game trying to keep the ball away from the other team until time ran out. This resulted in low scoring games with long periods of tedium that made for dull games.

To fix this loophole, officials introduced the 24 second rule where teams had to shoot the ball and hit the rim within 24 seconds or lose possession of the ball. This forced teams to shoot more often, resulting in higher scores and far more engaging games for both players and spectators alike.

Because rules define what's allowed, they can directly affect player decisions and actions. Until basketball introduced the 24 second rule, players had a greater incentive to hold on to the ball for as long as possible while their team was ahead. The 24 second rule forced players to change their tactics and their action.

Because rules define what's allowed, they give players two specific choices. First, players can follow the rules (and the assumptions behind the rules) to determine the best way to win. Second, players can look for loopholes in the rules and take actions not explicitly banned by the rules to gain an advantage.

For example, baseball assumes pitchers will try to get batters out by striking them out or getting them to hit a ball to a fielder who can catch the ball or throw the batter out. Thus the assumption is that pitchers will try to get a batter out.

However, a pitcher can subtly subvert the assumption of this rule by deliberately walking a batter to face a weaker batter. Intentional walks are not usually part of the game, but are allowed because the rules specifically do not ban deliberate walks.

When defining rules for a game, it's not enough to define what's allowed. It's equally crucial to understand how players might subvert any assumptions behind each rule. Otherwise players might follow the rules but exploit a loophole, which could give them an unfair advantage or create an unintentional outcome in a game, such as the case where basketball players would hold on to a ball for long periods of time after their team was ahead.

Following the rules (or exploiting loopholes within the rules) defines the actions players can take to win the game. In sports, referees or umpires enforce the rules (not always accurately) while in video games, the computer enforces the rules. Because the rules are hidden in a video game, players can often discover loopholes that they can exploit until the game developers patch the game to close this flaw.

Rules define how players can win a game by defining the difficulty levels of the actions players can take within a game. In soccer, the rules make the game more challenging by forcing players to hit the ball using any part of their body except their hands (the goalie is the exception). In chess, the rules define how each piece can move and attack, forcing players to calculate the arrangement of their pieces to attack and defend to win the game.

Because rules explicitly define what's allowed, it's crucial to look for any unintended consequences of rules that players can exploit. In ice hockey, players are allowed to stand in front of an opposing goalie to block their line of sight. However, the assumption is that players will turn their back to the opposing goalie while watching the play in front of them. One player broke this assumption and exploited this rule by standing in front of the opposing goalie and waving his arms and stick while spewing out insults. Officials had to add a new rule specifically forbidding this practice.

In some multiplayer video games, players appear at specific spawn points. Therefore enemies often look for these spawn points so they can kill new players the moment they enter or spawn into the game. Such a practice is known as "spawn camping" and can be minimized by keeping enemies a fixed distance away from spawn points (giving players time and space to react) or by making newly spawned players temporarily immune from any attacks (giving players time to stay alive). In any case, video games often must define new rules specifically to either ban or minimize the effect of unwanted behavior such as spawn camping.

The key to writing rules is to make them as short as possible and as complete as possible. The fewer rules, the easier the game will be to learn, but the more likely players will find a way to exploit the rules. The more rules, the harder the game will be to learn, but the less likely players can find a way to exploit the rules.

Every rule contains an assumption about how it affects the game so identify this assumption and imagine that the assumption is completely wrong. Now does the rule still affect the game the same way? By examining the assumption behind every rule, designers can minimize the risk that players can exploit a rule and negatively affect the way the game works.

Thought Exercise

Examine the rules in several different types of game such as a sport, a board game, and a video game. Pick one rule to eliminate and identify how that would change the physical or mental difficulty level. Pick one rule to modify and identify how that changes the physical or mental difficulty level.

Make up a new rule for each game and identify how your new rule would change the physical or mental difficulty level. Strive to make up a rule that drastically changes the physical or mental difficulty level.

The Game Opponents

In a game like Solitaire, the playing pieces (the cards), the boundaries (52 cards), and the rules (the player can only play cards based on previously played cards) all work together to make the game difficult to win. However, the playing pieces, boundaries, and rules passively block the player. What makes games far more interesting is when other players (or artificially intelligent non-player characters) actively block the player from reaching a goal.

In a video game, the simplest non-player characters (NPCs) often provide obstacles for players to overcome. Such NPCs challenge the player by sheer numbers and/or by directly confronting and attacking the player. In many zombie video games, zombie NPCs aren't much of a challenge by themselves, but when collected in a group, their large numbers create an obstacle players must either avoid or destroy.

On a more challenging level, NPCs may be controlled by an artificial intelligence (AI) algorithm that gives NPCs seemingly intelligent behavior. Now rather than blocking a player's progress through sheer numbers or random movement, AI-controlled NPCs behave intelligently and threaten players by appearing to respond to their actions.

However, even AI-controlled NPCs can feel limited and predictable. That's why human players make the best opponents since every person has different skill levels with different methods for making decisions. This means humans can strategize and act in ways that AI algorithms often fail to duplicate. Human opponents can analyze your reactions and respond by deliberately targeting your weakness. Even more entertaining (or frustrating) is that human players can taunt players to create an additional emotional challenge to winning the game as well.

One human opponent can be hard enough to defeat, but many games allow multiple people to play at the same time. Trying to outwit a single human opponent may be hard, but trying to defeat multiple human opponents, who all have different playing styles, can prove even more difficult.

Unlike AI-controlled NPCs, human opponents can make alliances with others, betray friends, and deceive everyone through misdirection or outright lies. Such an unpredictable element makes playing with and against human opponents most challenging of all.

Thought Exercise

A goal and the playing pieces needed to reach that goal define the physical and mental challenges players face.

The boundaries of a playing field increase or decrease the physical and mental challenges defined by the goal and playing pieces.

Rules adjust the difficulty level of the physical and mental challenges needed to reach a goal.

Opponents (whether AI-controlled or human) directly block a goal or force players in a race against time to reach a goal before their opponent can do so.

Pick any game and change the following to see how it affects the overall gameplay:

- Change the goal or playing pieces
- Change the boundaries of the playing field
- Add or subtract a rule
- Add or subtract the number of opponents

The Time Element

One factor that defines gameplay is the element of time. Specifically, does the game have a time limit when the game ends? In some games, there is no time limit. In baseball, a game can take however long it takes two teams to complete nine innings. In other games, there's a fixed time limit, which forces players to achieve their goal before time runs out.

Time can create greater excitement because it forces players to take desperate action before they run out of time. Besides the end of a game, time can also increase play at the end of specific divisions of a game such as the end of each quarter or, in the case of basketball, at the end of 24 seconds each time a team gains possession of the ball. Time keeps players active because if they don't take any action, they'll lose automatically at the end of the time limit.

Players can also slow down time as well. In many sports, teams can call a time out where they can stop the clock and plan their next move. In the video game Superhot, players can slow down or even stop time by stopping their own movement so they can analyze the current situation. When the player starts moving again, the clock in the game starts ticking once more.

Time plays a crucial role in many games. To increase the pace in speed chess, players each get an equal amount of time. The longer they take to make a move, the more time they'll consume, which means less time they'll have to make moves in the future. Just adding a time limit in speed chess alters the game considerably where players used to regular chess may not necessarily excel in timed chess matches and vice versa.

By adding a time limit to the entire game, to individual divisions of a game, or to specific events within a game, designers can alter the pace of a game that can affect the entire experience of the game.

Thought Exercise

Choose a game with a time limit (such as basketball) and imagine how the game would change if the time limit didn't exist. Choose a game without a time limit (such as golf) and imagine how the game would change if there was a fixed time limit for the entire game. For equal division of the game. For individual events within the game.

For games with time limits, how do time outs affect the game by stopping time temporarily? How does the lack of time outs affect a game with time limits?

One-Time Play vs. Repeated Play

Most sports, card, and board games are meant for repeat play. With these types of games, the challenge comes from playing multiple opponents who each bring different skills and strategies, which keeps the game fresh.

With the advent of video games, a different type of game has emerged that emphasizes one-time, solitary play. These types of games are more like novels or movies where part of the enjoyment lies in discovering a new world for the first-time. As soon as players finish these types of games, they can still play the game again, but the excitement of the unknown will be gone.

Such one-time playable games are meant to be consumed and enjoyed, but once you're done, you can move on to another game. Many video games with a strong narrative and puzzle solving emphasis lean towards one-time play.

However, once you unlock the game's various puzzles and explore most of the game world, you've essentially finished the game. Nobody can claim they've "finished" playing Go or baseball where they've mastered everything the game has to offer. Yet people can claim they've finished solitary video games once they've visited every part of the game world and completed all available tasks.

In general, the larger the emphasis on stories and puzzles, the more likely the game will be limited to one-time play. The more the emphasis involves playing against others, the more likely the game will offer repeat play that creates the same experience, but with different players, each time.

The reason why sports championships are popular year after year is because the two teams bring different players with their own stories to the game. This provides different challenges for their opponents to solve and for spectators to enjoy.

There's a market for both one-time play games and repeatable play games. By knowing which type of game you want to create, you can design all elements of your game to support one type of game emphasis or the other.

Thought Exercise

Pick a sport and apply a story and multiple puzzles players must solve. How does the addition of a story and puzzle alter play and lessen the chance of repeat playing?

Pick a solitary video game, minimize the story, strip away the puzzles, and imagine how you could play against multiple players. How does playing against others while minimizing a game story and puzzles increase the chance of repeat playing?

Summary

Playing a game means manipulating playing pieces in pursuit of a goal, staying within the boundaries of a playing field, following rules, and competing against opponents. Added to all this may be time limits to increase pressure on players to reach their goals.

Some games are meant to be played just once. These games are often solitary games that immerse players in another world that's controlled by a computer. While this world may feel fresh the first time players encounter it, the game never changes afterward. This means the game is rarely as exciting to play a second time as it was to play the first time.

Other games, especially sports, card, and board games, are meant to be played multiple times where the challenge lies in playing different opponents.

The combination of all these elements define a game. Altering these elements in various ways can subtly or drastically change the way the game works. Even a simple change can have a ripple effect throughout the game. Great games depend on multiple elements that combine to create a satisfying experience.

Further Reading

"Building Blocks of Tabletop Game Design: An Encyclopedia of Mechanisms", Geoffrey Engelstein, CRC Press, 2022.

Chapter 5
Understanding Game Loops

Every game is repetitive. The challenge in designing any game is to make every repetitive loop interesting no matter how many times someone may play it. The moment a game's repetitive loop stops being interesting, people will stop playing the game.

What makes a game's repetitive loop interesting are challenges. Look at the difference between Tic-Tac-Toe and chess. The limited number of options in Tic-Tac-Toe makes that game far less interesting once you understand the basic choices to avoid losing. Once you can avoid losing with 100% success, the entire game ceases to be fun anymore.

On the other hand, chess offers an exponentially number of choices in every game. This makes chess fascinating for people to continue playing for entire lifetimes. Both Tic-Tac-Toe and chess offer repetitive loops, but the repetitive loop in chess offers far more choices to consider, making that game far more interesting as a result. Repetition is unavoidable in any loop, but the key is to avoid identical repetition where a game fails to show the player anything new.

In every game, there's a core repetitive loop. In board and card games, this core loop occurs in each player's turn. Each turn in chess and checkers, players must decide which piece to move. In poker, players must make choices based on the cards they have, the money they have, and the choices and behavior of the other players. Games that offer more choices create a more interesting experience.

In real-time video games, this core loop occurs every second. In a racing game, players need to decide where to steer and how fast (or slow) to go. In a first-person shooter game, players need to decide where to move and what to shoot at. Because these choices change each second, the game provides an ongoing challenge for players to resolve.

W. Wang, *The Structure of Game Design*, International Series on Computer, Entertainment and Media Technology, https://doi.org/10.1007/978-3-031-32202-0_5

All game loops consist of the following repetitive steps:

1. Identify the objective
2. Collect information
3. Form a hypothesis to reach the objective
4. Test the hypothesis
5. Observe results
6. Interpret data from the results
7. Return to step 3 to form a new hypothesis

At the start of every loop, players must know their objective. What are they trying to do? In the main core loop of every game, players are trying to win, but they must know exactly what they need to do to win the game. In sports, the object is to score more points. In board and video games, the object might be to defeat an enemy or be the first to reach a specific location. Whatever the goal might be, players must have a clear path to reaching that goal.

Once players know what they need to do, they need to evaluate their options by collecting information. Where is the goal? What is in the way? Where are they located in relation to the goal? What can they do to reach the goal?

This initial information gathering stage involves players evaluating their current state to understand what they can do to get closer to the ultimate goal. When they know where they are, what they can do, and where the goal is, they can create a hypothesis (plan) for how to get there.

Players must test their hypothesis by implementing their initial plan. Most likely, players will find their actions will either fail outright or simply prove more difficult than they anticipated. In either case, players can see the results of their actions and then decide what they can change. Did they fail because their plan itself was faulty or because they simply failed to execute a good plan correctly?

Based on their actions and the results, players can learn from their mistakes. Then they can form a new hypothesis and repeat the loop until they finally achieve their objective.

Thought Exercise

Pick a board or card game and identify its core game loop that occurs every turn. Pick different video game types (such as a sport game, a vehicle simulation game, or a horror survival game) and identify its core game loop that occurs every second or every turn.

Why are the choices in the board or card game interesting? Why are the choices in a video game interesting?

The core game loop (by turn or by seconds) defines the main action of the game. Make sure this main action is fun, challenging, and interesting by offering players options that keep changing. Either new options appear (and old options disappear) or the same options remain but in different and changed circumstances. Pick a game that you do not like. What about its main action is not fun, challenging, or interesting to you?

Identifying Macro and Micro Game Loops

Every game consists of multiple game loops. There's the core game loop that defines the entire purpose for playing the game. In chess, the purpose of the game is to checkmate your opponent's king. In soccer, the purpose of the game is to score the most goals. In any game, there are macro loops and micro loops.

Macro loops contain the major repetitive loops in a game. In a video game, there might be an inventory management loop, a movement loop, and a combat loop. In a board game like Battleship, there's an initial ship placement loop and an attack loop. In a card game like poker, there's a card dealing loop, a card exchange loop, and a decision loop whether to stay in the game or not. Macro loops define the major, repetitive loops that make up the entire core game loop.

The core game loop of Monopoly involves driving all the other players into bankruptcy. To achieve this goal, the macro loops consist of these repetitive tasks as shown in Fig. 5.1:

- Move
- Buy property, pay rent, draw a card, or do nothing
- Collect rent from other players

Within each macro loop are one or more micro loops. In Monopoly, buying property represents one micro loop where players can decide to buy a property, pay money, and then receive the title for that property. The micro loops define the steps players take within the macro loop.

The core game loop for most first-person shooter video games involves reaching a goal by defeating all enemies in the way. The macro loops that make up this core game loop looks like this as shown in Fig. 5.2:

- Move
- Shoot
- Collect loot to upgrade player

Fig. 5.1 The macro loops of Monopoly

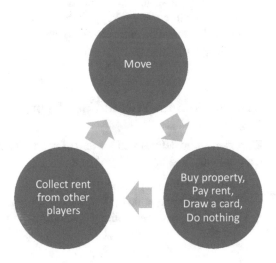

Fig. 5.2 The core loop of
a first-person shooter
video game

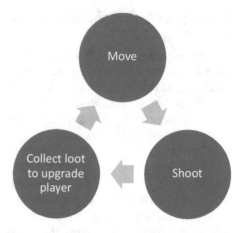

Within the shoot macro loop, players might go through several micro loops such as choosing which weapon to use, where to aim, and how many shots to fire.

Each game loop contains its own objective. Within the Move macro loop, the objective is to find the best position. Within the Shoot macro loop, the objective is to defeat an enemy. Within the Collect loot macro loop, the objective is to decide which loot is valuable enough to keep and use.

By defining the various loops that make up a game, you can better understand how different parts of a game work together to create a single unified experience for the player. Ideally, each micro loop should be fun to do and work together to support the larger macro loop of the game.

Thought Exercise

Pick a card or board game and identify its macro game loops. Then identify the micro game loops within one of its macro loops. Do the same for a video game.

How do the micro loops support the macro loop? Does each micro loop present players with interesting and ever-changing choices? If so, how? If not, how does this affect the game?

Defining Actions Within Each Loop

Each game loop defines a single unit of action. To take action, players need to know their options:

- Where does this loop take place? (Describes the playing field)
- What can the player do? (Describes the options the player must choose)
- How can players do something? (Describes how the player implements an option)

In Monopoly, the Move loop answers these questions like this:

- (Where does this take place?) Moves take place on a board divided into properties and random chance spots
- (What can the player do?) Each player must move clockwise around the board
- (How can players do something?) Players throw dice and move the amount determined by the dice total

By defining the main parts of each game loop, it's easy to define the overall actions within the game without getting bogged down with details too soon.

In a first-person shooter video game, the Move loop answers these questions like this:

- (Where does this take place?) Moves take place within the game world that can be inside a building or outside in a city
- (What can the player do?) Walk, run, duck, jump
- (How can players do something?) Press buttons on a controller, press keys on the keyboard, move the mouse, slide a finger on a touch screen

The various tasks that make up the core game loop must be fun or as short as possible. If any task within a loop is not fun or takes too much time, players will quickly tire of the game and abandon it.

Thought Exercise

Pick a sport and identify its core game loop, its macro loops (that make up the core game loop), and its micro loops (that make up each macro loop). In each loop, identify where the loop takes place, what the player can do, and how the player can do it.

For example, a baseball team has a management loop. This loop occurs before the game plays (Where does this take place?) and lets players choose the players and the order they'll bat (What can the player do?). A baseball simulation video game would also let players select players using a mouse, keyboard or game controller (How can players do something?).

Pick a board game and a video game (such as a real-time strategy or puzzle game) and identify its core game loop, macro loops, and micro loops.

Common Types of Game Loops

Every loop must challenge the player. Games often contain multiple repetitive loops that serve different purposes and create unique challenges for the player to overcome:

- The goal loop
- The inventory loop
- The movement loop
- The combat loop

The Goal Loop

The goal loop defines the overall objective within that loop. Specifically, what is the player trying to achieve?

In a first-person shooter, the goal might be to reach a specific location. However, reaching that location would be boring if players could simply walk there with nothing getting in their way. That's why every goal loop needs obstacles.

Obstacles can be as simple as pits to jump over, doors to open, and tunnels to crawl through. Obstacles must threaten to stop the player from reaching their goal within that game loop. To make obstacles more challenging, games can:

- Increase the number of obstacles
- Increase the danger of each obstacle
- Introduce a time limit for getting past all the obstacles

Each successive loop must make the player's goal harder to reach. Obstacles can be static, physical objects but the most challenging obstacles of all are other characters.

In a multiplayer game, other players represent obstacles to keep you from reaching a goal. In some cases, other players can also be allies to help you reach a goal. Non-player characters (NPCs) provide other challenges for players to defeat in direct combat, avoid, or to negotiate to get them out of the way or even to help you. The sole purpose of obstacles is to keep players from completing the goal loop.

Thought Exercise

Pick any game and identify a game loop. What is the goal players are trying to achieve? What obstacles try to stop players from reaching their goal and how do they try to stop players? How do the obstacles change as the main goal loop repeats?

The Inventory Loop

One common loop, especially in the beginning of a game, is an inventory loop. An inventory loop lets players manage their current resources and possessions. During the inventory loop, players can identify what they have, which items are more valuable than others, and which items to use (and which items to abandon if necessary).

Every loop needs something to change to make it interesting and with an inventory loop, a game must constantly give players something new to find. This forces players to decide whether to use the new items and whether to discard any old items. If the player must discard an old item, the challenge lies in choosing which items to abandon, never knowing for sure if that item might be useful in the near future.

In some games, players have the option of carrying more items at the expense of moving slower and getting tired more often. Now players must decide whether being overburdened is worth the possible advantage of having items you may need.

Another variation might give players options on where to store specific items such as in a backpack, jacket pockets, or in your hands. The location of specific items can determine how quickly players can access that item. Having a gun in a backpack will take time to grab if you get ambushed but if you had kept the gun in your jacket pocket, you could retrieve it faster.

Inventory systems commonly limit players to a fixed number of items they can carry, but others may limit players by weight. Thus you can carry lots of small, light items but only one or two heavy items.

Besides weight, inventory systems might also limit items by size. Carrying three daggers should be easy but carrying three battle axes would be much clumsier because of the greater weight and size. By using weight, size, and quantities, inventory systems can provide different types of challenges as puzzles for players to solve.

Just remember that inventory management is rarely the purpose of the game, but a way to improve a player's chances of reaching the goal of the game. The easier and simpler the inventory system is to learn and use, the better it will be for the overall game design. In the inventory loop, players want to feel rich based on the items they've collected.

Thought Exercise

Pick a non-children's board game (such as Monopoly or the Settlers of Catan) and a video game, then identify its inventory loop. What makes the inventory loop different each time players repeat it?

Pick a team sport (like hockey) and an individual sport (like golf) and identify the inventory loop in each game. What changes occur that make the inventory loop different each time players repeat it?

The Movement Loop

In a game, players must do something and that usually means moving within the playing field. Movement is the most repetitive loop in most games, so the challenge lies in keeping movement interesting.

In video games, the most common way to keep movement interesting are obstacles that need to be navigated around or avoided. When obstacles are other players or NPCs, those other players and NPCs may be moving too. That means players must either intercept them or plan ahead for how to avoid them. Where obstacles are static, they can be easy to find and avoid but other players and NPCs are dynamics, which makes them harder to find and avoid.

Even in the absence of obstacles, movement should be enjoyable because players can choose different movement options to express themselves. Walking, running, flying, climbing, jumping, and riding an animal or vehicle should all be fun and unique experiences in themselves.

Beyond obstacles and interactions with others players and NPCs, another way to make movement interesting is through scenery. Constantly changing scenery can make movement interesting, allowing players to explore the world around them.

Another option for making movement interesting is to provide a setting that teaches players how to use different movement options to navigate the environment. A swamp might force players to practice jumping from one log to another, a forest could teach players how to climb trees, a lake could give players a chance to swim, and an open field could teach players how to ride and control an animal such as a horse.

Movement should be more than just getting a player from one place to another. Movement should let players practice their options and explore the game world to learn more about how it works as well. That way players can develop their movement skills in a safe area before risking doing it in combat. In the movement loop, players want to feel in control.

Thought Exercise

Pick a video game and identify its movement loop. How do obstacles change over time? How do other players and NPCs interact with the player while the player moves? How can the player explore the gaming world through movement? What ways can the player practice different movement options?

The Combat Loop

Combat is how players deal with other players or NPCs who get in the way. Combat can mean fighting but can also mean avoiding enemies. The combat loop is about confronting enemies and choosing options to deal with them.

To make combat interesting, games give players different options for fighting where each option lets players express themselves in a visually expressive way. When players defeat an enemy, they want to see a satisfying confirmation that the enemy is either defeated, wounded, or still a threat.

When players dispatch enemies from a distance using a ranged weapon like a gun or a crossbow, enemies should fall over with a different visual confirmation than when players attack enemies at close range using sword or an axe. The more ways enemies can show they've been defeated, the more emotionally satisfying defeating enemies will be.

Each weapon should dispatch enemies in a distinct and memorable style. A club should smash enemies apart while a sword should cut enemies apart. A pistol should visually cause damage to an enemy far differently than a shotgun or a rocket propelled grenade. Variations in how weapons affect enemies and how enemies fall apart with each weapon can make combat interesting.

During the combat loop, players want to feel powerful. Each weapon and each method of attack (ranged, close combat, hand to hand) should give players choices for how to attack. By combining different weapons with a variety of different ways those weapons affect enemies, games can provide variation so the combat loop remains visually interesting and challenging.

Thought Exercise

Pick a video game and identify its combat loop. What variations in weapons does the game offer to keep the combat loop interesting? What variations does the game offer in how the player can attack enemies? What variations does the game offer for showing successful results in dispatching enemies?

Summary

Every game consists of loops. The main goal loop represents the purpose of that loop. When a player reaches this goal, the loop ends. Each time a loop ends, another loop begins.

Inside the core game loop are smaller macro loops, and inside each macro loop are even smaller micro loops that run multiple times. The inventory loop makes players feel wealthy by collecting valuables. The movement loop gives players a feeling of control as they navigate through the game world. The combat loop lets players feel powerful as they dispatch enemies using a variety of weapons and combat tactics.

Identify the loops in a game, make the loops interesting in themselves, and then make sure the loops support the overall goal of the game. The key to game loops is that they must constantly change and offer different challenges to hold the player's interest no matter how many times they may repeat.

Further Readings

"Core Loops & Prototyping", Dan Spaventa, https://youtu.be/Mep4_w8qxeE.

"Go From Ideas To Gameplay Using Gameplay Loops", Game Design with Michael, https://youtu.be/MIMMJ4xHYR8.

"How Gameplay Loops Keep You Playing", Adam Millard, https://youtu.be/Sk-nbAtIUko.

"The Real Core Loop - What Every Game Has In Common", Extra Credits, https://youtu.be/mGL5YGcAxEI.

"What Are Loops In Game Design?", Game Design with Michael, https://youtu.be/PMj8Q4ViKzs.

Chapter 6
Randomness in Games

Randomness adds uncertainty in games. Some games have no randomness whatsoever such as pure skill games like chess or Go. Other games are completely random such as children's games like Candy Land or Chutes and Ladders. When games lack randomness, the game outcome depends entirely on each player's skill. When games embrace total randomness, the game outcome depends entirely on chance.

Most games are not completely skill-based or completely random but a variation of both. For example, poker uses randomness to determine the cards each player receives, but players can then use their skill to make the most of their cards based on their knowledge of the cards held by other players.

The combination and amount of skill and randomness in a game defines different playing experiences. Too much reliance on skill can discourage novices from learning the game. Too much reliance on randomness can make a game less interesting to play beyond children.

The purpose of randomness in any game is to add a level of uncertainty to an outcome. Given a choice between choosing a certain option or a less certain option that may be affected by chance, there's no reason for anyone to choose the less certain option. Therefore, games balance uncertainty with reward. The more certain the option, the lower the reward. The less certain the option, the higher the reward.

This risk/reward option often occurs in sports. In basketball, players can opt for a close range shot and get 2 points, or take a chance for a longer range shot and get 3 points. The closer range shot offers more certainty of success, but the longer range shot offers a higher reward with less chance of success. By offering higher rewards in exchange for greater uncertainty, games force players to make difficult choices that can make the game more challenging.

© The Author(s), under exclusive license to Springer Nature
Switzerland AG 2023
W. Wang, *The Structure of Game Design*, International Series on Computer,
Entertainment and Media Technology,
https://doi.org/10.1007/978-3-031-32202-0_6

Dealing with the Imperfection of Randomness

In a perfect world, every option would have an equal chance of success. However in the real world, every form of randomness does not offer an equal chance of success. A typical die might display numbers from 1 to 6, but because of physical imperfections of the die, all numbers will not have the same chance to appear. This chance may be minuscule but it still exists.

Since few players want to lose a game due to a single flip of a coin, games often minimize the effect of randomness by multiplying the amount of randomness in a game. The chance of a single flip of a coin going against you is 50%, but the chance that twenty coin flips will all go against you is much less. Thus by offering multiple opportunities for randomness, games minimize the chance that players will lose due to one bad roll of the die.

Games often make players roll two or more die instead of one die to minimize the chance of getting an extremely low or extremely high value. Since rolling a 2 or a 12 on two die is least likely to occur (1 in 36 chance), some games provide extreme punishment or rewards. A roll of 2 on two die might represent really bad luck such as your weapon breaking. A roll of 12 on two die might represent extremely good luck where your attack hits a vital spot in an enemy and causes greater damage than normal. In this way, randomness can work both for and against the player in equal amounts.

Six-sided die are common in games, but to ensure that every number has an equal chance of appearing, role-playing games often use multi-sided die such as a 4-sided, 8-sided, 12-sided, and 20-sided die. Rolling a single 12-sided die means every number from 1 to 12 has an equal chance of appearing. Contrast this with rolling two six-sided die where a 7 is most likely to occur and a 2 or 12 is least likely to occur. Figure 6.1 shows different types of multi-sided die.

Besides die, other random number generators include cards and spinners. With video games, randomness relies on a random number generator (RNG) algorithm. Just like the minute imperfections of a die can make some numbers appear more often than others, computer-generated random numbers are also not truly random.

Computer random number generators rely on a seed value. Based on this seed value, the random number generator algorithm can generate multiple numbers. While these numbers appear random, the limitation is that giving a random number generator the same seed results in the same list of random numbers.

If you know the seed used by a random number generator, you can predict the list of random numbers it generates. This fatal flaw means that if a player can identify the pattern of a random number generator, they can predict the next number that the random number generator creates.

To make a seed value as random as possible, random number generators often use the current time, measured in seconds or even milliseconds combined with other factors such as the movement of a computer mouse in the player's hand. This essentially makes it difficult for anyone to predict the seed value while also ensuring that the seed value itself will be unpredictable.

Fig. 6.1 Multi-sided dice give each number an equal chance of occurring. (https://www.opencli-part.org)

Besides using a seed value that's unpredictable and essentially random by basing it on the milliseconds of the current time, another key component to create random numbers is to use algorithms optimized for randomness. (Since it's impossible to create true random numbers, computer-generated random number generators are often called pseudorandom number generators.)

One popular algorithm for creating random numbers is called Xorshift (https://prng.di.unimi.it). To randomize a list of items, such as shuffling cards, many video games rely on a randomizing algorithm called the Fisher-Yates shuffle (https://en.wikipedia.org/wiki/Fisher–Yates_shuffle). By using an algorithm optimized for creating random numbers, a video game can create random numbers that are as fair as possible.

When randomizing numbers, computer algorithms might define a range between 2 and 12. However, this creates completely different probabilities than rolling two die, much like rolling a single 12-sided die. That's because defining a random number between a range of 2 and 12 means that all numbers have an equal (theoretically) chance of appearing. On the other hand, rolling two die means a 7 has a greater chance of occurring (6 + 1, 5 + 2, and 4 + 3) while a 2 (1 + 1) or 12 (6 + 6) are much less likely to appear since there's only a 1 in 36 chance that both die will have an identical 1 or 6.

So rather than choosing a random number from 2 to 12, video games might generate two random numbers from 1 to 6 and then add them together. This mimics the same probabilities as throwing two die.

Remember, there are no such things as truly random numbers but through different techniques (mimicking multiple die) and choosing optimized randomization algorithms, you can use various shades of randomization to influence the design of a game.

Thought Exercise

Nobody wants to play a game that can be decided on a single bad roll of the dice or turn of a card. Pick several games that include randomness and identify how these games minimize the risk that a single random event will decide the winner.

In a video game, what elements include randomness? For example, moving from side to side may be certain, but jumping to a distant ledge may involve randomness because the jump may or may not be successful. In general, the riskier the move in a video game, the more likely it will use randomness to determine the outcome.

(Video games often slant the odds in favor of the player. If a player takes a risky shot from a long distance, they'll be happy if it succeeds but they won't be upset if they fail. On the other hand, if players perform a move that seems certain but incorporates randomness, there's a small chance that move could fail.

Since the odds are high the move will succeed, failing may be mathematically possible but infuriating to players who may feel the video game is working against them. For that reason, video games tend to make low risk options more likely to succeed even though this can eliminate randomness.)

Using Randomization in Games

Not all games need randomization, such as pure skill games like chess and Go. The purpose of randomization in any game is to create unpredictability. That way playing the same game multiple times can create a different outcome each time, enhancing the enjoyment in playing that game.

For example, most adults tire of Tic-Tac-Toe as soon as they spot the limitations of the game. However, few sports fans ever tire of seeing the same sport because the game will never play exactly the same way as before, even between two teams that previously played each other.

Several ways randomization can create unpredictability in a game include:

- Creation
- Movcment
- Combat
- Chance events

Creation involves introducing something new into the game such as new characters, new items (such as treasures or enemies), new actions (such as a non-player character attacking an enemy), or new events that could affect the game (such as storms or droughts).

Randomization can alter amounts, quantities, and positions. For example, randomizing amounts can alter the value of treasures found in a given area such as a loot box. The contents of a loot box can be randomized so players have no idea what it contains until they actually open it.

Randomizing quantities can alter the number of enemies that spawn at a specific area while randomizing their positions can alter their locations. Such randomization makes replaying a game enjoyable because the challenges are always different.

When creating video games, developers must manually design the entire gaming world, which limits how large that game world can be. To avoid this problem, developers rely on procedural generation where the computer can create new areas based on randomization. Through procedural generation of new areas, video games can offer new, limitless worlds for players to explore, which increases re-playability of a game.

When players move, they want certainty. Without this certainty, players would feel like they couldn't control the game. However when enemies appear in a video game, they shouldn't move in predictable patterns. Thus randomization ensures they move in unpredictable ways that can make a game more challenging. This also gives computer-controlled enemies the appearance of intelligence since they seem to be making decisions instead of choosing the same movement each time.

In skill-based games like chess or checkers, combat is always certain. In many other games, initiating combat may be certain, but the outcome involves an element of chance. This means that even overwhelming force may fail occasionally while outnumbered forces can sometimes emerge victorious.

Adding uncertainty in combat gives players a dilemma. Should they risk moving closer to an enemy to increase their chance of hitting (and getting hit in return)? Or should they stay further back to decrease the chance of an enemy fighting back but also decreasing the chance that they will hit the enemy at all?

Uncertainty forces players to make tough decisions. While a lucky break might help occasionally, more skillful players should win most of the time. Chance simply keeps a game interesting since players could still lose despite all the odds in their favor. This forces good players to adapt to unlucky breaks that further challenges their skill.

Randomization can also control events in games, such as the weather or actions of non-player characters. In a fantasy game, players might need to hire a boat to take them across the ocean, but if a random storm occurs, this can delay their journey or even cancel it altogether, forcing players to look for an alternate path to their goal.

If players transport spices from one area to another, a war breaking out between two kingdoms can threaten their trade route, their trading business, or even their lives as warring armies either block trade temporarily or permanently, or force players to choose sides to fight on. Random events keep a game from being too predictable.

Thought Exercise

Pick a skill-based game with no randomization, such as chess, and find ways to add randomization to the game's initial setup, movement, combat, and random events. How does this alter gameplay?

Pick a children's game that relies on randomness and replace the randomness with skill. How does this alter gameplay and make the game more difficult to play?

Input vs. Output Randomization

Randomization can occur in two ways: input or output. Input randomization occurs before the player can take action. Output randomization occurs after the player has already taken action.

An example of input randomization is any card game such as poker. The cards each person gets is random, but it's up to the players to use their skill to make the most out of the cards they have. Skilled players can succeed, or at least minimize their losses, even after receiving a bad hand.

An example of output randomization occurs in many games where players choose to attack an enemy where the outcome of that combat depends on probabilities. If the player has a massive advantage in combat, the attack will likely succeed, but could still fail. If the player has a tremendous disadvantage in combat, the attack will likely fail, but still has a chance to succeed.

Input randomization forces players to react to chance and then use skill. Output randomization forces players to use skill first and then take a chance that all their skill and planning could still fail in the end.

For that reason, players are often more accepting of input randomization (getting dealt a bad hand) than they are of output randomization (doing everything right only to still fail anyway).

When adding randomness to a game, decide whether you want to use input or output randomization because each type of randomization will give players a slightly different experience.

In board games, players can often see their odds of success ahead of time, such as displayed in a Combat Results Table (CRT) as shown in Fig. 6.2. Seeing the odds and rolling die to determine the outcome makes the entire process transparent. Because all possible outcomes are clearly visible, players are less likely to get upset with an unlucky roll of the die.

COMBAT RESULTS TABLE									
Die Roll	1-5 or less	1-4	1-3	1-2	1-1	2-1	3-1	4-1	5-1	6-1 or more
1	--	--	--	DX	DE	DE	DE	DE	DE	DE
2	AE	--	--	--	DX	DE	DE	DE	DE	DE
3	AE	AE	AX	--	--	DX	DE	DE	DE	DE
4	AE	AE	AE	AX	--	--	DX	DE	DE	DE
5	AE	AE	AE	AE	AX	--	--	DX	DE	DE
6	AE	AE	AE	AE	AE	AX	--	--	DX	DE

Explanation of Results:
AE: All attacking units are eliminated
DE: All defending units are eliminated
AX: All attacking units are eliminated first, and then one or more defending units whose Combat Strength is equal to or greater than that of the attacking units are eliminated.
DX: All defending units are eliminated first, and then these must be matched by eliminated attacking units.
--: No result.

Fig. 6.2 A Combat Results Table shows the odds of success when attacking

In video games, these lists of odds are not visible. As a result, players may have a distorted (optimistic) view of their chances of success that may not be realistic. If they fail, they may not understand why, which can prove upsetting.

For that reason, video games may skewer the odds. When there's a slight chance of success, the video game may report less favorable odds of success. That way if the player does fail, they will think the odds weren't that high anyway and accept the result.

When the odds are in the player's favor (such as 90%), the video game may actually give the player a greater chance of success (such as 99%) to better match the player's perception of their odds. When a player's perception matches the outcome, they'll be less likely to get upset and accept the hidden and opaque random calculation inside a video game.

Thought Exercise

Pick a game based on input randomization, such as poker where randomness defines the cards each player receives. Change this game to output randomization where the outcome of each player's actions offers varying degrees of chance. How does this alter gameplay?

Pick a game based on output randomization, such as a sport like a penalty kick in soccer. Change this game to input randomization where players must adapt to random situations before making a decision. How does this alter gameplay?

Independent vs. Dependent Probability

Another type of randomization involves independent or dependent probability. Independent probability means every moment has the exact same odds. For example, when you flip a coin, the odds are always 50–50 (assuming a fair coin). Often times with independent probability, people create irrational beliefs.

If you flip a coin ten times, it's perfectly possible to flip heads ten times in a row with the same chance as flipping heads five times and tails five times in various combinations. When one possibility occurs too often, people erroneously believe that the next coin flip must be tails because heads appeared too often. Yet this is not true because each coin flip is completely independent of the previous coin flip. This belief that independent probabilities are related is known as the "Gambler's fallacy" because gamblers cling to this belief when betting on casino games such as roulette, craps, or even slot machines.

Dependent probability occurs when the outcome of a random event directly affects the odds of succeeding random events. In many card games such as blackjack, the odds of drawing two queens are 4 in 52. That's because there are four queens in a deck and fifty-two cards available.

If you draw two queens, the odds of drawing two more queens is not 4 in 52 (7.7%) anymore because both the number of queens and the number of total cards has changed. The odds are now 2 in 50 (4%) because there are only two more queens remaining out of fifty cards.

Each time you draw a card, the odds immediately change based on the type of card you drew and the number of cards remaining in the deck. That's dependent probability.

Dependent probability gives players a chance to calculate their odds based on what has already happened. This can give players a greater sense of control and increases their chances of success, which is why card counting in blackjack can dramatically improve your chances of winning.

If you know which cards have already been played and which cards are left, you can better guess which cards are most likely to appear next. If all the aces have been played, then you know you can never expect an ace until the deck gets shuffled once more.

Independent probability (sometimes called white noise) makes every outcome feel completely random. Dependent probability (sometimes called brown noise) makes every outcome somewhat predictable. A combination of the two is referred to as pink noise where outcomes are generally predictable but can occasionally get out of control.

To resolve combat, a game might require players to throw two die. Since rolling a 2 or a 12 is less likely than any other number, one or both of these could trigger additional dice rolls, creating dramatically different results than normal.

Independent probability (white noise) can make players feel out of control. Dependent probability (brown noise) can make events somewhat predictable. However, the combination of the two (pink noise) can provide the most surprises since outcomes are largely predictable but can occasionally inject a massive surprise (good or bad) that keeps any outcome from feeling too certain.

Thought Exercise

Pick a game that relies on independent probability such as a casino game. How would this game change if it relied on dependent probability?

Pick a game that relies on dependent probability, such as blackjack. How does independent probability make the game less predictable and how does this alter gameplay?

Look for an example of pink noise randomization in a game. How does this game allow for occasional wild deviations from the norm?

Summary

Randomness adds an element of uncertainty to a game. Too much randomness creates a feeling of helplessness in players since they have no chance of affecting the outcome of the game. Pure randomness is best for children's games so children have an equal chance to win against adults. Otherwise purely random games are unlikely to hold most people's interest for long unless they're gambling such as in any casino game.

Randomness can occur before a player can do anything or after a player has already made a decision. When randomness occurs before a player does anything, the game forces players to react to their situation whether it's good or bad. When randomness occurs after a player has already made a decision, failure can often upset players if they don't understand how the game calculated and resolved the odds.

Randomness is meant to create variety in a game so every game plays slightly differently. By altering the amount and number of random events, you can modify the way players experience a game and increase the appeal of playing the game again.

Further Readings

"The Two Types of Random in Game Design", Game Maker's Toolkit, https://youtu.be/
    dwI5b-wRLic.
"Uncertainty in Games" Randomness, Information and Luck in Game Design", The Game
    Overanalyser, https://youtu.be/Srgva9gEJDw.
"White, Brown, and Pink: The Flavors of Tabletop Game Randomness", Geoffrey Engelstein,
    https://youtu.be/qXn3tGBztVc.
"Uncertainty in Games", Greg Costikyan, The MIT Press, 2015.

Chapter 7
Psychology in Games

Every game must attract players to buy and then play the game. While playing the game, players need to follow rules. In the process of following those rules, players must receive some type of enjoyment from playing. This emotional experience can give players a reason to keep playing the game as long as possible and encourage them to play multiple times.

To achieve all of these goals, game designers often rely on psychology. Psychology in a video game can:

- Aid navigation
- Create emotional experiences
- Motivate players
- Minimize conflict between players

Aiding Navigation

All games give players choices. However, games must necessarily restrict player's choices to valid options. In sports, referees and umpires enforce game rules while in card or board games, players enforce the rules themselves. In video games, the computer enforces the rules, but since players cannot read the video game rules, they have no idea what they can and cannot do.

Since video games hide their rules, video games need to let players know their valid options. However, video games must make discovering valid options easy and intuitive. Failure to do that can make discovering valid options frustrating.

Early text-based video games, such as Zork, forced players to type in commands for what they wanted to do. However, there was no clue what valid commands the

© The Author(s), under exclusive license to Springer Nature
Switzerland AG 2023
W. Wang, *The Structure of Game Design*, International Series on Computer,
Entertainment and Media Technology,
https://doi.org/10.1007/978-3-031-32202-0_7

game would accept. If players typed in an invalid command, the video game might simply reply, "That sentence isn't one I recognize."

Such trial and error methods for finding valid options can not only be frustrating, but can interrupt the game. The more times the game fails to respond to the player, the more frustrating the game and the less likely anyone will want to keep playing it.

One solution is to display a list of valid options so players can never choose invalid options. This is the method often used in point and click video games, but such restrictions can also limit the player's sense of freedom.

To give players apparent freedom to choose without artificial restrictions on their options, video games often rely on psychology to manipulate players. Psychology lets players feel in control while subtly manipulating players to choose only valid options.

In most video games, players cannot roam anywhere they want. A simple solution is to block players from moving too far out of the game boundaries by using obstacles such as walls, mountains, or large bodies of water.

Since such physical boundaries can feel artificial and provide negative feedback, video games often use psychology to provide positive encouragement. Rather than restrict players through walls or oceans, video games might simply create empty expenses as boundaries. Players can freely roam through such empty expanses, but there's nothing to see or do in those areas, which encourages players to move back within the playing area.

Video games often use positive enticement based on theme park designs. In Disneyland, Walt Disney wanted visual landmarks to make it easy for people to find their way around. That's why Sleeping Beauty's Castle appears in the center of Disneyland so no matter where people might be, they can see the spires of the castle and head towards it.

In contrast, think of a casino that's purposely designed to keep people confused so they cannot easily find the exits. Such a confusing layout encourages people to stay as long as possible because the longer someone stays in a casino, the more likely they'll gamble (and lose money).

Video games use these same principles to provide navigation guides. To create a sense of disorientation and helplessness, horror video games create maze-like areas that keep players confused. To create a sense of direction, video games often display prominent landmarks so players can easily see where they should head towards.

In many video games, prominent landmarks such as a large mountain shows players which direction they need to go as shown in Fig. 7.1.

Some video games use arrows to point players where they should go, but a better solution is to identify certain areas in the game using colors or light. Colors can help guide players through the game world. Green might identify safe places where players can land while red might identify valid passages for players to follow. When players are navigating around a dark area, any form of light will be easily visible and help direct players where they can go.

Through color, light, roads, paths, prominent landmarks, and empty areas, video games can subtly guide players where they should go so they don't feel lost and always have a sense of direction of where to go next without feeling artificially constrained as shown in Fig. 7.2.

Fig. 7.1 A mountain in a video game can provide a constant landmark helping direct players towards a specific goal

Fig. 7.2 Scenes in a video game can guide players towards a specific goal using roads, landmarks, and light. (Image courtesy of Ravenscourt https://ravenscourt.games)

Thought Exercise

Pick a video game and identify how the game helps you navigate around the game area. What immediately catches your attention? How can you tell what your choices are at any given time? What does the video game do to keep you from feeling lost and directionless?

Creating Emotional Experiences

Everyone plays games for different reasons. While everyone's different, people tend to fall into recognizable categories. To provide a framework to classify different players, professor and game researcher, Richard Bartle, organized players into four general categories:

- Achievers
- Explorers
- Socializers
- Killers

Achievers play games because they enjoy the challenge of increasing their skills and completing the game. In multi-player games, achievers enjoy comparing themselves and showing off to others on leaderboards that rank their status.

Explorers play games to satisfy their curiosity in learning about a new world. These types of players prefer to take their time investigating every possible area of a game until they're satisfied they've experienced everything within the game. With explorers, combat and achievements are less important than simply fully experiencing the game world as much as possible.

Socializers play games to connect to others. Thus the enjoyment of the game comes from their interaction with other players in addition to the game itself. Socializers are more likely to help others and interact with them both in the game and outside the game in real life.

Killers enjoy competition by proving they're better than everyone else. They want to challenge and defeat others, which can sometimes get to the point of ruining the fun for other players. Killers want to win and enjoy the thrill of overcoming everyone around them.

Most people exhibit traits of all four categories in varying degrees. A first-person shooter game might appeal to killers, but it can also appeal to explorers if the game challenges players to search a world for clues to solve a mystery. Such a game might also appeal to achievers who may enjoy trying to reach a specific goal, and socializers who may enjoy working in a team to protect each other.

By understanding different ways people enjoy games, you can create a game that satisfies as many playing styles as possible. Ideally, a game can satisfy all playing styles in different ways. For example, a game might let players attack enemies (Killer) or negotiate their way out of a fight (Socializer). The more options a game gives players to achieve a goal, the more freedom players can enjoy as they experiment with the way they like best.

While people may have different reasons for playing a game, nearly all people share a common trait known as loss aversion. Basically, loss aversion occurs when people fear losing something more than they desire gaining something.

Given a choice between losing $100 or gaining $100, people feel the sting of losing far more than they feel the excitement of winning. When given a choice between losing something or gaining something, losing something is far more emotionally memorable. That means games can use loss aversion to maximize a player's emotional response.

The classic example of loss aversion in a video game comes from Portal where players are tasked with carrying around a companion cube with a heart on it. To help players emotionally bond to their companion cube, the hearts make it appear different from all other cubes players have seen before.

In addition, players see graffiti on the walls supposedly written by other people talking about how much they loved their companion cube. The purpose of this graffiti is to help players bond with their companion cube. After all, if other people (supposedly) felt emotionally attached to their companion cube, players will feel permission to emotionally bond to their companion cube as well.

Finally at one point in the game, players have no choice but to incinerate their companion cube. No matter how long players take to finally toss their companion cube in the incinerator, the game tells them that they took the least amount of time to decide to euthanize their companion cube, which evokes further feelings of guilt that strengthens the emotional bond the players had with their companion cube. Because of the way Portal exploits a player's natural tendency to feel bad over loss aversion, the game heightens a player's emotional experience playing the game.

Loss aversion is most often used in the inventory portion of a game where players must give up items they already possess. In Monopoly, nothing feels worse than having to give up hotels, houses, or even properties to pay a debt. For that reason, many horror games use loss aversion to limit what players can hold. By forcing players to either abandon their current items or ignore newly found items, loss aversion in horror games can help players feel a greater sense of helplessness and emotional turmoil. In romance games, loss aversion can force players to make difficult decisions to choose one partner over another, knowing they won't have a chance to reverse their decision later. This increases the emotion impact no matter how the decision turns out.

Loss aversion is partly what can make games so addictive such as slot machines. After spending enough money or time doing something, players don't want to quit until they get the reward they've been pursuing. Therefore, people will keep playing longer than they originally intended.

Sometimes loss aversion can have an unintended effect in a game. In League of Legends, players were rated by their win/loss ratio. However, if a game started going against a team, players on that losing team often quit the game rather than risk hurting their win/loss ratio. This created a poor playing experience for the players who remained in a losing game since they're now outnumbered and far more likely to lose after their teammates abandoned them prematurely.

Loss aversion can play an important role in designing a game. By understanding how loss aversion works, game designers can create games that influence the way players experience a game.

Thought Exercise

Pick a favorite game and identify which player style would find the game most appealing? The least appealing? Identify if your favorite game uses loss aversion in any way. If so, how does loss aversion influence a player's behavior?

Since all players are a mix of different styles (Achiever, Explorer, Socializer, or Killer), which playing style do you embrace most often? Which playing style do you embrace least often?

Motivating Players

Every game designer wants people to buy their game, play for long periods of time, and play the game over and over again. The longer people play a game, the more likely they'll convince their friends to play or buy items within the game to provide additional revenue to the game publisher.

People often play a game because they find it interesting, which is known as intrinsic motivation. However, they may play a game longer than they might normally do because of rewards, achievements, and leaderboards, which are known as extrinsic motivation.

Few people will play a game they dislike just to get a high score and brag to their friends. However, people may enjoy a game more if they already like the game and they can brag to their friends about their high score later. That's how extrinsic motivation can keep people playing games longer.

Rewards are often valuables that players get for completing tasks such as defeating a monster or unlocking a treasure chest. However, the frequency of rewards can determine how successful they are in motivating players. Common types of reward schedules are listed (from worst to best):

- Continuous (worst)
- Fixed interval
- Fixed ratio
- Variable interval
- Variable ratio (best)

Continuous rewards mean the game rewards players every time they complete a task. Imagine a rat in a cage getting a pellet of food each time it pushes down a lever. You might think rats would find a continuous reward schedule appealing because it's predictable. Yet, continuous rewards are actually the worst form of motivation.

Because rewards are so predictable, it's far too easy for people to tire of the rewards and the task needed to receive them. This may seem counter-intuitive but part of the fun in games lies in uncertainty. If we don't know when we might receive a reward, we'll be far more motivated to keep playing until we do get the reward. If we know we can get a reward reliably by performing a certain task, there's no uncertainty and thus no excitement.

Fixed interval schedules reward players after a certain amount of time has passed. That means players don't receive rewards immediately after completing a task, but receive rewards at periodic intervals afterwards. This is the second worst reward schedule since players soon adjust to getting rewarded on a regular basis and quickly lose interest in completing the necessary tasks to start a new reward schedule all over again.

Fixed ratio schedules reward players after they complete a ratio of tasks, such as every time they complete three tasks no matter how long (or short) it takes them. A fixed ratio schedule is better than a continuous and fixed interval schedule, but players often lose motivation to keep playing as soon as they receive their reward.

Variable interval schedules reward players at ever-changing time intervals. Because the game rewards players in an unpredictable manner, players feel a sense of anticipation and excitement waiting for the next reward.

Variable ratio schedules are the most motivating because they reward players far less predictably free from time intervals. Since players never know when they might receive a reward, they tend to keep playing until they receive a reward. Then when they receive a reward, there's new anticipation wondering how soon the next reward will arrive.

Because variable ratio schedules are the least predictable, they're the most motivating in keeping people playing longer. Slot machines use this unpredictable reward schedule to keep players anticipating a jackpot so they'll keep playing.

Many video games use one or more of these techniques to keep people playing. For example, a game might reward players each time they play (fixed interval). Then while they're playing, the game may provide rewards based on their performance (fixed/variable ratio/interval). Through a combination of predictable and unpredictable rewards, games can keep people playing the game longer.

Similar to rewards are achievements. Where rewards occur when players complete certain tasks, achievements acknowledge a player's longer term goals such as completing a certain number of levels within a game. Achievements occur less often than rewards but occur based on the player's performance. Thus achievements acknowledge a player's growing skill, which can encourage them to continue playing to reach the next achievement level.

Once someone has reached one achievement level, there's often the desire to complete all of the remaining achievement levels. This desire for completeness is known as the Zeigarnik effect.

Imagine receiving a loyalty card from your favorite restaurant that gives you a free meal after you buy ten meals. Yet the card comes with two meals already credited so you only have to buy eight additional meals to get the free meal.

Because the card is already partially completed, people are nearly twice as likely to buy the remaining meals than if they were given a blank card that required them to buy eight meals. Video games can use this the Zeigarnik effect to entice players to continue playing so they complete any necessary tasks.

Instead of the video game acknowledging players for completing the first two levels, the video game may do nothing. Once players complete the first two levels, then the video game displays a list showing their two completed levels along with the remaining eight levels. Because players see they've already completed two levels, they'll be more motivated to complete the remaining eight levels.

Yet if the video game had simply displayed all ten empty levels as uncompleted right from the start, players would be less motivated to even complete the first level. Thus the Zeigarnik effect can be a way to keep people playing longer.

Another form of extrinsic motivation occurs through leaderboards, which posts the highest scores of players for everyone to see. However, novices often find leaderboards intimidating because there's a vast difference between a beginner and an expert who has been playing for years.

Instead of displaying a leaderboard for all possible players, games typically display leaderboards for a much smaller group such as players with similar levels of experience. From a psychological point of view, people prefer to be near the top of a lower performing group than at the bottom of a higher performing group. So leaderboards often display your position among similar players. That way everyone can feel like they have a chance to move up the leaderboard.

Leaderboards can be particularly appealing when players can compare their rankings with their friends. This competitive aspect encourages both players to keep playing so they can surpass their friend's rankings, which in turn encourages their friends to keep playing as well.

Thought Exercise

Pick a video game and identify all the different ways this video game rewards players. Which types of rewards do you find most appealing? Which types of rewards do you find less motivating?

What types of achievements does the game give players? If the game allows multiple players, how does it display a leaderboard so you can compare your ranking to others? How does this leaderboard keep novices from comparing themselves to experts?

The Appeal of Near Misses

People are more likely to quit any game when they're losing by an overwhelming amount. That's why video games often disguise failure by showing players almost succeeding. These near misses are rarely seen as losses. Instead they're usually seen as near successes. Because players feel they almost succeeded, they feel the urge to try one more time.

Slot machines use this concept of near misses to make players feel like they're close to success. No matter how many times people lose, the slot machine makes them feel like they almost won. Similarly, video games use this idea of near misses to make players feel like if they just try one more time, they'll succeed. Since players feel like they're on the verge of success, they won't want to give up.

Seeing near misses as a sign of success instead of failure is the key to making games addictive. After all, nobody wants to quit when they're ahead and nobody wants to quit when they keep getting so close to winning.

Video games use near misses to motivate players in combat, movement, and even economics. In combat, players may lose, but they almost defeated the enemy. In movement, players may fail at jumping from one ledge to another, but they almost made it. In economics, players may need a certain amount of money or other resources to purchase a much needed item, but they're just short.

The dangling appeal of near misses makes players keep trying one more time because success seems just barely out of their reach. The end result is that players wind up spending more time playing the game in pursuit of this illusionary success.

Thought Exercise

Pick a video game and look for ways that the game makes failure look more like a near success. How does the game make you feel when you almost succeed? How would the game make you feel if it was blatantly obvious that you failed?

Dealing with Toxic Behavior

When playing any game, players must deal with toxic behavior of others. In card or board games, players often know each other and since they're sitting in the same room, there's less of a chance that one player's behavior will get so obnoxious that the others will simply abandon the game rather than tolerate one person's behavior any longer.

However, with online video games, toxic behavior is far more common. Part of that reason stems from the anonymous nature of online video games where people can hide their face and real names from others. When you're anonymous, it's far easier to behave the way you want with much less risk of any consequences whatsoever.

Besides the anonymity that online video games offer, there's also the opportunity to play with people you don't even know. With card or board games, you're physically sitting in the same room as the other players, even if you've only met them for the first time so there's a social element encouraging people to get along. With online video games, the combination of anonymity and complete strangers you may never meet again further encourages toxic behavior because there are no consequences.

Any video game that allows social interaction with others must deal with the problem of toxic behavior. One solution is to remove anonymity from players by forcing them to use their real names and possibly entering other personal information such as their home address so the game publisher can identify players.

Even if other players cannot see the real names and personal information of other players, the game publisher can. Remove complete anonymity and players will more likely behave better among others.

To further enforce acceptable behavior, many online games allow players to report certain players for abusive language and unacceptable behavior. Players typically receive warnings of their behavior but if it continues, the game publisher will often ban those players for a limited time. If their behavior still doesn't change, they may get banned for good.

By allowing players to report and identify problem players, the gaming community as a whole can (hopefully) self-regulate itself. Even with these safeguards, toxic player behavior can still pop up far too often. The long-term solution is to use psychology to get toxic players from misbehaving in the first place.

Riot Games dealt with toxic behavior in League of Legends by disabling the cross chat option by default. That meant players could not talk to people on other teams but could only talk to their own team members.

Just this simple change reduced negative chats by 32.7% and increased positive chats by 34.5%. Because members on the same team needed to help each other, there was more of an incentive to remain positive to increase their chances of winning. By simply removing the default option to trash talk opponents, Riot Games found they could drastically reduce toxic behavior among all players.

Another psychological tactic Riot Games used was by displaying chat logs of reported players so the community could see exactly what players were accused of doing and then vote on whether that behavior was toxic or not.

By identifying behavior that the publisher tagged as toxic, accused players got clear feedback on what they did wrong. Once toxic players saw what they did, they often apologized and changed their behavior to avoid making the same mistakes again.

To further increase the chances that people would regulate themselves, Riot Games tested in-game tips to encourage positive behavior. Using both messages and colors, Riot Games found that specific messages displayed in different colors has a measurable effect on player behavior.

Stating "X% of players punished by the Tribunal improved their behavior and are never punished again" decreased verbal abuse by 6.35%. Displaying "Teammates perform worse if you harass them after a mistake" in the color red decreased verbal abuse by 6.22% However, displaying that same message in white caused no changes in behavior.

Stating "Players who cooperate with their teammates win X% more games" in the color blue decreased verbal abuse by 3.64%, but that same message displayed in red caused no changes in behavior.

Ultimately, Riot Games found that various psychological tactics showed measurable differences in player behavior. Combining multiple tactics can dramatically lower toxic player behavior within an online video game as toxic players find psychological reasons to regulate themselves.

Thought Exercise

Pick an online, multiplayer video game and identify all the ways the game tries to defuse toxic behavior among players. Which methods are most effective with you and why?

Summary

In any game, players want freedom but enjoying a game depends on following a constrained boundary and rules. Coercing players into following specific behavior will likely create resentment and rebellion. So a far better solution is to use psychological tactics to gently guide players into specific behaviors that can make a game more enjoyable. Such psychological tactics give players freedom of choice while directing them into behaviors that will increase their enjoyment of the game.

Whether players need help navigating around a game world or want to experience emotions from their actions, psychological tactics can make a game more enjoyable without the players even realizing they're being guided. Psychology can further motivate players to keep playing through a system of rewards, achievements, and leaderboards.

Finally, psychology can help reduce toxic behavior from others by helping players regulate themselves. Such self-regulation will be far more effective than outright coercive techniques that risk generating resentment from players who feel they're being forced to take certain actions. By using psychology, games can get players to do what the game designers want them to do while the players themselves cheerfully do it.

Further Readings

"Achievement Relocked: Loss Aversion and Game Design", Geoffrey Engelstein, The MIT Press, 2020.

"Elements of Game Design", Robert Zubek, The MIT Press, 2020.

"Getting Gamers: The Psychology Of Video Games And Their Impact On The People Who Play Them", Jamie Madigan, Rowman & Littlefield Publishers, 2019.

"Loss Aversion And Game Design", Chariot Rider, https://youtu.be/eAHDU9BDHyo.

"This Psychological Trick Makes Rewards Backfire", Game Maker's Toolkit, https://youtu.be/1ypOUn6rThM.

"How Your Personality Affects What You Play", Daryl Talks Games, https://youtu.be/gvjVP56r0BA.

"The Science Behind the Shaping Player Behavior in Online Games", Jeffrey Lin, https://archive.org/details/GDC2013Lin.

"How Riot Games Used Science to Curb Toxic Behavior in League of Legends", Katie Zigelman, https://www.spectrumlabsai.com/the-blog/how-riot-games-is-used-behavior-science-to-curb-league-of-legends-toxicity#:~:text=At%20GDC%202013%2C%20Jeff%20Lin,million%20 active%20players%20every%20day.

"7 Ways Games Use Psychology To Control You", Logitech G, https://youtu.be/A2gIE5gyA6s.

"Designing Addiction: The Twisted Psychology Of Game Design", goukigod, https://youtu.be/ K0M1PuQaE8s.

"Spies, Lies, and Algorithms: The History and Future of American Intelligence", Amy B. Zegart, Princeton University Press, 2022.

"Ambiguity of Play", Brian Sutton-Smith, Harvard University Press, 2001.

"Seven Rhetorics of Play – Game Design Basics", Godot Tutorials, https://youtu. be/0ReATHQHiD4.

Chapter 8
Game Balance

"The perception of balance is more powerful than balance itself."

– Jeff Kaplan, Overwatch game designer

The game Rock, Paper, Scissors perfectly defines game balance. Rock can defeat Scissors, Scissors can defeat Paper, but Paper can defeat Rock as shown in Fig. 8.1. That means no one option has more advantages over any other option. Thus the goal in game balancing is to make every option exactly equal.

Except for simple games like Rock, Paper, Scissors, perfect game balance is impossible. One reason for this is that simple games can be symmetric. That means each player can choose from the exact same set of options (Rock, Paper, or Scissors). Most sports, card, and board games are symmetric where players have the exact same options, but even then games can be slightly skewered to one side or the other. For example, the person who moves first in chess has a slight advantage while in baseball, the home team bats last so they have a slight advantage.

However, most games are asymmetric, which means that players may choose different options to compete against each other. It's relatively easy to balance a game with a limited number of options where each player has the exact same choices (Rock, Paper, Scissors). When there are a large number of options and players do not have the exact same choices, then game balancing becomes much harder.

In many historical wargames, each side may have different equipment and similar types of equipment can have drastically different features. A game simulating a battle between British tanks and German tanks is already inherently unbalanced because the forces are not exactly the same since one side may have more or less tanks than the other side.

Even more confusing is that German tanks have different advantages and disadvantages than British tanks. So even if the number of tanks are equal, the capabilities of each tank differ. Asymmetric games force players to use different strategies and tactics to exploit advantages of their forces while exploiting the disadvantages of the enemy forces.

W. Wang, *The Structure of Game Design*, International Series on Computer, Entertainment and Media Technology, https://doi.org/10.1007/978-3-031-32202-0_8

Fig. 8.1 Rock, Paper, Scissors represents a perfectly balanced game

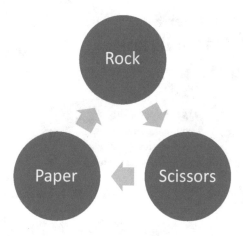

If one side has too much of an advantage (called overpowered or OP), this unbalances the game because there's no point in choosing any other side. If some playing units offer too little of an advantage, this can also unbalance a game because no one will bother even considering any option that can't help win the game.

So there's a risk that some units may be overpowered and some units may be too weak. In either case, players will either gravitate towards the overpowered options and completely ignore the much weaker options. In an ideally balanced game, every option must be equally useful or else there's no point in offering that option in the game.

Game balancing is all about making sure every part of a game can be useful in different situations. If certain options are never useful in any situation, then that option either should be cut from the game or modified so it can be useful in certain situations. When every option is just as useful as any other option, a game will be completely balanced.

Thought Exercise

Pick a card, board, or video game and identify if it's symmetric (all players start with the exact same options) or asymmetric (each player starts with a different set of options). If the game is symmetric, does one side have an advantage anyway?

If the game is asymmetric, are there certain (overpowered) options that are always good no matter what? Are there certain options that are never any good no matter what?

Balancing Quantity vs. Quality

At the simplest level, game balance is about making sure each player has the exact same choices at all times such as in chess, Go, checkers, or any sport. However balance is more than making sure players have the same quantity of options. In asymmetric games, each player has an unequal number of options so the only way to balance the game is to equalize the quality of each option.

One popular type of video game are tower defense games where the player controls a handful of weapons mounted on towers while the computer controls an infinite number of enemies. Even though the player is clearly outnumbered at all times, the player's weapons are vastly more powerful than the computer enemies, balancing out the numeric differences.

Balancing a game numerically involves making sure each side has the exact same quantity of options. However when each option is unequal, balancing a game is much harder because each unequal option can affect the others in unpredictable ways.

In many fighting games (Mortal Kombat, Street Fighter, etc.), each player can choose a fighter with different abilities. Unless both players choose the exact same character, the game will be asymmetric. The challenge lies in making sure that no matter which character players choose (out of dozens of available characters), the game must still give each player an equal chance to win.

Some fighters might rely on speed but the force of their attacks is much weaker. Other fighters might rely on strength, but they attack at a much slower rate. Some fighters are good at punching while others are better at kicking. Then each fighter has a unique move that's hard to do but gives massive damage to an enemy. Thus changing the abilities of each fighter is a delicate balancing act like building a house of cards. If even one character's abilities are too weak or too overpowering, the whole balance of the game falls completely apart.

Preventing games from getting unbalanced is hard with asymmetric games that offer multiple options of varying power. Change one characteristic and it may inadvertently affect another part of the game. Sometimes the answer lies in varying the quality of each option, but sometimes the answer lies in changing the quality of completely different options. Sometimes the answer might be eliminating an option altogether.

Because multiple, unequal options can interact in so many different ways, the number of possible interactions increases exponentially. This makes finding the imbalance difficult and correcting the imbalance even harder.

When designers find a game mechanic that's unbalanced, they'll often increase its power, which is called "buffing." An alternative is to weaken the powers of other game mechanics to bring them down to the level of the weaker game mechanic, which is called "nerfing."

This constant balance between increasing and decreasing power of different game mechanics can keep a game feeling fair to all players at all times based on feedback from the players.

Thought Exercise

Card and board games are usually symmetric games where all players start with the same options. Despite this, every game typically gives one or more players an advantage by when they take their turns (first, last, after another player, etc.).

Identify the advantage in a card or board game. How would the game change if this advantage did not exist? How could you eliminate this advantage?

Some video games are also symmetric, such as battle royale games where players on opposing teams may have the exact same options. However, many video games are asymmetric where players start with different options. How do such asymmetric video games balance the different, unequal options? Are there some options that are overpowered? Some options that are underpowered and totally pointless to choose?

Game Balance Is About Risk vs. Reward

Achieving absolute balance in any game is impossible. However, the real goal is to make players believe every option can be useful in the right circumstances. Thus game balance is really about making players feel their skill and choices can determine their chance of winning. The more choices available that all seem useful at any given time, the more the game will feel balanced. Victory depends partly on the game design but more on the player's skill in choosing the right combination of options.

Suppose you flip a fair coin that always has a 50–50 chance that it will land as Heads or Tails. Now players must choose between Heads or Tails. If they choose Heads and the coin lands on Heads, they win $1. Likewise, if they choose Tails and the coin lands on Tails, they also win $1. This game is completely balanced but boring. Because the choices between Heads or Tails is equal, winning (making money) is more a matter of luck than decision-making.

Suppose the game changes by letting players decide how much to wager each time. The game is still balanced, but because players can control the amount they bet, they feel more in control of the game results. If they lose all their money, it's because they made bad decisions. If they make a lot of money, it's because they made good decisions.

Change the game some more and suppose if a player wins, they have the option of tripling their money if they bet their winnings on the next coin flip. Because players have the additional freedom of another choice, they feel more in control of the game's outcome.

Suppose we unbalance the game and use a rigged coin that comes up Heads 75% of the time but only Tails 25% of the time. Now if the player bets on Heads, they only double their money (betting $1 gives them $2 in return) but if they bet on Tails, they get ten times the amount they bet (betting $1 gives them $10 in return).

Even though this game is completely unbalanced mechanically (the chances of Heads or Tails is not equal), the game is still balanced in the player's mind because they have the freedom to choose either option.

Mechanically a game may be unbalanced, but if the rewards are large enough, players will accept the higher risks in return for higher rewards. So one way to solve an unbalanced game mechanic is to change the game so the mechanic becomes balanced (50–50 chances of Heads or Tails). A second way to balance a game is to change the ratio of risk vs. rewards. Now players will accept an unbalanced game mechanic if it gives them a chance to risk higher rewards in exchange for a lower chance of success.

Games of chance (casino games) are always unbalanced in favor of the house. People still play these games because the rewards (hitting a jackpot) seem far more appealing than the risk of seemingly minor losses. The challenge in playing an unbalanced game comes from the player trying to win despite the unbalanced nature of the game.

The more choices players can make, the more they feel in control of the outcome no matter how unbalanced a game might be (such as craps or roulette). Even though an unbalanced game works against players, most players will accept their losses due to their own decisions rather than to the stacked odds against them.

Ironically, few people would play casino games for free. Even though there's no chance they could lose, there's also nothing to gain. The promise of money makes casino games appealing to large numbers of people despite the odds against them.

Thought Exercise

Pick a game and identify an unbalanced part of the game. Why is that unbalanced part still in the game? Is there a high reward for choosing that unbalanced option? How do the number of choices make an unbalanced game appealing?

Study a casino game like roulette or craps and count the number of choices players can make. If the casino game only gave players one choice, would the casino game still be interesting and appealing to play?

Defining the Cost of Advantages and Disadvantages

Every game will be unbalanced in one form or another. Designers can nerf or buff the various game options to balance the game out, but this risks simply unbalancing the game in other areas. Designers can also give greater rewards for choosing options with lower chances of success as another way to balance the game. A third way to balance a game is to add costs.

If a particular item in a game provides too great an advantage, give that advantage an added cost. For example, a certain gun in a first-person shooter might be too powerful so some ways to adjust its cost could be:

- Weight
- Size
- Available ammunition

Adding a weight cost could make such a powerful weapon less appealing because players might have to carry fewer supplies such as food or water. Adding a size cost could be another way to limit the weapon's effectiveness. Perhaps the gun is simply too big to use in narrow hallways and corridors in the same way that a submachine gun or a pistol makes a better weapon for trench warfare than a shoulder-fired missile launcher.

Limiting the amount of ammunition available for a powerful weapon can be another way to reduce its effectiveness. Lugging a powerful gun around might dispatch enemies easily, but if you only have two shots, then players must decide if the carrying that gun instead of another, less powerful weapon, is really worth the risk of running out of ammunition and becoming defenseless.

Adding costs can be one way to balance a game. Another is to give discounts to less powerful options.

In a fantasy combat game, players might choose a sword as a standard weapon. If they want a more powerful pike ax, the length of the pike ax will be less practical in confined spaces and the weight of the pike ax might mean carrying less supplies.

So players could simply arm themselves with daggers instead of a sword. Daggers would cause far less damage and be harder to hit enemies, but their smaller size means players could move faster. This increased speed represents a discount to make up for the dagger's lower combat effectiveness.

A dagger would also weigh less, meaning players could carry more items such as food, healing potions, or another small weapon. Thus players could deliberately choose the weaker option (a dagger) to gain additional benefits (less weight and smaller size).

By manipulating the costs and discounts of various items, designers have another way to balance a game.

Thought Exercise

Pick a game and identify which part of the game is unbalanced. Does the game correct this imbalance by imposing higher costs on powerful items and discounts on weaker items? If not, would costs and discounts balance the game better?

Analyzing for Game Balance

Balancing a game is a combination of art and science. The art portion focuses on keeping players happy whether the game is actually balanced or not. In many video games, the game is actually unbalanced in favor of players so they'll have a more enjoyable experience. As long as players feel that the game is fair, the actual balance of the game won't make much of a difference.

The science portion focuses on the numbers that give designers information on how well different parts of a game work based on the reaction of players. One common way to measure game balance is to identify the following:

- Win rate
- Pick rate

The win rate refers to different game items and how often those items lead to a win. In a fighting game, the win rate measures how often each fighter character wins. Ideally, this win rate should be close to 50%.

By examining the win rate for multiple characters played by a large number of people, designers can identify which characters seem to be winning more often and which characters seem to be losing more often. Then they can tweak the game to bring this win rate closer to 50%.

The pick rate refers to how many times players choose a particular game item or character. The idea is that if almost everyone chooses an item, it's because that item gives players an enormous (and possibly unfair) advantage. Likewise, if players consistently avoid choosing specific items or characters in a game, that could be a huge clue that something is wrong with that item.

The pick rate for every item should also be around 50%, which means people are no more or less likely to choose that item. By adjusting a game so the pick rate of every item is close to 50%, designers can make games that feel fair and give every option in the game the same chance of winning.

To capture the win rate and pick rate of every item in a game requires lots of data. Knowing how ten people behave isn't statistically valid but knowing how ten million people behave can give you a much clearer view of how people generally play a particular game.

The win rate is not just a single number but a number for every possible combination. For example, fighting games offer dozens of characters. Therefore it's important to know the win rate of one character against all the other characters. As long as the win rate against every other character is roughly 50%, the game is balanced. It's entirely possible that the win rate might be roughly 50% against most characters but suddenly rise or drop against a single character. That drastic difference can signal where the imbalance occurs.

Calculating the win rate and pick rate requires tracking the behavior of large numbers of people and analyzing every major decision they make. Such exhaustive research can be time-consuming to collect and examine, but it's another tool designers can use to ensure their game is properly balanced.

Thought Exercise

Pick a game and identify one item, either a possession (such as a weapon) or a character. Based on your own experience with the game, is this item or character overpowered (higher win rate) or underpowered (lower win rate) against another other similar item or character?

Which item or character in a game is your favorite (pick rate) and why? Which item or character is your least favorite (pick rate) and why? Can you identify any evidence that could justify why something is your favorite and something is your least favorite?

The Mathematics of Game Balancing

To balance games, designers often rely on probabilities such as the win rate or pick rate. The easiest data for game designers to manipulate are numeric data. For example, identifying popular choices boils down to counting what percentage of people might choose a particular item. Without numeric data, it's difficult to compare one set of data to another.

The first step to gathering numeric data is to identify what type of numeric data to use. Pick rates and win rates are often defined as percentages because it's easy to see that a 73% win rate is unbalanced (not near 50%). On the other hand, saying 24,902 players won with a specific fighting character means nothing if you don't also know the number of players who won with other fighting characters.

Numeric data can often be represented as percentages or fractions, depending on which would make the data easier to understand. When rolling a fair six-sided die, there are six possible outcomes so getting one particular outcome (such as a 5) has a 1 in 6 chance of occurring. Since every other number also has a 1 in 6 chance of occurring, that means all numbers have an equal chance of appearing on a single die throw.

Notice that stating a number has a 1 in 6 chance of appearing can sometimes be clearer than saying a number has a 16.7% chance (1/6) of occurring, even though it's the exact same value. By viewing probabilities as a fraction, it's easy to see at a glance the number of all possibilities (6).

Probabilities can appear as either fractions or percentages, but the range of probabilities always ranges from 0 to 1 (or 0% to 100%). That means something may have zero probability of occurring or certain probability of occurring. However, there's no way anything can have a negative probability or a higher probability than certainty (100%).

Probabilities typically identify what can happen, but the opposite can also identify how that same chance might not happen. For example, throwing a 3 on a six-sided die has a 1 in 6 chance of occurring. To determine the chances of not throwing a 3, simply subtract from 1 such as:

Chance of throwing a 3 on a six-sided die = 1/6
Chance of not throwing a 3 on a six-sided die = 1–1/6 or 5/6

Seeing the chances of something not occurring simply gives another perspective on the exact same probability. At any given time, the probability of something occurring and the probability of something not occurring must always equal 1 (100%).

In many cases, probabilities define the chance that a single outcome will occur. However, sometimes you may want to know the chance that two or more, mutually exclusive outcomes might occur. For example, what if you wanted to know if a six-sided die throw will come up 1 or 6?

Mutually exclusive probabilities can be represented by the Boolean logic operator OR, which means calculating the odds that either a 1 or a 6 will occur by throwing a six-sided die.

When calculating mutually exclusive probabilities (OR), calculate each probability separately and then add them together. So the chance that a six-sided die will display 1 is 1/6. Likewise, the chance that a six-sided die will display 6 is also 1/6. Add these two probabilities together to get the total probability that a six-sided die will display 1 or 6:

$$1/6 + 1/6 = 2/6 \left(1/3 \, \text{or} \, 33.33\%\right)$$

By examining the fraction, it's easy to understand that this probability is accurate. Since we want a 1 or 6 to appear, those represent two possible numbers out of six possible numbers (2/6).

Instead of calculating the chances of two separate, mutually-exclusive outcomes, what if you wanted to calculate the chances of two or more outcomes occurring one after another? For example, what is the chance that throwing a six-sided die will display a 1 on the first throw and another 1 on the second throw?

Since the outcome of each throw of the die is completely independent (the outcome of one die throw does not affect the outcome of the second die throw), multiply the probabilities. The odds of throwing a 1 on the first throw of a six-sided die is 1/6. Then the odds of throwing a 1 on the second throw is also 1/6 so the total probability is:

$$1/6 \times 1/6 = 1/36$$

Completely independent outcomes must occur sequentially in the correct order, which makes the odds much lower. Horse race betting uses this to offer bettors greater rewards in return for lower chances of success. A daily double forces bettors to guess the winning horse in two consecutive races.

The odds of picking one winning horse is low, but the odds of picking the winning horse in the next race is equally low. Combined, the total odds of picking two winning horses in back to back races are extremely low, but that's why daily doubles pay so well when they do occur. Someone always wins a daily double but the odds will always be against you being that winner.

While it's possible to calculate and store data by hand, it's far more common to use a spreadsheet. Spreadsheets not only make it easy to organize and calculate data, but create charts from that data as well. Visually examining data can help you spot trends. Then you can examine the actual numeric data that makes up that chart to get specific details.

Numeric data helps you identify imbalances in a game. By adjusting numeric values, designers can balance a game until it "feels" right regardless of the numeric data. The numeric probability data simply helps designers identify and balance a game, but choosing the exact numeric values to make that game balanced relies on the designer's intuition and player feedback. In many cases, games that skewer results slightly in the player's favor will create a more enjoyable game experience.

Thought Exercise

Pick a game and identify the probabilities of different outcomes. State the probability as a fraction and as a percentage. State the probabilities of an outcome not happening. Store the results in a spreadsheet and create a chart displaying the probabilities.

Calculate two or more mutually exclusive outcomes. Calculate two or more dependent outcomes.

Summary

At the simplest level, game balancing is similar to the Rock, Paper, Scissors game where no single option holds an advantage over all other options. Instead, each option is better than others but also weaker in different situations.

Ideally, games should be completely balanced using numeric data such as win rate or pick rate. Symmetric games are easiest to balance while asymmetric games are much harder because of different starting conditions.

Game balance involves risk vs. reward. The lower the risk, the lower the reward. The higher the risk, the higher the reward. Every option often has a cost and a disadvantage. By adjusting the cost and/or disadvantage of each item in a game, designers can achieve a fair balance.

Designers use numeric data to identify probabilities as fractions or percentages. The lowest probability is always 0 and the highest probability is always 1 (100%). The probability of something not happening can be calculated by subtracting from 1 such as:

Probability of 2 appearing on a six-sided die = 1/6
Probably of 2 not appearing on a six-sided die = 1–1/6–5/6

When calculating mutually exclusive probabilities, add them together. When calculating sequential probabilities that are independent from one another, multiple them together.

Ultimately, game balance is all about adjusting a game towards achieving a specific goal, whatever the purpose of the game might be.

Further Readings

"Balancing Mechanics for Your Game's Power Curve", GDC, https://youtu.be/ul1MSQ8aW00.

"Game Balance", Ian Schreiber, CRC Press, 2021.

"How Games Get Balanced", Game Maker's Toolkit, https://www.youtube.com/watch?v=WXQzdXPTb2A.

"Top 10 Tips On How To Balance Your Game", Jonas Tyroller, https://youtu.be/uo9qIDbJvT8.

Part II
Finding the Fun in Games

No matter how well designed a game might be, games can only succeed if people find them fun to play. Yet the definition of "fun" is entirely subjective. One person might enjoy the thrill of running around while someone else might prefer the challenge of outwitting an opponent. Not all games will appeal to everyone, but every type of game must appeal to a target niche.

So what makes a game fun? Beyond superficial appearances of fancy graphics and imaginary settings in history, fantasy, or the present day, games provide a structured challenge for players to achieve. Sometimes players may compete against others, sometimes players may cooperate with others, and sometimes players may do both. In any game, overcoming challenges is what defines the fun in a game.

This part of the book divides different types of challenges, how they work, and why players find them interesting. Simple games may only provide a single element of fun such as in children's games like tag, where the fun lies in running around. More complex games provide multiple elements of fun to provide greater and more complicated challenges that makes the game appealing to play over and over again.

Games can only succeed when they're fun to play, so understanding how to create fun is what game design is all about.

Chapter 9
Understanding Fun

Games should be fun, but everyone has a different idea what fun means. One person might like the thrill of escaping zombies or serial killers in a horror game while someone else might enjoy solving complicated word puzzles. Some people might find both types of games fun but may also like playing sports simulation games as well.

Although everyone enjoys different types of games, games are fun because of the challenges they pose to players. The way each game appeals to people depends on a combination of:

- Expectation
- Predictability
- Exploration of new worlds
- Choice and control
- Achievement
- Community

Expectation in Games

There are literally thousands of possible games anyone can buy and play at any given time. To help people identify the types of games they might enjoy, games target distinct genres where each game genre offers specific experiences so players can easily choose the game they want to play based on the emotion they want to feel.

A horror game focuses on fear and survival in a hostile environment while a vehicle simulation game focuses on letting players fantasize about controlling actual machines in real situations such as flying World War II fighter planes in the

© The Author(s), under exclusive license to Springer Nature
Switzerland AG 2023
W. Wang, *The Structure of Game Design*, International Series on Computer,
Entertainment and Media Technology,
https://doi.org/10.1007/978-3-031-32202-0_9

Battle of Britain or driving Formula One race cars on the famous Le Mans racetrack in France.

No matter what game people play, they want to feel powerful. That means players want to experience mastery over a game by developing their skills needed to reach the end of the game or whatever goal players might have set for themselves.

The following lists common game genres and the main emotional experience players expect from them:

- Action – Excitement and power in speed and combat.
- Horror – Fear by trying to run and escape from monsters.
- Stealth – Cleverness by trying to sneak past obstacles without being detected.
- Sports – Fantasy in controlling athletes in a popular sport.
- Vehicle simulator – Fantasy in controlling real or imaginary machines in combat or sports.
- Strategy – Fantasy in controlling a large organization.
- Puzzle – Intellectual challenge in solving difficult problems.
- Role-playing – Fantasy in pretending to be another person in another world.
- Comedy – Laughter in mocking something.
- Open world/sandbox – Curiosity in exploring a new world.

Every game genre promises a certain experience so any game within that genre must deliver on that experience. If you violate that genre's expectations, you'll disappoint players regardless of the quality of the game.

Consider a game with a title like "Kitten Rampage." The title alone hints that it's a comedy game but if the actual game showed a kitten tearing people apart with realistic bloody images while players try to hide and escape, then the game would emphasize horror instead of comedy. This would disappoint players just as much as if they were expecting a horror game but got a comedy or puzzle game instead.

Players seek fun in games that promise to recreate past experiences that players have enjoyed in other games. Genres act like shortcuts to help players quickly find which games they'll most likely find enjoyable.

Thought Exercise

Pick a video game at random and based on the title, trailer, and art, can you guess what type of experience the game promises players? If not, what is not clear?

Pick any game and imagine it fitting in a completely different genre. How would the gameplay need to change to match this new genre?

Pick a game in a genre you don't normally enjoy. What could a game do in that genre that would appeal to you and make you want to play it?

Predictability in Games

There's a saying in Hollywood that explains why studios constantly remake movies and TV shows along with making sequels to popular films: "Give me the same thing, only different."

Essentially people want what they already like, but they also want something new. These seemingly contradictory goals work in the gaming industry as well. People want games similar to what they already like, but they also want a slightly different experience.

If someone likes playing simulation games where they can pretend to manage an amusement park, they might also like a similar simulation game where they can pretend to manage a football team. When people play games, they often enjoy certain genres and play games within the same genres.

That means players expect other games, within the same genre, to give the same type of experience, but in a different setting. For a game designer, it's crucial to study games within the genre of your own game design, and see what works and what could be improved.

By mimicking the best features of popular games, your own game can be easy for new players to learn as long as they're familiar with that genre. By improving on existing features (or creating entirely new ones), you can make your game different while still being nearly the same. Basically, games must be predictable enough to fit within a specific genre, but different enough to entice people to buy and play it.

Players find fun in games they can predict and thus understand easily. By playing the same game or same type of game, players can gradually develop their skills and gain a sense of mastery, and that makes the entire process fun and enjoyable.

Thought Exercise

Pick two or more video games in any genre and identify what features they share. What makes each game different?

Pick two video games in different genres. What features do these two games share? What features are unique to each genre?

Exploring New Worlds in Games

Games, like movies, books, and music, help us ignore real life if only for a moment. The more we can ignore reality, the more appealing any form of entertainment can be. Unlike real life, games provide boundaries that define a safe area that encourages experimentation (and failure) by offering a clear path towards overcoming obstacles and reaching a specific achievement. Games provide a sense of clarity and certainty that's not always easy to find in the real world.

Role-playing games let players pretend to be another person, either an enhanced version of themselves or an alter ego of who they wish they could be. Simulation games let players fantasize about controlling actual vehicles in realistic situations, or controlling large organizations to see if their choices could run a city or business successfully.

First-person shooter games let players pretend to be powerful heroes while sports games let players fantasize about playing at a professional level. Horror and survival games let players explore mysteries and test their wits to survive against the odds. Puzzle, stealth, and mystery games challenge players to find non-obvious ways to solve different types of problems.

The more a game can tap into a player's fantasies by putting them in a world outside their regular life, the more appealing the game will be. The more a game gives players the feeling of controlling events in another world, the more the game will be fun to play.

Part of the fun in any game comes from learning, playing, and eventually mastering skills in an alternate world whether that alternate world is just a playing field in a stadium, a location in our own world that most people never experience (such as crime scenes), or a complete fantasy world populated by dragons and elves. New worlds essentially let people play "let's pretend" in a structured and safe environment.

Thought Exercise

Pick a game in a genre you don't enjoy and ask yourself why games in that genre would appeal to anyone. Then pick a game in a genre that you do enjoy and identify all the reasons why you like games from that genre.

Can you think of any game that does not create a different or alternate world for people to play in?

Choice and Control in Games

Games provide clear goals for players to achieve. To reach these goals, games define rules that force players to choose from different options. By offering a fixed set of options for players to choose from at any given time, games let players control their actions in ways that's not always possible in the real world.

Clear choices combined with a feeling of control gives players a sense of mastery within the artificial world of a game. If a game only offered two choices, players would likely find the game too limiting. However, if a game offers multiple choices, then players can analyze their different options and choose what they think is the best option. Choosing from multiple options gives players a feeling of control within the game.

Even better, players should see the results of their choices. Such feedback lets players know whether their choices are helping or hindering them in pursuit of whatever goal they want to achieve. This feeling of control increases fun by letting players experiment with different choices just to see what might happen.

The more choices you give players, the more they can feel in control. The more players feel in control, the more they'll play around to see what they're capable of doing. Once players know what they can do, they'll focus their control towards helping them achieve a specific goal.

Choice can be fun by giving players options. Too few options make a game boring like Tic-Tac-Toe. Too many options can make a game feel overwhelming, which is what often frustrates novices learning a complicated game for the first time. The key is offering just enough choices to make players feel in control but not too many choices that players feel out of control.

More importantly, each choice should feel meaningful by creating predictable outcomes. The more predictable the choices, the more players will feel in control. Games aren't just about what players can do, but about understanding when and why they should choose different choices to affect the outcome of a game.

The fun in choices comes from trying to make the best choice at any given time and seeing whether you did it or not.

Thought Exercise

Pick your favorite game and identify how many choices you can select in the beginning of the game. How many choices can you choose in the middle of the game? How many choices can you choose near the end of the game?

When you make choices in a favorite game, how do those choices give you more control over the game? How does this control make the game more (or even less) fun to play?

Pick a game you don't like and examine the choices the game offers. What do you not like about the available choices? What do you like about the available choices?

Achievement in Games

When playing any game, people want to feel their activities have a purpose. If it's a puzzle, people want to find the solution. If it's an action game, people want to wipe out all the enemies and reach a goal. If it's a vehicle simulation, people want to explore all the different ways to control the simulated vehicle while trying to achieve a result. In all games, players want a reason to justify their actions.

A reason gives every player a purpose for playing a game. This purpose is the whole point of the game, so striving to achieve this purpose can give players a sense of triumph when they finally reach the game's goal.

Part of the fun in a game comes from striving towards a clearly defined goal and getting acknowledged for your accomplishments along the way. Achievements often appear in a game as badges, titles, on leaderboards, or by custom appearances for an avatar within a game to provide a visual acknowledgement of a player's progress.

Constantly acknowledging a player's achievements gives players motivation to continue playing the game. Players rarely continue playing to get more recognition, but recognition rewards players for how far they've gotten in the game. Each achievement recognition shows how much closer the player is to their ultimate goal, which can spur them on to keep playing until they finally complete the game's goal.

People don't play to receive achievements but recognition of any kind helps validate a player's time spent playing the game. However, achieving both minor and major goals within a game provides a challenge for players and a sense of accomplishment when they finally reach it. The more challenging a game, the more emotional satisfaction players will experience when they finally master it.

The fun comes from the activity in the game. Any rewards or recognition for having fun is just an extra bonus to reward players for the time they've already spent playing the game.

Thought Exercise

Pick a video game and identify how the game rewards a player's progress while playing. How often does the game acknowledge a player's progress? Does the game provide the player with any benefits or just recognition (or both)?

Pick a favorite video game that you play frequently and identify whether the game's acknowledgements of your progress make the game better or worse to play.

Community in Games

People play board and card games for social reasons. Games give people a common goal to pursue while enjoying each other's company in the process. Although it's possible to play a board or card game by yourself, it's rarely as entertaining as playing with others.

Because a computer can substitute for a human opponent, video games have the option of letting players enjoy the game all by themselves. On the other extreme, the Internet now gives players the option of playing with people all over the world.

Yet even if someone enjoys playing a video game by themselves, they still have the chance of being part of a larger community, and that represents another way games can be fun. Communities centered around specific games can help people meet other opponents so they can play together, or just provide them with a new pool of possible friends who at least share the same interest in a particular game.

Popular video games often encourage fans to create art or stories based on the game, or even create their own modifications (mods) and levels to expand the game for others to enjoy as well. The more popular a game, the larger its supportive community and the more active the game modifications, making the game even more interesting to play.

The fun in communities comes from using a game as a social tool to reach out and connect with others. By playing together or simply sharing a common interest, communities centered around games can make people feel less isolated so they can find friends no matter what part of the world they may live in.

Thought Exercise

Pick a board or card game and identify how that game makes it easy for people to interact. Pick a video game, meant to be played alone, and identify how this game can provide a community for players to join. Pick a video game, meant to include multiple players online, and identify how this game provides a community for players.

What ways do communities make a game more enjoyable to play? How easy is it to find a community around a video game? Around a board or card game? Around a sport?

What benefits do people get from belonging to a community centered around a game? Could they get these benefits without the game?

Summary

The whole purpose of a game is to entertain people. Games do this by offering different ways to have fun. Players can have fun through a game that's similar to what they already know, look for something different, immerse themselves in a new world, exhibit control and mastery over skills, strive for regular achievements, and join a community of like-minded individuals to create a shared experience.

Fun is relative but there's always a way for everyone to enjoy themselves with the right game. To increase its appeal, games should emphasize different aspects of fun such as emphasizing community or realistic new worlds to explore. By emphasizing different aspects of fun, a game can be similar enough to attract attention but different enough to stand out. Ultimately, games are fun because they provide multiple ways to keep people entertained.

Further Reading

"A Theory of Fun for Game Design", Raph Koster, O'Reilly Media, 2013.

Chapter 10
Fun in Movement

All games involve movement. Either the players themselves move (such as in sports) or the players move pieces that act as surrogates for the player (such as playing pieces in a board game or a digital avatar in a video game).

Movement changes the player's state. Through movement, players can get closer towards achieving the goal of the game. In addition, movement can also block other players from achieving the goal of the game first. In some games, players must always move, such as in chess or in sports like marathon running. In other games, such as in first-person shooter video games, players have the option to do nothing.

Remaining stationary can be useful to plan the next move, rest and regain health, lie in wait to ambush another player, or reload or change weapons in safety. However, players must eventually move if they want to win the game.

Movement can be discrete or continuous. Discrete movement defines fixed intervals for both time and space. In many board games, players take turns moving their playing pieces. Board games, and some video games, may also constrain movement of playing pieces to specific areas. These areas may be irregularly shaped but often consist of uniformly shaped grids of squares or hexagons that define valid spaces where playing pieces can move as shown in Fig. 10.1.

In contrast to discrete movement, other games allow continuous movement in time and space. In many sports, such as boxing or horse racing, players can move whenever they want at any speed that they choose. The distances players move can vary but is not constrained to artificial areas so players can move at any time, in any direction, and stop wherever they wish.

Discrete movement sacrifices realism for preciseness in the game. In this way, players can easily understand the position of their pieces in relation to other objects on the playing field at all times. Turn-based and strategy games often use discrete time so players can analyze the game before making their next move.

Continuous movement sacrifices clarity for realism. Real-time, action games often use continuous movement to provide greater control and freedom within the

© The Author(s), under exclusive license to Springer Nature Switzerland AG 2023
W. Wang, *The Structure of Game Design*, International Series on Computer, Entertainment and Media Technology,
https://doi.org/10.1007/978-3-031-32202-0_10

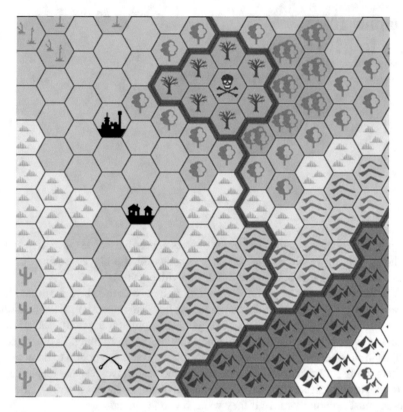

Fig. 10.1 Hexagons divide a map into discrete areas that regulate movement of game pieces

boundaries of the playing field. Continuous time puts players under pressure to respond because if they take too long making a decision, the game and the other players will move on without them.

Thought Exercise

Pick a turn-based game that divides movement within a regular grid overlaid on a map. How would this game change by making movement less discrete? How would this game change by forcing all players to react in real-time?

Pick a real-time game that allows continuous movement on a playing field. How would this game change by forcing movement into discrete areas such as squares or hexagons? How would this game change by forcing players to take turns?

Controlling Movement

In real-time games such as sports and video games, players strive to control their movements precisely and reliably. In sports, physical movement requires constant practice and rigorous training, yet a player's physical performance can still degrade due to fatigue over time. In video games, players must map the movements of their digital avatars to the input devices of the computer or game console.

Such input devices often include a keyboard, mouse, trackpad, game controller, virtual reality (VR) headset, or even a motion detector. Unlike sports where players know how to run and jump, video games force players to learn how to perform basic movement through input devices.

On a keyboard, the cursor keys offer the most obvious way to move up, down, left, or right, but those same actions can often be duplicated by pressing the W, S, A, and D keys respectively. Since controlling players in a video game is so important, many video games allow players to customize keyboard and mouse keys and buttons to control specific movements in a video game as shown in Fig. 10.2.

In video games, input devices can be digital or analog. Digital controls are either on or off, such as pressing a key on the keyboard or holding down a button on the mouse. Analog controls, such as joysticks, can represent a continuous range of

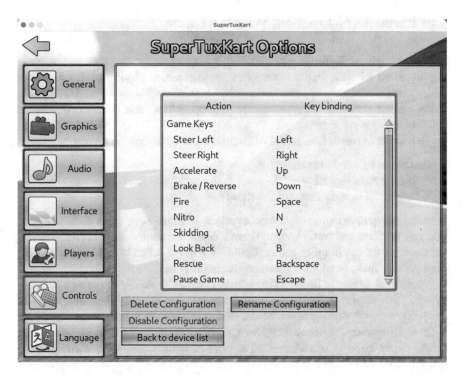

Fig. 10.2 Video games often let you customize the buttons and keys of the keyboard and mouse to specific actions

values, which can allow finer control. When designing video games, players can optimize input controls so games respond immediately to their commands. Often part of the fun in a video game comes from discovering and mastering various input shortcuts or combinations that allow greater control over digital avatars.

Real-time games such as sports and video games that rely on dexterity, physical movement plays a crucial role in determining success or failure. For that reason, movement plays a crucial role in how a game works and whether players enjoy it or not.

Thought Exercise

Pick a game that offers movement in discrete time and space such as a turn-based game that places units on a map overlaid with squares or hexagons. How would that game be different if players could move at the same time? How would that game be different if players did not conform to an artificial area on a map like squares or hexagons?

The Purpose of Movement Within a Game

Movement defines the fun in a game whether players are moving themselves, playing pieces on a board, digital avatars in a video game, or placing cards down on a table during a card game. Movement involves making decisions. By making consistently correct decisions (or more correct decisions than their opponents), players can eventually win the game.

To make movement fun, games often pose these questions to players:

- Can players even do the move?
- Is that the right move?
- What are the consequences of the move?

Movement in games can be certain or uncertain. In games such as checkers or poker, you can perform any valid move. There's never a question on whether you can choose a move, but in other games, choosing a move depends on the players skill (and perhaps luck) in whether they can successfully execute that move.

Sports and dexterity-based video games constantly challenge players to make moves. Thus players must choose between moves that are easy (but offer minimal rewards) or moves that are much harder (but offer greater rewards).

In fighting games (both real and virtual), players can make a simple move that causes slight damage, or risk making a more complicated move that could cause greater damage. The simple move may have an extremely high probability of success but the more complicated move may have a much lower probability of success.

Part of the fun in giving different types of movement various degrees of uncertainty is to encourage players to strive for mastery. The more players train and practice, the more likely they'll complete their chosen moves with much less risk of failure.

Mastery involves not only increasing the success rate for common moves, but also in performing moves that few people can do. The ability to perform rare moves gives players an added advantage in a game, especially if their opponents are unable to duplicate those same moves.

Beyond the certainty or uncertainty in completing a move, games provide additional fun in challenging players to make the right move. The greater the number of possible choices, the more challenging deciding the right move.

At all times, choosing a move means deciding on what players think is the right move. Since the game constantly changes, the right move at one time could be the wrong move at another time. In American football, teams that score a touchdown early in the game often choose the safe move of kicking 1 extra point afterwards, rather than take the risk of throwing or running the ball in the end zone for a 2 point conversion.

However late in the game when a team is trying to catch up before time runs out, they often choose the riskier 2 point conversion. Success increases their chance of winning while failure drastically decreases their chance of winning.

The more choices, the more challenging the game. Chess and Go offer astronomically number of possible moves players can choose at any given time. This makes chess and Go so appealing to so many people for centuries. On the other hand, games like Tic-Tac-Toe offer few possible moves and each additional move further narrows down the list of possible moves. The end result is that games like Tic-Tac-Toe reduce the challenge by progressively limiting the number of possible moves while chess and Go progressively increase the number of possible moves. The more possible moves, the more challenging it can be to choose the best possible move.

Being able to make a move and then choose the best possible move provides much of the fun in a game as players react to each other's choices. That's why the consequences of each move increases enjoyment and challenge in a game.

In fighting games, players have a choice between multiple types of attacks. If a player chooses a risky move and fails, that failure could leave them wide open to an easy counter-attack by their opponent. So not only do players risk failing in their move, but they also risk dramatically decreasing their chance of success in the future as well.

Even if players successfully complete a risky move, there might still be consequences afterwards. In a fighting game, successfully completing a risky move could add fatigue, limiting the possible choices of moves the player can make in the immediate future. In multi-player games, successfully completing a risky move could alert other players to your risk of winning, which could cause them to gang up against you as a result.

Completing a move with varying degrees of certainty, choosing the right move, and dealing with the consequences of each move is what makes games fun to play.

Thought Exercise

Pick a game where players are 100% certain in controlling their playing pieces. How does the game change if movement is less than 100% certain?

Pick a game where movement can be uncertain, such as sports like basketball or soccer. What happens if movement were suddenly changed to being 100% every time, how would that change the game?

Pick a favorite game and examine how the number of available options makes the game fun. Imagine cutting down the available options by 50% or more. Would that game still be fun to play?

Pick a game and identify two possible moves a player could make at any given time. Are there any consequences if the player should fail to make a move? Are there any consequences if the player should succeed in making a move?

What are the consequences if the player should fail in making that move? What are the consequences even if the player should succeed in making that move?

Making Movement Fun

On a basic level, movement within a game gets players one step closer towards a goal. The most common way to move characters in a video game is through walking, yet walking long distances can be boring. To make walking more interesting, video games offer several options:

- Allow users to vary their pace
- Display interesting settings to discover
- Threaten the user

The more options a game offers, the more freedom players have. For that reason, video games often give players the option to walk, jog, run, or sprint so they can choose the method they like best. While walking may seem the slowest, video games often provide different types of rewards for moving slower.

One technique is to display interesting settings for players to explore. These settings can simply further immerse players in the game world (such as a fantasy or science fiction world) or provide additional clues or supplies players need to reach their goal. By walking, players can increase their chance of finding something useful. By running, players may get somewhere faster but risk overlooking crucial clues or useful items such as weapons or food.

Another way to make movement interesting is to threaten the player. Horror games force players to move slowly to avoid making noise and attracting attention. Similarly, stealth video games encourage players to duck in and out of shadows while avoiding patrolling enemies. By giving different types of movement meaning and consequences, video games give players greater choices in how they want to play the game.

However, movement can serve multiple purposes than simply transporting players or playing pieces from one place to another.

Movement is often involved in combat. Players can either move closer (or farther away from) opponents, and that movement alone can be interesting since it can be part of the player's strategy within the game. Sometimes movement itself is the combat, such as checker pieces jumping over each other or video game characters, such as Mario, who moves side to side and jumps on top of enemies to destroy them.

Whether movement is part of combat or not, players must first learn how to move in a game. This means knowing what they can do as well as knowing what they cannot do. Initially, every player must learn the specific movements in a game, but eventually they'll move to the next stage where they practice mastery of the moves capable of helping them win the game.

In sports, this might mean mastering throwing, hitting, or catching a ball. In video games, this might mean mastering the controls needed to make a digital avatar move exactly the way you want. First, players must learn how to move. Second, players must learn to master their movements.

The stages for learning movement in a game typically involves:

- Learning how to move
- Mastering the movement
- Understanding how to apply different types of movement to overcome obstacles and challenges

In video games, movement can be an enjoyable feature in itself. Once players learn to move and start mastering their movements, they can tackle progressively more difficult game challenges that involve:

- Chaining moves
- Timing
- Using the environment

Chaining moves involves performing two or more individual moves in rapid succession, which can create unique outcomes. In baseball, left-handed hitters can perform a drag bunt. Unlike a normal bunt that simply drops the ball down on the infield, a drag bunt lets a left-handed hitter run and bunt at the same time. This knocks the ball down on the infield while giving the batter a head start in trying to reach first base.

In many fighting video games, players can duck, jump, move, punch, or kick. Novices often do one action at a time such as move and punch or jump and then kick. However, each fighter can respond to multiple input that creates a fighting combination unique to that specific fighter.

Of course, it doesn't do players any good just to learn any special combinations. Once they learn how to unlock special abilities, they must practice timing these moves for maximum effect against an opponent.

Any move done at the right time can succeed. Conversely, the right move done at the wrong time won't help the player and may even set the player further back from winning. After mastering movement, players must then master their ability to choose any movement at the optimum time, which takes practice and experience.

In many video games, players can time their different movements to move faster. Giving players options for moving and chaining multiple moves at specific times can challenge players to move in visually interesting ways that can be appealing in itself.

Just as movement can be an integral part of combat, so can movement change depending on the environment. Certain moves that may work in an open area may not be as effective (or may even be impossible to do) in a confined room.

Players may find they can move faster or move in ways to avoid enemies or obstacles by exploiting elements in their environment such as railings, wires, walls, or pillars. Now players can master movement and explore further advantages of those movements when paired with unique parts of the world around them.

Moving while taking advantage of the environment is the appeal of parkour, where players jump on railings and scale walls to get from one point to another. Similar ways of expressing movement can be found in games that allow players to use their environment for maximum effect like parkour, which makes moving fun in itself. Many players enjoy speed running, which involves completing a level or task as quickly as possible. Now the goal isn't just to reach goal, but to reach that goal faster than anyone else. Speed running adds a time limit to make movement even more challenging and fun.

Movement as combat and movement taking advantage of objects in the environment can keep players further engaged in exploring what they can do in a game. Rather than just offer movement as a way to get from one place to another, games can offer multiple purposes for movement to give players greater freedom and expression. These greater movement options give players something to discover, explore, and ultimately master.

Thought Exercise

Pick a video game that allows players to walk in the gaming world. How many other options for moving does the game offer besides walking? If players choose to just walk, how does the game make walking interesting?

Pick a video game that allows multiple purposes for movement. How do players discover these additional uses for movement? How does the environment help or hinder movement?

In many board games, players move and then fight. How would the game change if the game forced players to fight first and then move?

Video games often let players combine multiple movements to create something more powerful than each individual movement. How could you apply this idea to a board game?

Summary

Movement can involve just getting playing pieces or a digital avatar from one place to another, but movement can be so much more. Movement can involve walking, running, jumping, ducking, or climbing. In addition, movement can include combat where moving can attack enemies.

With multiple movements combined in rapid succession, players might be able to unlock capabilities unique to their particular digital avatar in a video game. Movement represents a major part of any game and should be fun, interesting, and useful.

Players must learn how to move in a game and then master those moves. Finally, players must control their movements to do precisely what they want exactly when they need it. These multiple challenges to controlling moving is what makes movement a large part of what makes a game enjoyable.

Further Readings

"How to Turn Movement into a Game Mechanic", Game Maker's Toolkit, https://youtu.be/rlmVxrq-3Go.

"How Game Designers Create Meaningful Mechanics", The Game Overanalyser, https://youtu.be/KkdPxZbUNSw.

"Good Game Design – Movement", Snoman Gaming, https://youtu.be/tAE2H5qJ8A8.

Chapter 11
Fun in Puzzles

Puzzles appeal to our need for order. When a puzzle confronts us with a problem, its lack of a visible solution creates internal discomfort. The greater our unease, the greater our emotional need to put life back in order by solving that puzzle. Solving a puzzle removes uncertainty and chaos and replaces it with order and predictability, which provides a sense of psychological satisfaction.

Puzzles often consist of two parts. The first part misleads us with a seemingly obvious (but incorrect or difficult) solution. The second part is the actual way to solve the puzzle, which is often disguised so it's easy to overlook.

This puzzle structure entices people to solve the puzzle using the most visible and seemingly obvious path, which leads to a dead end. Only by looking at the puzzle from a different perspective can people find the actual solution.

Consider this puzzle:

Two people ride a bicycle at 10 miles per hour heading in opposite directions. When both riders are 20 miles from each other, they ride towards each other in a straight line. At that moment, a fly on one bicycle heads towards the other bicycle. The fly travels at 15 miles per hour. Each time the fly reaches a bicycle, it turns around and heads towards the other bicycle. How far does the fly travel before the two bicycles meet?

The misdirection leads people to focus on the distance that the bicycles travel, decreasing the gap between them as the fly bounces back and forth. This seemingly obvious solution can work, but relies on a lot of complicated mathematics.

However, the real solution isn't to focus on the distance but the time. If both bicycles travel at 10 miles per hour and start 20 miles from each other, they'll meet after each has travelled 10 miles. Since they travel at 10 miles per hour, that means it will take them 1 hour before they meet.

Since the fly travels 15 miles an hour, after 1 hour, it will have travelled 15 miles, which is the answer.

© The Author(s), under exclusive license to Springer Nature Switzerland AG 2023
W. Wang, *The Structure of Game Design*, International Series on Computer, Entertainment and Media Technology,
https://doi.org/10.1007/978-3-031-32202-0_11

Puzzles may be a challenge by themselves or as part of a game. Crossword puzzles, Rubik's cubes, and sudoku puzzles are meant to be enjoyed on their own. The moment you solve the puzzle, you need new puzzles to continue playing. In the case of Rubik's cube or jigsaw puzzles, you can scramble the pieces to create a new puzzle although solving the same puzzle a second time is rarely as challenging as trying to solve it the first time.

In some video games, the puzzle itself is the main purpose of the game. For example, mystery video games challenge players to solve a crime by collecting clues and interrogating suspects. Based on this information, players must deduce who the criminal might be.

In other types of video games, puzzles act like locked doors that block access. Solving the puzzle unblocks access like a key. These types of puzzles are meant to be solved once so the player can continue progressing towards a larger goal.

Some of the different ways puzzles can block access include:

- Access to areas (such as a locked room or hallway leading to another area)
- Access to information (such as finding and reading a diary containing clues to a murder)
- Access to items (such as a magical shield or ammunition for a gun)

The Risks of Puzzles

Because puzzles often block access within a video game, there's the risk that if a player fails to solve a puzzle, that puzzle could completely stop a player's progress. That means a puzzle should never be too difficult for the average person to solve. Some ways to ensure that a player can get past a puzzle include:

- Offer multiple ways to gain access besides solving the puzzle
- Offer multiple ways to solve the puzzle
- Offer hints for the player
- Provide different difficulty levels for puzzles
- Make the puzzle solvable with items visible near the puzzle

No matter how well you design a puzzle, someone will find it too frustrating to solve. To avoid stopping these types of players from completing a game, offer several options for achieving access. Instead of solving a puzzle, players might be able to find a key to unlock a door instead. They may also be able to find an alternate path around the puzzle. The more options to bypass a puzzle, the less likely the puzzle will completely frustrate any player unable to solve the puzzle.

Since a puzzle can block access, another option is to provide multiple solutions to a puzzle. In chess, there are numerous ways to checkmate a king using two different pieces. You could use a king and a pawn, a bishop and a knight, a rook and a queen, and so on. So if your puzzle focuses on a specific outcome regardless of the exact method needed to achieve that outcome, players have a greater chance of solving that puzzle.

One possible solution for dealing with any puzzle might even be not to solve it at all. If your game makes a puzzle optional, players can choose to solve the puzzle or skip it altogether. By giving players the option to skip a puzzle, the game ensures players can never get stuck. By not solving a puzzle, players might miss out on additional money, weapons, or treasures, but they'll still be able to continue playing the game.

If a puzzle can only be solved one way, your game can offer hints if the player asks. These hints keep a player from getting stuck. That way they can still gain access despite not solving the puzzle on their own. Remember, the purpose of a puzzle isn't to stop players but just to slow them down and (ideally) force them to learn something about the game and the game world at the same time.

Since not everyone enjoys puzzles, another option is to give players an option to set a difficulty level for the puzzles within a game such as Easy, Medium, or Hard. That way players who want a challenge can choose the Hard option while players who aren't as good at solving puzzles can choose the Easy option.

Multiple difficulty levels for puzzles can also increase re-playability. If players enjoy the game, they might replay it using a different difficulty level. Now the game will be different enough to challenge them.

When choosing a puzzle solution, some games scatter clues in different areas. This can frustrate players if they miss a particular clue and need to leave the puzzle and travel somewhere else just to retrieve that one clue.

A better option is to put all clues near the puzzle itself. That way players know they have all the tools needed to solve the puzzle. Now they can exhaustively try every possible combination until they find the answer. As long as you ensure that a puzzle doesn't completely ruin a game for players unable to solve that puzzle, you can make sure everyone can enjoy your game.

Thought Exercise

Pick a game where a puzzle completely frustrated you. Why did this happen? Pick a game where you could solve a puzzle. How did the game make it easier to solve the puzzle?

Designing a Puzzle

When designing any puzzle, start with the solution first so you know the answer. Then work backwards to the beginning state of the puzzle. By defining the beginning state of a puzzle, you'll know exactly what the puzzle will look like when players see it for the first time. By defining the ending state of the puzzle, you'll know what the solution looks like.

Once you know both the beginning state to the ending state of a puzzle, the next step is to define how the player can get from the beginning state to the ending state. Specifically, what does the player need to do?

There are two types of activities needed to solve any puzzle:

- The number of steps needed
- The time needed

The fewer the steps needed, the easier the puzzle. Similarly, the less time needed for each step, the easier the puzzle.

Think of a combination lock. Normally a combination locks displays numbers ranging from 1 to 36 and you have to turn them clockwise, counter-clockwise, and then clockwise again to three specific numbers. This makes guessing the right three number combination extremely difficult.

Instead of three steps (clockwise, counter-clockwise, and clockwise), what if a combination lock only required one step (clockwise) to spin the dial to the correct number? Since there are 36 different possible numbers, someone could eventually open this combination lock by exhaustively trying every number. Thus the reduced number of steps makes it easier to guess the right combination (a single number).

Spinning a dial to exhaustively try each number takes a minimal amount of time. What if the combination lock only let you make one guess every hour? In a worst case scenario, this would mean exhaustively trying 36 different numbers, which would take 35 hours (1 hour for each failed attempt). By increasing the amount of time needed, guessing the right combination suddenly becomes much harder.

When designing a puzzle, you can adjust the puzzle difficult by adjusting the number of steps needed and the time needed for each step. Once you know how to solve the puzzle, the next step is to mislead people.

Misdirection can work in two ways. First, play on people's assumptions and desire to try the most obvious idea first, which will lead to a dead end. Second, create assumptions in the player's mind that they must break to find the right answer. Breaking this assumption forces the player to follow a completely different path. As long as they stick with the obvious path, they'll never find the answer.

Consider the puzzle of connecting nine dots using four lines without lifting your pencil off the paper as shown in Fig. 11.1.

The misdirection comes from the nine dots forming a rectangle, so people naturally assume you can't draw a line past these artificial boundaries of this non-existent rectangle. That's why the solution requires breaking this assumption, as shown in Fig. 11.2, like this:

Puzzles consist of two parts: a key and a lock. The key is any element needed to solve the puzzle. The lock is where the key must go. By matching the key to the lock, players can solve a puzzle.

Suppose a puzzle forces players to collect three masks and then arrange those masks in a certain order to solve the puzzle. In this case, the masks are the keys and the area where players must place and arrange the masks are the lock.

If the three masks are near the lock, then players can just focus on arranging the masks in different orders until they solve the puzzle. However, if the three masks are

Fig. 11.1 The nine dot
puzzle problem

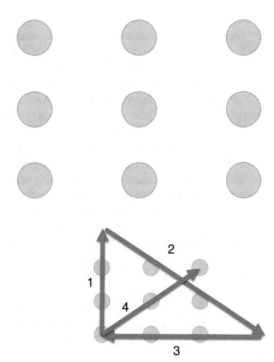

Fig. 11.2 One possible
solution to the nine dot
puzzle problem

scattered in different areas of a map, players must take time to find and collect them all, then bring them to the key. All of these extra steps make the puzzle harder to solve just because of the added amount of time needed to retrieve all the keys and bring them to the lock.

So another way to adjust the difficulty of a puzzle is by defining how far the keys are located away from the lock.

Most importantly, make it obvious how to find a key that belongs to a specific lock. If players never know how to find and arrange three masks to unlock a puzzle, they'll get stuck and wind up frustrated.

Similarly, make the key logical and integral to your game. In Metal Gear 2, players must sneak into a military base surrounded by an electric fence. However, there's no way to get over, under, or through that electric fence.

The solution is that the guards will shut the electric fence off at night. Unfortunately, the game never changes from day to night. To convince the guards that it's night, players must find an owl and carry the owl near the guards. Once the owl hoots, the guards will think it's night time and shut off the electric fence, allowing you to sneak in.

Huh?

Note the numerous problems with this puzzle. First of all, it's odd that guards in a military base will shut off a protective electric fence at night. Second, finding an owl as a key doesn't fit into the military setting of the game. Third, using the hooting of an owl to convince guards that it's night so they'll shut off the electric fence seems completely illogical.

Puzzles must remain logical within the game world and setting. In real life, moving traps can never remain a danger around archeological sites for centuries, but in the game setting of Tomb Raider or the movie setting of Raiders of the Lost Ark, these puzzles make sense because they fit within the immersive world of that game or movie. The puzzle example with the owl in Metal Gear 2 does not.

Perhaps the most important part of any puzzle is to provide feedback. The first time players face a puzzle, they'll have no idea how to solve it and their first attempt likely won't be the correct solution. To help players gradually find the correct solution, it's important for puzzles to provide feedback.

In the game Cows and Bulls (marketed commercially as the game Mastermind), one player picks four numbers (from 0 to 9) and arranges them in a specific order (such as 4278). The other player must guess those four numbers in the exact order.

Trying to guess four different numbers in the right order is nearly impossible, so the game provides feedback to let players know how close they're getting to the solution. If the number is 4278 and the player guesses 1564, only the number 4 is correct but it's in the wrong position. Any correctly guessed number in the wrong location is called a Cow as shown in Fig. 11.3.

If the player now guesses 0472, the 4 and the 2 are correct numbers but in the wrong position, that's two Cows. However, if the 7 is correct and in the right position, that's a Bull. Thus by giving players feedback that they guessed the right number but in the wrong position (Cow) or they guessed the right number in the right position (Bull), players can gradually deduce the correct four numbers in the right order as shown in Fig. 11.4.

Without such feedback, the only way players could solve this puzzle would be to guess the exact four numbers in the precise order, which is nearly impossible. With feedback, players can keep getting closer to a solution without feeling completely lost and frustrated.

Thought Exercise

Pick a puzzle and identify the seemingly obvious, but misleading direction that will lead to a dead end. Identify the assumption that leads players into a dead end.

Pick a puzzle and identify how it gives feedback that you're getting closer to solving it. Now imagine taking away this feedback. How would this make the puzzle harder to solve?

Target: 4278

Guess #1: 1564 (1 Cow)

Fig. 11.3 A Cow occurs when the player guesses a right number but in the wrong location

Fig. 11.4 A Bull occurs
when the player guesses a
right number in the right
location

Target: 4278

Guess #1: 1564 (1 Cow)

Guess #2: 0472 (1 Bull, 2 Cows)

The Purpose of Puzzles

At the simplest level, puzzles act like locked doors that slow players down and force
them to find a way to solve them. However, another purpose of puzzles is to force
players to learn new capabilities within the game. In this way, puzzles can act like a
more engaging tutorial.

In Angry Birds, players must use a slingshot to fling cartoon birds at pigs hiding
in a structure made out of various materials such as wood, glass, and stone. The first
level teaches players the basic gameplay in shooting birds at the pigs, but each successive level adds more complications, thus acting like a puzzle.

If players try to solve each successive level the same way they did in the previous
level, they'll likely fail. Instead, players must understand how the new structures are
built that are protecting the pigs, and how the material of the structure works. Then
using this knowledge, players gradually learn more about what different birds are
capable of doing and the strengths and weaknesses of different structures.

So puzzles can serve several purposes:

- As a challenge in itself
- As a locked door
- As a tutorial

Most importantly, players must recognize a puzzle when they see it. If players don't
recognize a puzzle, they won't even bother trying to solve it since they won't know
it exists. The appearance of a puzzle must make it obvious it must be solved, which
can be provided with feedback.

Puzzles often get progressively harder and more challenging. Often times, solving an earlier puzzle can give hints on how to solve a newer puzzle. Puzzles work
best when they allow anyone to solve them eventually.

Thought Exercise

Pick a puzzle and identify its purpose in the game. How does the game make the
puzzle's purpose obvious to the player?

Types of Puzzles

Every puzzle forces players to do something. The action needed to solve a puzzle is the puzzle's mechanics. The combination of mechanics, misdirection, and a solution that involves non-linear thinking defines the puzzle.

Puzzles often fall into categories that define the main mechanics:

- Word puzzles – Scrabble, crossword puzzles, Wordle, hangman
- Number puzzles – Sudoku, magic squares
- Spatial puzzles – Rubik's cube, mazes
- Pattern matching puzzles – Candy Crush, Bejeweled, Tetris
- Logic puzzles – Clue, mysteries

Word puzzlesrely on a player's knowledge of vocabulary in a language that uses an alphabet. (Chinese and other language that use characters that represent entire words, are often not suitable for the same types of word games as alphabet-based languages like English.) In word puzzles, players must examine letters or spaces to create or deduce the right word.

Cryptography is a unique type of word puzzle that involves taking plaintext and following a fixed set of rules to scramble words and/or letters around to create cipher text. Now the challenge is to decipher the cipher text and identify the original message stored in the plaintext.

The rules for scrambling data are called encryption algorithms and often include a mix of substitution and transposition. Substitution replaces one character with another, such as replacing the letter "E" with the number "9" so the phrase "The red dog" becomes "Th9 r9d dog".

Transposition moves a character a fixed distance from its original location, such as moving the letter "E" two places to the left. So the phrase "The red dog" becomes "eTher d dog". By applying both substitution and transposition to each character, encryption algorithms can scramble data beyond recognition.

Number puzzles, like Sudoku, require knowledge of number values and sometimes simple arithmetic. Solving a number puzzle involves arranging numbers in specific patterns where the number values themselves restrict the placement of neighboring numbers.

Spatial puzzles rely on observing or manipulating objects such as shapes or colors. Moving different objects in various patterns is how players can arrive at the puzzle's solution, such as manipulating a Rubik's cube.

Rather than manipulate objects, spatial puzzles may require players to maneuver around objects, such as racing around a track to avoid obstacles, or tracing a path through a maze. Solving a spatial puzzle involves understanding the position of multiple objects.

Pattern matching puzzles are a variation of spatial puzzles except they rely on identifying patterns among shapes. The challenge often involves spotting patterns within a limited time frame. If players fail to spot a pattern, the opportunity will be lost for good, such as trying to manipulate geometric shapes in Tetris before they hit another object and stop moving. One common pattern matching feature is called Match 3, which gets its name because players often have to match three similar items.

Puzzles may combine features. Tetris is a pattern matching puzzle that involves spatial puzzle features. Scrabble is a word puzzle that also involves spatial puzzle features. In video games, puzzles often involve spatial challenges in either moving a character to the right position or moving one or more objects in a specific pattern.

Logic puzzles provide information and define relationships between separate items to force players to deduce facts using a process of elimination. Such logic puzzles define detective mysteries that challenge players to gather clues and use this knowledge to identify the criminal among several suspects. Logic puzzles, such as in Myst, also define mysteries that force players to search for clues to determine what's going on, where they might be, or who they can trust in a completely unknown environment.

The difficulty of logic puzzles depends on two items:

- The number of facts provided
- The number of relationships possible

When the number of facts provided is small, the logic puzzle is easier to solve. Suppose someone showed you a red ball and a blue ball and then dropped both balls in a bag. If you pull out the red ball, you can easily conclude that the ball remaining in the bag must be blue. In this case, the number of facts is 2 (red or blue) and the number of relationships is 2 (a ball is either in the bag or out of the bag).

Logic puzzles get more challenging when the number of facts increase. Suppose there are now 20 blue balls and 10 red balls in a bag. Each time you can pull out two balls at a time. If they're the same color, add a blue ball to the bag. If they're different colors, add a red ball to the bag. What will be the color of the last ball left in the bag?

Note: Assume you have a big supply of Blue and Red balls for this purpose. When you take the two balls out, you don't put them back in, so the number of balls in the bag keeps decreasing. (Answer: A blue ball.)

When the number of relationships between facts increases, players must use known facts and relationships to deduce additional facts, which is the basis for solving mysteries. Suppose Bob, Alice, and Selina hold the position of CEO, engineer, and secretary in a company, but not necessarily in that order. The secretary is an only child and earns the least. Selina, who is married to Bob's brother, earns more than the engineer. What position does each person hold?

(Answer: Bob = engineer, Alice = secretary, Selina = CEO)

Logic puzzles require players to juggle multiple chunks of seemingly unrelated information and use this information to discover new facts, which can then be used to uncover more facts until players eventually find the right answer. Logic puzzles give players all the information they need so they can either find the answer through deduction or exhaustively test all possibilities until they find the right answer.

When designing puzzles for your game idea, keep in mind that word puzzles are the most limiting since they're not playable the same way in different languages. As a result, word puzzles are the hardest to translate for a global market.

Spatial and pattern matching puzzles are usually best for reaching a universal audience since everyone can understand colors, shapes and positions. The best puzzles are those that offer simple rules that spawn a nearly limitless number of combinations to play.

Thought Exercise

Pick a puzzle and identify the puzzle type (word, logic, spatial, etc.). What makes this puzzle appealing and challenging?

Summary

Designing puzzles can almost be a puzzle in itself. When creating puzzles for others to solve, identify the solution to your puzzle and the starting state of that puzzle. Then make sure there's one or more possible solutions to get from the starting state to the solution.

Ideally, the solution should be integral to the game and teach players additional capabilities they can use in later parts of the game. Once you've created one or more solutions, focus on misleading players so they look for an obvious solution that will lead them to a dead end.

Consider how to help players if they get stuck solving the puzzle. Will you provide hints? Adjustable difficulty levels? Ways to solve the puzzle another way? You must make sure puzzles don't stop progress completely or players will get frustrated.

Spatial and pattern matching puzzles can appeal to the widest possible audience since they do not rely on knowledge of language like word puzzles. Logic puzzles can eventually be solved by everyone as long as they take enough time. The best puzzles are the ones that challenge players, provide feedback to guide players, and offer multiple solutions so players of all skill levels can ultimately find a solution.

Further Readings

"The Puzzle Instinct: The Meaning of Puzzles in Human Life", Marcel Danesi, Indiana University Press, 2004.
"Level Design Workshop: Solving Puzzle Design", GDC, https://youtu.be/0xBJwrm9C8w.
"The Art of Puzzle Design", The Game Overanalyser, https://www.youtube.com/watch?v=hCOHjTX4GYE.

Chapter 12
Fun in Combat

Combat directly attacks enemies and opponents to stop them from attacking you or keeping you from achieving your goals. Combat can range from simply making enemies disappear to showing blood squirting out of open wounds in slow motion as you tear their heads off for a final killing blow.

Even in romance games, there's combat where a player might strive to win over a love interest while other characters may try to block this goal (or convince the player to fall in love with them instead). Whatever form combat may take in a game, its whole purpose is to clear enemies from the playing field. On an emotional level, combat is meant to make players feel powerful.

In some games, such as first-person shooters, combat represents the main appeal of the game. In other games, such as stealth or horror games, players must actually avoid combat as much as possible to win. Some games, such as realistic simulations, may not appear to offer any combat at all. Yet even in simulation games, there is still a form of combat where players must make decisions to overcome obstacles or opponents in their way. Any time an enemy tries to keep a player from achieving a goal, there's conflict and that creates some form of combat.

The essence of combat lies in choice. Players must choose:

- Which enemy to hit
- Where to position themselves
- Which attack to use
- When to attack
- How to react against enemy attacks

The more choices players have, the more interesting combat will be. Think of combat as a puzzle that forces players to maximize their odds of success by using:

- Their arsenal
- Their positioning
- Their environment
- Their skill

W. Wang, *The Structure of Game Design*, International Series on Computer, Entertainment and Media Technology, https://doi.org/10.1007/978-3-031-32202-0_12

The Weapons Arsenal

To increase the appeal of combat, games typically give players options for choosing one or more weapons. Now the challenge lies in choosing the best weapon based on the player's playing style and the pros and cons inherent in every weapon. Some weapons can attack from a distance (crossbow, rifle, hand grenade) while other weapons are meant for close combat fighting (axe, fists, club).

Some weapons can be used with one hand (club, pistol, whip) while others require two hands (broadsword, heavy machine gun, bow). Some weapons inflict massive damage but take time to prepare, manipulate, or reload (cannons, chainsaw, flamethrower) while others inflict low amounts of damage but can be used in rapid succession (dagger, brass knuckles, feet).

When designing combat in a game, ask the following questions:

• How many ways can a player attack enemies?
• How do different enemies respond to each type of attack?

The more ways a player can attack an enemy, the more choices the player must make to choose the best type of attack. Initially, player need to learn a basic way to attack, but that type of attack should never work on all types of enemies. As players encounter different types of enemies, they'll be forced to learn other ways to attack.

In Super Mario Brothers, players fight enemies by jumping on their heads. However, some enemies have spikes on their backs, which actually hurt players if they jump on them. Now players must learn and use a different way to attack these spiked enemies since jumping on them will no longer work.

In many first-person shooters, players can carry a variety of weapons, but the tradeoff involves being able to carry a limited number of weapons and ammunition. Then players must decide on the right mix of weapons to take and eventually learn which weapons work best on different enemies. The fun in combat comes from deciding the best weapon to use at any given time.

Thought Exercise

Pick an action video game and identify all the different weapons players can choose to attack an enemy. What are the pros and cons of each weapon?

Pick a video game that does not emphasize combat such as a horror, stealth, or simulation game. What are different ways players can still attack enemies?

Positioning for Combat

Choosing from an arsenal of weapons can be like a kid choosing which sweets to eat in a candy store. Yet another challenge in combat involves moving within the game to advance or retreat from enemies.

Advancing can be as simple as charging straight towards an enemy, or as compli-cated as maneuvering around a playing field to get in the best position possible before attacking an enemy. Retreating could be just running quickly away from an enemy, or it could involve retreating, attacking, then retreating some more.

Combat often involves various distances. Ranged combat allows players to attack with much less chance of getting hurt in return. Ranged combat might involve guns, crossbows, thrown spears, or magic spells that throw fireballs.

Close combat forces players to stand in front of an enemy and hit using weapons like swords, clubs, or staffs. With close combat, players increase their chance of hitting the enemy but with the risk that the enemy also has a greater chance of hit-ting back.

Similar to close combat is hand to hand combat, which involves attacking an enemy by punching, kicking, or wrestling. Unlike close combat where players can often attack (or defend against) multiple enemies, hand to hand combat generally allows players to attack a single enemy at a time, which can make them vulnerable to attacks from other nearby enemies.

Positioning can involve changing the distance between the player and an enemy, but positioning can also mean where the player is in relation to the enemy. If the player attacks an enemy from the front, there will be less chance of success (because the enemy can see the player) than if the player attacks from behind (where the enemy might not see the player until it's too late).

Players might also position themselves towards the side to attack an enemy or position themselves vertically such as in a tree or on the third floor of a building so they can shoot down on enemies. Positioning gives players a way to increase their odds of successfully attacking an enemy while minimizing the chance that the enemy can defend or fight back.

A player's position can also be important for defense. In close combat, a player might duck, dodge, or jump to avoid getting hit. In ranged combat, a player can duck behind obstacles to avoid being seen and hit, and then move to get in a more favorable position to attack.

Fighting games often emphasize finishing moves to knock out an enemy using dramatically stylistic gestures. Such finishing moves further immerse the player in the gameplay experience even if that movement serves little practical use in the game.

Movement can be a way to position players to a more advantageous location to attack, move the player away from danger, or simply let players enjoy the aesthetic experience of moving with visual flair. Since players will spend more time moving than fighting, games must make moving intuitive and emotionally satisfying as well practical.

In any video game, identify the core movement that players do most often during combat. Make sure this core movement by itself is fun and interesting, then add variation to this core movement.

In Angry Birds, the core movement is simply shooting birds through the air using a slingshot. Players can adjust the angle and velocity that defines how the birds fly through the air to knock down targets. Once players learn and master this core movement, variations give players a choice of which birds to shoot (who all have different abilities), but the core movement remains the same (adjusting angles and velocities).

Thought Exercise

Pick a simple video game and identify all the ways players can control movement. What makes movement fun and interesting?

Pick a more complex video game (such as a AAA title) and identify all the ways players can control movement. Are there ways to move in a AAA game title that could be adopted for a much simpler casual video game? Are there ways to move in a AAA game title that could not be easily duplicated in a simpler casual video game?

In any video game, what's the core movement that players do most often? What variations in this core movement does the game offer?

Fighting in Different Environments

Almost every game contains different settings. Within a single game, players might go from an open field to an isolated dungeon to a bustling city. Different settings exist not just for variety but because they provide different challenges. Specifically, each setting provides different ways for players to fight.

In an open field, ranged combat might dominate since players can attack enemies from a distance. Move players into the narrow confines of a subway station and this forces combat to occur in shorter distances because players have less room to maneuver. However, a subway can provide different ways for players to take advantage of their surroundings such as hiding behind pillars, knocking over trash cans to use as weapons, or pushing enemies in front of moving subway trains.

Terrain plays a crucial role in combat. Rivers and mountains keep players from moving in certain areas, forcing combat within a smaller range. Mud or sand can restrict movement, making fighting more difficult while forests provide plenty of cover for players to hide behind to set ambushes.

Every setting should provide new challenges that both limits and increases the available choices players can fight. Each new environment introduces players to additional ways to fight. Knowing more ways to fight increases the game challenge as players must master all the different combat options against different enemies in ever changing environments.

Thought Exercise

Pick a video game and identify at least three different environments that players visit. What advantages does each new setting provide players for movement? What disadvantages does each new setting create that inhibits movement?

If a game offers different environments that do not alter combat in any way, what is the purpose of having a different setting?

Using Skill in Combat

Beginners must always learn how to fight in a game. Once players learn the basics, the next step is to master these various combat options. Skill in combat involves:

- Precision
- Timing
- Speed

Precision means aiming (with ranged weapons) or striking specific parts of a target in close combat (such as stabbing a vulnerable spot on an enemy). By aiming an attack, players can hit weak spots and cause more damage than normal.

Timing means attacking at the optimal moment. In many fighting games, performing a fighting move too soon gives away your intentions, allowing an enemy to retreat or defend against the attack. On the other hand, performing a fighting move too late will likely miss or make the player vulnerable to a counter attack. Timing means choosing the right moment to strike with the right combat option. Get the timing wrong and there's a chance the attack won't succeed at all, or may even leave players vulnerable to a counter attack.

Related to timing is speed. Attacking an enemy in rapid succession increases the chance of landing a blow, but at the risk of expending too much energy or ammunition. Attacking an enemy slowly increases the chance of hitting accurately, but risks getting hit in return before even getting a chance to attack.

Combat skill focuses on both attack and defense. On defense, players can block, parry, or dodge attacks. Defense isn't just about avoiding or minimizing attacks, but in setting yourself up for a counter attack.

Enemies in a game serve several purposes:

- Block a player's progress towards a goal
- Test the player's offensive skills
- Test the player's defensive skills

Different enemies offer different challenges to players. More versatile enemies can adapt to a player's behavior to force players to change their methods of attack and defense so gameplay doesn't become repetitive and dull over time.

In some cases, players can actually use enemies to help them in some way. In 2D platform games, players can often jump on top of enemies to help them reach heights they wouldn't be able to reach otherwise. Discovering how to exploit enemies rather than destroy them can be another way to make combat interesting and challenging.

Players can develop skill in precision, timing, and speed so they choose the right combat option at the right time and use it to cause the maximum amount of damage. Precision, timing, and speed can also be used to develop defensive skills in a game as well. When players feel that their skill can give them greater control over the game, they'll find the game more enjoyable to play.

Thought Exercise

Pick a children's game that relies entirely on luck. Notice how your knowledge of the game has no effect on the game. Now pick a video game that relies on fast reflexes and physical dexterity. Notice that in the beginning, novices are at a disadvantage because they're still learning to control the game. However as players gain more experience and skill, they can develop greater control over the game outcome. How does the video game accommodate novices playing with more experienced players (if it does at all)?

Creating Depth in Combat

There should never be a single dominant strategy that defeats enemies every time or else players will simply choose that one method. Any type of repetitive gameplay will create a dull game.

To make combat exciting and challenging, players must constantly be challenged in several ways:

• Different enemies that must be attacked in different ways
• Different environments that force players to adapt different combat strategies
• Enemies that change behavior based on the player's actions

Enemies must always challenge the player. Early enemies can teach players basic combat moves while later enemies can teach players more complicated types of attacks. By constantly varying the skills players need to defeat enemies, a game can increase tension and gradually ramp up the difficulty level without overwhelming the player.

Besides challenging players with enemies of different abilities, games must also challenge players with different environments. This forces players to learn new ways to move and fight as they encounter new types of terrain and obstacles.

Combined with fighting different enemies, new terrain keeps combat challenging so players must keep learning what they can do to survive and eventually thrive.

As players learn how to defeat enemies, those enemies can further challenge players by altering their behavior as well. Attacks that previously worked on one type of enemy may suddenly fail to work or work less effectively in a new situation. An enemy might change their movement, defense, and attack strategies to force the player to adapt to this new behavior.

Ultimately games can make combat satisfying by letting players feel in control. That means giving players choices for how to fight. If there's only one way to defeat an enemy, the game may be exciting until players discover this one solution. After that, the game won't feel as exciting anymore.

Ideally, games should offer a wide variety of combat options that test the player's knowledge and mastery. Knowing all available combat options challenges the player to understand the pros and cons of each option. Then players must learn when to use a specific combat option for each situation. This combination of facing different enemies and environments, while trying to choose the best combat option, keeps a game challenging.

Strategy forces players to evaluate their enemies and environment. Tactics forces players to choose the best combat option to defeat their enemies in that particular situation.

The best games don't overwhelm players with too many combat options, but offer a handful of options with subtle variations. Ideally, all combat options should be easy to learn but difficult to master.

In chess, it's relatively easy to teach novices how the different chess pieces move. However, it can take a lifetime to master how to move these various pieces in a coordinated attack and defense.

Board games need simple rules to make it easy to attract new players. Wargames often sacrificed simplicity for complexity to provide greater realism. Thus learning the rules to play many wargames required reading thick rule books that discouraged many people from even playing.

Even though video games mask much of the complexity in rules, they too need to make combat options simple to understand but difficult to master. One way video games do this is by allowing players to chain multiple, basic moves together to create a unique attack or defense ability that no single combat option can offer.

Fighting games like Street Fighter or Mortal Kombat give each player unique moves that players must master for that particular character. Thus the challenge lies in not only learning each unique move and using it at the right time, but defending against the unique moves of other players as well.

Suppose a game offers players just two options for combat. This makes learning to fight easy, but ultimately repetitive and dull. Now give each option just three different variations and suddenly the number of choices increases from 2^1 (2) to 2^3 (8) possible options.

In other words, what makes combat challenging isn't just the number of fighting options available, but the number of variations for each combat options. The more combat option variations, the more interesting and challenging the game can be as players strive to master the best time to use each possible variation.

The more combat options available, the more players can express themselves within the game. Some players might prefer a more conservative approach to combat while others might embrace a wilder combat style. The key is that neither approach is right or wrong but dependent on the situation and the player's choices at the time. This provides players with a nearly endless amount of challenges for fighting.

Thought Exercise

Pick a video game that offers minimal choices for fighting, such as the simple jumping mechanic in Super Mario Brothers. How does the game provide variations on this simple jump combat mechanic?

Pick a video game that offers a wide variety of fighting options. Does having so many fighting options make the game easier or harder to learn? Identify how many variations each fighting option offers. Does this make the game more challenging to play or not?

Real-Time vs. Turn-Based Combat

In video games, there's a choice between real-time or turn-based combat. Real-time combat emphasizes player dexterity in responding to enemy actions. As a result, real-time combat video games let players feel their skill can determine the success (or failure) of any attack.

Turn-based combat emphasizes player strategy because they can take time to analyze each situation and choose their best options to attack and defend. Turn-based combat gives fighting more of a strategic emphasis at the sacrifice of less realism. Choosing from a menu of different options can slow combat down in a turn-based combat game. In addition, gameplay can slow down since everyone must choose an action before the video game determines the result.

Since turn-based combat doesn't rely on the familiarity of input controls or game enemies, turn-based combat can be easier and less intimidating for beginners to learn. Also since turn-based combat gives players time to analyze every combat situation, turn-based combat places less stress on players.

However, real-time combat can be more visually appealing and exciting. Whether your game uses real-time combat or turn-based combat, the combat system must be engaging to make players eager to play it multiple times. The more engaging the combat system of a game, the more people will continue replaying a game.

Thought Exercise

Pick a video game that uses real-time combat and imagine how the game would change if its combat system was turn-based. Pick a video game that uses turn-based combat and imagine how the game would change if its combat system was real-time.

The Consequences of Combat

In some games, waves of enemies exist solely for the player to mow them all down in as creative and emotionally satisfying ways possible. However, many games create consequences for combat to make a game more interesting so each attack affects the future in some way.

Depending on how players treat non-player characters (NPCs), those NPCs may later be friendly or hostile in the future. That means if players rely on sheer violence to solve their problems, killing so many NPCs will likely make other NPCs leery and suspicious of the player so they'll least likely to help them and may even attack them instead.

Consequences help link individual battles together so they don't feel like endless waves of combat for no reason. Instead, combat with consequences helps tell a story. What players do now has repercussions in the near and far future.

This gives players another way to think about their options. Should they fight? Negotiate? Retreat? Sometimes combat means fighting and sometimes it means not fighting, which can give players more options than blindly charging into a bunch of enemies just to blast them away.

Thought Exercise

Pick a video game that lets players fight enemies using weapons or hand to hand combat. Is there a story that links the consequences of one battle to the next? If so, how does this affect the gameplay? If not, would the game be better or worse if the consequences of one battle affected the next in some way?

Summary

Combat has competing goals. On the one hand, if combat is too easy to learn, it risks being quick to get boring as well. On the other hand, if combat offers too many choices, it's too hard to learn and use.

The ideal balance lies in creating combat options that are easy to learn but hard to master. That means combat options should offer few fighting options but provide variations for each option that provides a seemingly endless amount of options for players to learn, explore, and master.

Ultimately, combat is meant to challenge players by testing their skills and knowledge. The more challenging the combat against different enemies and environments, the more players can feel powerful. Combat is nothing more than a way for players to exhibit mastery of their skills so they have the freedom to express themselves by their choices.

Further Readings

"Embracing Push Forward Combat in DOOM", GDC, https://youtu.be/2KQNpQD8Ayo.

"What Makes a Good Combat System?", Game Maker's Toolkit, https://youtu.be/8X4fx-YncqA.

"How Platinum Design a Combat System", Adam Millard – The Architect of Games, https://youtu.be/D689ZBdOAuw.

"How To Make RPG Combat More Interesting", Adam Millard – The Architect of Games, https://youtu.be/ZwlT0fMIiXo.

"What is 'Perfect' Video Game Combat?", CircleToonsHD, https://youtu.be/JwPPxNM3cHM.

Chapter 13
Fun in Strategy

Every game challenges players to achieve an objective using a combination of different skills (along with a little bit of luck). Video games often emphasize dexterity and quick reflexes but board games and some video games emphasize long-term planning instead. Such games fall under the category of strategy games.

Strategy is about choosing how to achieve a goal while tactics are the collective actions needed to support that strategy. As a result, strategy games are a type of puzzle game that offers a wide variety of possible solutions where all solutions are equally valid. The challenge lies in choosing the best solution (strategy) based on the current game conditions and the actions (and reactions) of the other players. Since game conditions and player actions will always change, strategy games provide an endless variety of situations for players to analyze and react to.

The fun in strategy games comes from selecting one of many options and taking action to maximize the chance of that option winning the game while minimizing the consequences of that option helping other players winning the game. Maximizing your odds while minimizing an opponent's odds is known as minimax theory as shown in Fig. 13.1.

In this minimax figure, the player has two choices. One choice offers a + 6 benefit while the other offers a + 2 benefit. Initially, the seemingly obvious choice would be the +6 option.

However, if the player chooses the +6 option, the opponent will choose an option to change the game state that minimizes the game state against the player. In this case, choosing the +6 option might look like the best choice, but then the opponent will likely choose the option that sets the game state against the player at −1.

On the other hand, if the player initially chooses the +2 option, the worst the opponent can choose in reaction is a + 1 option. Thus it appears that the +2 option could actually be the better move.

The deeper players can go in their analysis, the better they can anticipate an opponent's possible choices. Part of the fun in strategy games lies in:

© The Author(s), under exclusive license to Springer Nature
Switzerland AG 2023
W. Wang, *The Structure of Game Design*, International Series on Computer,
Entertainment and Media Technology,
https://doi.org/10.1007/978-3-031-32202-0_13

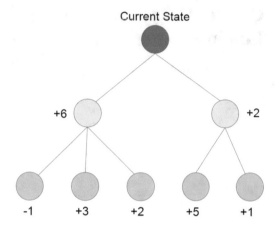

Fig. 13.1 Minimax tries to maximize options that also minimize an opponent's possible reactions

- Understanding the game rules
- Evaluating all possible choices to determine the best option
- Evaluating possible consequences of each option
- Identifying the opponent's strategy to defeat your own strategy

Understanding the Game Rules

Strategy games involve analyzing current game states to determine the best possible move. To do this, players need a comprehensive understanding of the game rules (so they know what their options are and the consequences of each possible move).

In chess, it's not enough to know how the individual pieces move. Players must also understand how the position of the various game pieces (both the player's and the opponent's) can interact on the board to create different types of challenges.

Board and card games must make its rules available for all players to read and understand. However, video games often hide the rule details from players such as how the game calculates combat odds between units on different terrain. As a result, players must often play a game multiple times until they can fully understand how each game rule works.

Part of the fun in playing strategy games is learning what all the rules are and then knowing how to apply those rules to gain an advantage. By knowing all the rules, you know all your options. By knowing how to apply those rules, you know the best time to rely on certain rules.

In chess, beginners often overlook moves like castling and en passant that depend on specific circumstances. However, chess masters not only know all possible moves, but also the best times to castle as well.

In a video game, armies might fight well against one type of opponent but poorly against another. Terrain might also make a difference such as defending from a higher position or trying to force march through swamp land. Video games can also hide details of the battlefield so players won't know what the terrain is or what enemy units might be located there until they search that particular area.

The more players can understand the rules and how different game elements might affect these rules, the better players can choose their best option at any given time. For strategy game enthusiasts, part of the fun lies in deciphering the game's rules so they can fully master the game.

Thought Exercise

Pick a strategy board game and identify all the common rules and all the less common rules. Think of a game situation when a less common rule might give you an advantage.

Pick a video game and identify how you can infer the rules. What are some ways you can test your understanding of a rule in a video game?

Evaluating All Possible Choices

The more choices available, the more interesting the strategy game. Not only must players identify all possible choices, but they must also evaluate the best ones. In a good strategy game, some choices will be better than others, but in different circumstances, other choices might be better.

In making the first move in chess, players can move any of the pawns or the knights. Players cannot move the king, queen, bishops, or rooks because they're blocked in by the pawns. However, later in the game, moving a bishop or rook might be a far better choice than moving a pawn or a knight. Yet in other situations, moving a pawn might be better than moving a queen. By giving players so many choices where the "best" choice constantly changes based on circumstances, chess always challenges players so they'll keep playing the game.

The more valid options available to the player at any given time, the more interesting the game. Valid options are any choices that could bring the player closer to victory while invalid options are choices that do not bring the player closer to victory. In chess, an invalid option might be moving a queen so it can be captured the next turn by the enemy with no resulting benefit. Therefore it should be easy for players to ignore invalid options but hard for them to choose between seemingly equal valid options.

With so many available valid options, evaluating the best valid option involves tradeoffs. Tradeoffs mean that no option will universally be best. Instead, each option can be best depending on how an opponent reacts and which strategy they choose. Some of the different possible tradeoffs include:

- Offense vs. Defense
- Short-term gain vs. Long-term potential
- Low risk/Low reward vs. High risk/High reward
- Time vs. Resources
- Light vs. Heavy

The classic strategy choice forces players to emphasize whether they should focus on attacking opponents or build up their own resources and protect them against opponents. Thus the dilemma involves choosing a balanced mix of offensive and defensive capabilities.

Short-term gain promises immediate advantages while long-term potential promises advantages later in the game. This sets up a dilemma. Do you sacrifice short-term gain for long-term potential (and risk never reaching the long-term potential)? Or do you pursue short-term gain (and sacrifice any long-term potential gain)?

Sometimes the safe choice is to choose a low risk, low reward option. This often translates into a "sure" bet such as a financial game that forces players to choose between investing in bonds that pay a low interest rate but almost never go bankrupt. In comparison to bonds, players may have the option of investing in riskier stocks that could go bankrupt or skyrocket overnight.

The right answer is often a mix of both safe and riskier options, but which safe and risky options you choose and how many safe options you choose compared to risky ones keeps the game challenging.

Another tradeoff involves sacrificing time for resources, or expending resources to buy time. A game where you control a kingdom might force you to choose between spending time to farm or saving time by invading a neighboring country to steal their food supplies.

With a Light vs. Heavy tradeoff, players must choose between two extremes such as quality vs. quantity. Do you choose to build lots of weak units or a much smaller number of more powerful units? What about faster units that require more fuel or slower units that require less fuel?

A similar variation involves specialization vs. generalization. Should you build units that do one task well (and other tasks poorly), or should you build units that can do everything but none of it well?

The key to options is that there's never a clear "right" answer. Thus players must choose the strategy they want to pursue and then pick the options that give that strategy the best chance to succeed by sacrificing some types of benefits in exchange for other benefits instead.

Thought Exercise

Pick a strategy game and identify the available opening moves each player can make. What are the tradeoffs for each option? Under what circumstances would a player find one option more desirable than another?

If a player chooses one extreme option or another (such as focusing 100% on offense or 100% on defense), is there still a chance the player can win? Why or why not?

Evaluating Possible Consequences

Another key in strategy games is not only giving players multiple options at all times, but forcing them to evaluate the consequences of each option. Starting a war against a neighboring country might seem appealing, especially if the country is weak and easily conquered. However, this could turn other countries against the player, making future trade and negotiations difficult.

Consequences can be negative but they can also be positive as well. If players have a choice of attacking a country that's already invading a weaker country, the player's attack could increase the chance other countries will want to trade and support the player. In chess, it's possible to sacrifice a queen to gain a positional advantage several moves later.

Part of the challenge lies in evaluating possible consequences for each decision, and hoping you evaluated each consequence accurately. It's entirely possible to choose an option that seems to have minimal consequences, only to find out later that your decision actually creates massive problems that you overlooked.

To evaluate consequences, players need to decide how their choices might affect the game and how their opponent might react to each decision. Sometimes opponents might not respond rationally or may react in an unexpected manner because they're busy pursuing a different strategy that you may not recognize.

The inability to predict all possible consequences for each decision makes any strategy game interesting and unpredictable. Guess the consequences correctly and you can plan ahead. Guess the consequences poorly and even the best strategy can fall apart.

Ideally, every option should offer the player benefits and consequences. This forces the player to decide whether the benefits of a given option are worth the consequences or not.

Thought Exercise

Pick a strategy game and evaluate two different options. What are the consequences of each option? If the consequences are not predictable, how could they drastically change for better or worse?

Anticipating the Opponent's Strategy

Whether you play against a human opponent or a computer-controlled one, players must anticipate the opponent's moves. The opponent's moves can block the player's strategy or bring the opponent closer to victory, forcing the player to devote more energy towards stopping the opponent than trying to win themselves.

To defeat an opponent, players must plan their own strategy and understand what their opponent may be trying to do. The better players can understand their opponent's plans, the better players can defeat those plans or block them from interfering with the player's own plans.

Strategy games essentially force players to create and implement their own plan while also watching how an opponent's plan may be unfolding. When there are multiple players in a game, each player must interact with all the other players, which can lead to alliances (and broken agreements) and deception to fool others about each other's plan.

Interacting with multiple players also creates another level of gameplay where each player attempts to influence the others. By tricking one player into taking a certain action that winds up helping you, players can negotiate and backstab one another to gain an advantage, which can increase enjoyment of the overall game.

Strategy games work best when players can out think and out bluff an opponent rather than rely on faster reflexes and physical dexterity to win the game.

Thought Exercise

Pick a strategy video game where one player competes against the computer. Now pick a multiplayer strategy board game where multiple human players compete against each other. How can players foil the strategies of the computer? How can players foil the strategies of multiple human opponents?

Characteristics of Strategy Games

Action-oriented games emphasize reflexes and dexterity. On the other hand, strategy games emphasize analysis and planning. Some of the key characteristics of strategy games include:

- Multiple paths to victory'
- Dramatically changing gameplay each turn/loop
- Feedback loops

In some board and video games, there's only one way to achieve victory by reaching a specific goal. In strategy games, the fun lies in the fact that there is no single best way to win a game each time you play it. Winning the game depends partly on luck, but mostly on players correctly analyzing the game state and reacting as it changes. That means a strategy that worked while playing one game won't necessarily work while replaying that same game because the circumstances and opponent actions will likely change.

Besides offering multiple paths to victory, another way strategy games can alter victory conditions is by offering different ways a game could end. By offering multiple ways to win, strategy games offer players the freedom to choose the method they think is best.

Some common ways strategy games can end are:

- Acquisition – When one player collects a specific number or percentage of items or resources.
- Elimination – When all players are eliminated from the game. Also called "last man standing".
- Physical Goal – When one or more players reach a specific physical objective (like checkmating the king in chess).
- Points – When one player reaches a specific number of points.
- Spatial Endings – When one player controls a specific portion of space such as 50% of all territories or properties.
- Target – When one player captures, destroys, or collects an item or location.
- Turns – When a fixed number of turns has passed and one player has the lead in one of the above categories.

Because strategy games are much less action-oriented than first-person shooter or other action-oriented games, strategy games create variety by constantly changing the choices and challenges that confront each player in every turn. These new challenges are a direct result of the decisions each player made that interacts with other decisions, creating a constantly shifting landscape to analyze.

Part of the fun comes from studying each player's move to determine how it affects you and how best you can take advantage of this new situation. To make this work, strategy games provide constant feedback so players understand the consequences of each decision.

Feedback comes from studying the playing field and analyzing the resources each opponent may hold. Often times this information remains hidden but players can deduce their opponent's status by their current and past actions. In poker, players can memorize their opponent's past actions to deduce what they're more likely to do in the present, which adds an additional layer of intrigue (and fun) in the game.

Each turn in a strategy game typically offers new and different challenges. In some strategy games, players take turns, which means each player must analyze and respond to the opponent who plays before them. Then the player's actions directly affect the options available to the opponent who plays after them. Thus sequential play creates obstacles for players based on the actions of the opponent before them.

Instead of sequential play, strategy games may opt for simultaneous play, which means every player chooses an action without a chance to see what other players might do first. Simultaneous play creates a different layer of interaction by forcing players to make decisions in the absence of other player's choices.

Based on their available resources, players must choose the best options based on the current game state that's constantly changing from the choices of each player. This constantly changing interaction makes every turn in a strategy game act like a different puzzle to solve. Each player has full knowledge of their resources but only partial knowledge of their opponent's resources and goals.

Strategy games often offer three different play structures:

- Inclusive Play – All players remain in the game until the end.
- Exclusive Play – Players gradually drop out until only a single winner (or winners) are left.
- Cooperative Play – Players can cooperate with each other to work towards a single goal, work as a team against other teams, or work against time limit.

Inclusive play can work best with multiple human players, often in a board game so play becomes more of a social event. By keeping everyone involved in the game, everyone can keep playing. Card games such as poker or bridge let people play together, mostly for social reasons.

Exclusive play offers a more competitive game and can work when games are short so players who get eliminated early don't need to wait long before another game starts up again. Monopoly is a board game that's often criticized since the game often goes on for too long as players gradually drop out.

Cooperative play can involve players working together to solve a single problem, such as trying to control a disease in the game Pandemic. In this case, all players win or lose as a group. Other types of cooperative play puts players in teams where they compete against other teams. In this way, players on the same team can form friendships but the game may then scramble players on different teams later.

Video games can be particularly appealing to individuals who can't always get people to play in person, so they can play with online friends and strangers instead who may be located anywhere around the world.

Thought Exercise

The way a strategy game ends and the way it plays can greatly determine how players experience the game. Pick a strategy game and change the way it ends. Then change the player experience such as from inclusive play to exclusive play. How does each change alter the way the game works?

One hazard strategy games must avoid is an emergent, dominant strategy that wins all the time. Such a dominant strategy makes all other choices irrelevant to the point where players will no longer even consider them, which narrows the variety and scope of the game. Can you identify any emergent, dominant strategy in a strategy game? If so, how can this dominant strategy be fixed to keep the other game options attractive?

Summary

Strategy games are about making decisions that involve weighing the pros and cons of every choice. When played alone, strategy games are like fancy versions of Solitaire but where players have more control over their chances. When including multiple players, strategy games force everyone to consider not only their own decisions, but how to react to the decisions of the other players.

Multiple players can work together, work in teams, or work individually. Part of the fun in strategy games lies in analyzing the current state of a game and then choosing options from a constantly changing environment. Through thoughtful planning, bluffing, and deception, players can ultimately achieve success in a strategy game.

Further Readings

"How Do You Make a Strategy Game? Paradox and Firaxis Sound Off", GamesRadar, https://www.gamesradar.com/how-do-you-make-strategy-game-paradox-and-firaxis-sound.

"How to Make a Strategy Game – Practical Tactical Warfare", NPT156, https://www.instructables.com/How-to-Make-a-Strategy-Game-Practical-Tactical-War.

"Engineering The Perfect Enemy", Adam Millard – The Architect of Games, https://youtu.be/rqaTqI1XSWw.

Chapter 14
Fun in Economics

Economies within a game represent the movement of resources. Because resources can be valuable (within the game), game economies can influence player behavior. Players will find a way to get rich within a game economy so they can increase their chance of success within the game.

Many games have some form of economics where players gather resources, trade them, and convert them into other valuable items like weapons and armor. In many games, an economics system helps make the game more realistic but isn't the main focus of the game. However in some organization simulation games, the whole point of the game is to give players a chance to manage resources on a large scale such as running a city, a company, or an entire civilization.

Whether economics are the main focus of the game or just a small part of the game, economics forces players to make choices in managing resources. Any time players choose to buy one item, that means they can't buy a different item. Such choices force players to think strategically so they can maximize their chances of reaching their goals.

Economies in games often consist of the following parts:

- Taps
- Inventories
- Converters
- Drains
- Traders

Taps create resources. This can be something as simple as killing enemies and receiving money as a reward or something more complicated such as mining for gold. Taps are necessary to provide resources for the player to earn or collect.

Taps can appear within a game in several ways:

- Defeating enemies/challenges
- Random

© The Author(s), under exclusive license to Springer Nature
Switzerland AG 2023
W. Wang, *The Structure of Game Design*, International Series on Computer,
Entertainment and Media Technology,
https://doi.org/10.1007/978-3-031-32202-0_14

- Time
- Real money

Games often reward players for their actions, whether they win or lose. The more they play, the more rewards they get. This encourages players to take risks within the game and keep playing the game as many times as possible.

Sometimes players can find resources by exploring a new area of the game world. This encourages players to risk visiting new places. In some games, taps can appear at random, such as loot boxes that players can find.

Another source of resources can be time. The longer the player stays alive, the more points the player may earn. Thus the game rewards survival such as making it through an entire level without getting defeated by an enemy or obstacle.

Finally, many games even allow players to buy resources, trading real money for in-game items. Thus a player's own bank account in the real world can act as a tap within a video game. The more taps a game offers, the greater the variety of play within the game.

Inventories hold resources such as a backpack or a bank. In some games when a player dies, all items in the inventory are lost. In other games when a player dies, the items in the inventory remain scattered in the area where the player died, which gives the player a chance to revisit that area to retrieve any items. Inventories are necessary to hold any resources the player collects.

Converters let players exchange one type of resource for another, such as turning gold ore into money or exchanging experience points for greater abilities such as increased intelligence or dexterity. Converters are necessary so any resource can eventually be converted into in-game money for players to spend.

Drains are the opposite of taps. Where taps create new resources, drains destroy existing resources to prevent an overabundance of resources. The simplest drain is ammunition for a gun. Each time the player fires it, there's one less bullet available to use in the future. Drains can also force players to act if players gradually lose health over time and must replenish their health by eating food, which can cost money.

In a board game like Monopoly, drains are unexpected bills players must pay when they land on a certain space or draw an unlucky card. Drains exist to ensure there's never an unlimited number of resources within a game.

Traders are a variation of converters. Where converters let players exchange resources for other items at a fixed rate for clothing, weapons, or supplies, traders introduce varying prices and costs. This provides players with another source of income. Rather than mine, farm, or retrieve resources, players can simply trade resources.

One area of a gaming world might have an abundance of wheat or iron that play-ers can transport to another area to sell those resources at a large profit. Traders act like a combination of taps and converters. Traders are necessary to create additional risks and rewards for trading resources.

Economies can be zero-sum or positive sum. A zero-sum economy means there's a fixed number of resources available, which encourages players to fight each other for those scarce resources. A positive-sum economy means there's a constant generation of new resources so players have far less incentive to fight each other and more incentive to collect as many new resources as they arrive.

At the most basic level, economies need taps and drains where taps provide resources and drains eliminate those resources to keep them from becoming too numerous. By balancing taps and drains, designers can shape a game's economy.

Thought Exercise

Pick a board game and identify how resources are created and how they can be destroyed. Then identify if the game uses inventories, converters, and traders. How do these affect gameplay?

Pick a video game and repeat the above. The main difference between a board game and a video game is that a board game forces players to manage the game economics while in a video game, the computer takes care of managing the game economics.

What is the advantage of having players manage the game economy? What is the disadvantage?

What is the advantage of having the computer manage the game economy? What is the disadvantage?

Shaping Player Behavior

Money changes people's behavior and in-game currencies are no different. Because of this, one way games can influence players' behavior is through the use of its game economy.

If a game wants to encourage players to explore and fight enemies, the game can reward players by emphasizing taps. Scatter treasure chests and valuable items around the game world to encourage players to explore. Provide a variety of rewards each time players defeat enemies. By rewarding the behavior you want players to do, they'll likely do more of it.

If a game wants to encourage players to interact with others, including non-player characters (NPCs), then the game can emphasize converters and traders. Rather than give players valuable items directly, the game can force them to acquire resources, such as gold ore, that must be converted into something useful like food, clothes, or tools. Now players must collect resources and then travel to people who can convert their resources to what the players need.

To encourage players to trade, a game can emphasize various converters that have changing prices. As soon as players discover they can buy items at a low price and sell them at a higher price somewhere else, they'll be more likely to engage in trading and speculating.

Similar to trading is gambling. By offering gambling within a game, players can win (or lose) money. Gambling in-game currency gives players a chance to earn extra money quickly but at the risk of losing their money just as fast.

Games can also offer an investment system that forces players to expend resources now in hopes for a larger payoff later in the future. The challenge is that players must decide which long-term strategy to pursue. All may offer advantages but the advantages depend on the player's own strategy within the game.

Many management simulation games emphasize long-term planning. Should players plant crops to feed their people, but at the risk of inviting other players to attack them and steal their food? Or should players emphasize military power at the risk of not having enough resources left over to feed their population?

By offering a collection of resources, games can entice players to complete an entire collection, such as collecting all the monsters in Pokemon or all the cards in Magic: The Gathering. Collections of resources give players an incentive to complete their collection and provides another goal players can pursue within a game.

To increase a player's sense of despair and helplessness, especially in horror games, emphasize drains such as the player's health or supplies like limited ammunition. If players expend or lose resources faster than they get them, each resource will feel far more precious. This forces players to hoard their resources.

Emphasizing a player's inventory and how to spend resources essentially defines the basis for many strategy games or management simulation games. Now players must spend time analyzing the current situation and deciding how to allocate their resources to best pursue specific strategies.

Perhaps the greatest influence on player behavior occurs through the snowball effect, which can also be described as "the rich get richer and the poor get poorer." That means players in the lead often have more opportunities to get even further ahead. Conversely, players falling behind have fewer opportunities, which causes them to fall even further behind.

The classic example of this occurs in Monopoly. Richer players have more money to buy properties, houses, and hotels while being able to withstand unexpected expenses. Poor players have less money to buy properties, houses, and hotels, which means they can generate far less income. Because they have less money, unexpected bills can force poor players to sell houses, hotels, or even entire properties so they can pay their debt. This creates a downward spiral for poorer players with fewer resources to generate any future income.

One way to help players who are behind is to give them additional bonuses or advantages so they can catch up to the leader. A second away to help players who are behind is to give players in the lead fewer bonuses or advantages. In both cases, helping players who are behind or minimizing advantages to the leader will keep the leader from pulling so far ahead so that other players have no chance of winning and simply drop out of the game.

Letting the rich get richer and the poor get poorer creates an overall negative game experience for everyone but the winner. Ideally, games need to minimize a leader's advantage and aid players falling behind to keep the game outcome in doubt.

By simply emphasizing one part of an economy (taps, drains, converters, traders, inventories), games can greatly influence how players behave. By using resources as rewards, depending on whether players are ahead or not, games can keep a game challenging for all players from start to finish.

Thought Exercise

Pick a game with a game economy and identify which part the game emphasizes the most (taps, drains, converters, traders, or inventories). How does this emphasis change the gameplay? What would happen if this economic emphasis were reduced or eliminated altogether?

Types of Resources

Resources come in different forms. The most basic resource is money that players can spend to buy items. Through taps, money can be earned by doing jobs or finding them as treasures. Through drains, money can be spent to buy new items or repair current items.

Money may not be the only resource in a game. One other type of resource is subsistence, which can be represented as food or health points. While playing the game, players will consume (drain) subsistence, which forces the player to find or buy additional food or health points (taps). Where money represent resources that players can collect and hoard, subsistence resources represent consumables that players need on a regular basis just to keep playing the game.

Another type of resource are shortcuts, which typically provide a useful advantage to the player such as enhanced movement, combat, or healing abilities. Think of games where players can find a magic sword, a powerful gun, or a medical kit. Shortcut resources may be temporary (such as increasing a player's size for a limited amount of time) or permanent as long as the player possesses that item (such as enhanced armor that provides increased protection from attacks).

Players can often find shortcut resources by defeating enemies or finding them by chance (such as in loot boxes). Shortcut resources can increase a player's chance of success but may also be traded or sold so they also represent a type of money resource as well.

Sometimes resources simply enhances a player's overall character such as giving increased strength, dexterity, health, intelligence, or experience points. Increased strength may give the player the ability to use more powerful weapons while increased health may give the player the ability to withstand battle damage longer. Increased experience points may help boost a player's ability to access more powerful equipment.

Such enhancements or power-ups can vary in duration. Sometimes they last as long as the player owns the item (such a magical shield), sometimes they last for a limited time (such as the power-ups in Pac-Man that temporarily allow players to eat their enemies instead of the other way around), and sometimes they last until a certain event happens (such as getting hit a fixed number of times). By varying the duration of a power-up, games can prevent power-ups from dominating the game and making other resources less useful.

Some resources may serve little purpose other than to enhance a player's social status among other players. Such status enhancement resources might include "skins" for vehicles or customized graphics for clothing. Status resources exist so players can show off their achievements or just provide another way to enjoy the game through customization of a player's character or possessions.

By including and emphasizing different types of resources, a game can influence players' actions. A survival game might emphasize the constant need to find food while a casual game might emphasize winning shortcut resources to overcome difficult challenges. By offering different types of resources, games can create different experiences for players to enjoy.

Thought Exercise

Common resources in a game include:

- Money
- Shortcuts
- Power-ups

Pick a game and identify the types of resources available. Which type of resource does the game emphasize and how does this affect the actions of the players?

For example, Monopoly focuses solely on money so players strive to earn as much money as possible. On the other hand, a game like Dungeons and Dragons includes money (gold coins), shortcuts (magic swords), and power-ups (potions to increase strength). How do these different types of resources affect player actions? How long do power-ups last and how does this affect the value of the power-up?

The Psychology of Money

People don't like losing and they especially don't like losing money. To divorce people's emotional attachment to money, games use play money. Players exchange real money for play money and since play money isn't real money, they feel less emotionally attached to the value of play money.

This is why poker and other gambling games substitute real money with plastic chips that seem to have less value than the equivalent real money. Video games adopt this same principle by using in-game currency as a substitute for real money. To further divorce emotions from real money, many video games offer several types of in-game currency.

One type might represent real money. Another type of currency might just be rewards for completing tasks or finding treasure within the game. By getting players comfortable spending in-game currency that cannot be exchanged for real money, games help desensitize players to the idea of spending in-game currencies of all types.

In gambling games, players can always exchange plastic chips for real money at any time. However in many video games, the exchange can only go from trading real money for in-game currency, but never the other way around. Yet other video games, such as Entropia Universe, do allow players to exchange in-game currency for real money, which creates a real world opportunity for players to profit from their activities within the game.

Video games use in-game currency so players can buy items or powers as a short-cut. For players unwilling to pay for items or powers, they can still receive them but only after playing the game for a long period of time. Thus games give players the choice of spending either time or money to get further ahead.

Such an arrangement must be fair because if players can only buy special items or powers, they can essentially pay to win. Pay to win games put non-paying players at a disadvantage, causing them to drop out. Thus the game can eventually rely less on skill and experience and more on who's willing to pay the most to win the game.

In many video games, players know exactly what rewards they'll gain by performing certain actions. In other video games, rewards occur randomly. One variation of random rewards are loot boxes.

Loot boxes are essentially rewards that players receive periodically after playing a certain amount of time or by finding items scattered throughout the gaming world. Because loot boxes contain random items, many video games let players pay real money to purchase additional loot boxes. The catch is that the contents of each loot box can vary from trivial items to super rare and powerful items that can give players a huge advantage.

Because the value of loot boxes is unpredictable, paying for additional loot boxes is basically a form of gambling. When players find loot boxes for free through exploring the gaming world or as rewards for completing quests, the unpredictable nature of loot boxes doesn't matter. When video games encourage players, especially children, to spend real money to buy loot boxes, this can be an ethical and moral problem.

Essentially games replace real money with play money or use play money that players can earn within the game. This play money helps players think of it less as real money so they'll be willing to spend it more freely.

Thought Exercise

Pick a video game and identify all the in-game currencies the game offers. What are all the ways that players get more in-game currency? Does the video game let players exchange in-game currency for real money or does it only allow players to spend real money to get in-game currency? Can players simply spend enough money to win?

Pick a card game that allows players to buy additional cards using real money. How does this game prevent players from winning by simply spending more?

Summary

Economies are often just one part of a game but in management simulations, economies may represent the entire game. The most basic part of any economy involves taps and drains. Taps are anything that create resources while drains are anything that consumes and eliminates resources. Inventories hold resources, converters let players exchange resources for other items, and traders let players profit through moving resources from one area to another.

The way an economy works can influence player behavior. If resources are scarce (more drains than taps), players will likely play more cautiously. If resources are plentiful (more taps than drains), players will likely take more risks.

Resources can be money, shortcuts, or power-ups. Sometimes resources may need to be converted into another resource such as converting iron into armor and swords. Economies exist to influence player behavior in a game.

Further Readings

"Gamedev Economy Design", Fundamentally Games, https://youtu.be/75R0ezHWX_4.
"How Video Game Economies are Designed", Game Maker's Toolkit, https://youtu.be/Zrf1cou_yVo.

Chapter 15
Fun in Storytelling

*"Great stories agree with our world view. The best stories don't
teach people anything new. Instead, the best stories agree with
what the audience already believes and makes the members of
the audience feel smart and secure when reminded how right
they were in the first place."*
— Seth Godin, *"Tribes: We Need You to Lead Us."*

Every game tells a story. That story may be brief (run away from ghosts as Pac-Man) or extremely detailed (the sole survivor on a plane that crashes in the Atlantic Ocean discovers an underwater city in BioShock).

Games don't need stories, but stories can enhance a game through setting, graphics, and tone to create a specific experience for players to enjoy. Strip away the story and every first-person shooter looks no more exciting than running around a maze, shooting at different shaped enemies that pop up at random intervals.

Now add a story and those same shapes in a maze could be hordes of zombies trying to trap you in a shopping mall, a posse of cowboys hunting you down in the Old West, or swarms of orcs attacking you in a castle located in a fantasy world. Each of these conflicts might be identical but story makes each one unique and adds a different type of meaning to the gameplay.

At the simplest level, story can provide a background history that explains the purpose of the game. In a game about building a space station on Mars, the story can explain that the player represents the first colonists on Mars who must survive by terraforming the planet and overcome natural disasters. Once the story explains the game setting, the player is free to make choices that can send the game in a variety of directions.

On a more complicated level, story defines the direction and experience of the player from start to finish. In many horror survival games, the story defines a specific order of events that players must follow in gathering information, meeting people, and solving puzzles. In these types of games, story shepherds the player from one scene to another with little freedom to deviate from the story's plot. Although players have much less freedom, story-driven games give players a

W. Wang, *The Structure of Game Design*, International Series on Computer,
Entertainment and Media Technology,
https://doi.org/10.1007/978-3-031-32202-0_15

specific type of experience that's not possible to get from games that give players more choices and freedom.

Ultimately, story defines the player's emotional experience in the game.

Thought Exercise

Pick a board game that does not have a story (such as backgammon, checkers, or chess). Does the lack of story help or hurt the game? How would adding a story to a board game make it better (or worse)?

Pick an old arcade game and identify its story. Imagine if this arcade game did not have a story. How would that affect the player's experience playing the game?

Pick a more current video game and identify its story. How does this story shape the experience in playing the game?

The Elements of a Game Story

In the world of fiction (books, TV shows, and movies), a story highlights a hero striving to reach a goal while overcoming obstacles. At all times, fiction strives to tell a story by showing a hero in action.

In the world of games (board games and video games), a story also highlights a hero striving to reach a goal while overcoming obstacles. The main difference is that instead of seeing a hero in action, games let players control the hero's actions. While fiction lets people experience a story by reading or seeing it, games let people experience a story by acting in it.

As a result, storytelling through a game revolves around the core game mechanic that players do most often. In both Tomb Raider and Uncharted, the story revolves around visiting exotic locations, battling enemies, and searching for treasure. So the main, repetitive action players perform in these games involve exploring, fighting, and solving puzzles to find the treasure.

To help players bond more easily with characters in a video game, many games rely on the crutch that the hero has amnesia. This lets the player and the character learn the elements of the gaming world together so there's no possibility that the hero will possess any character traits that the player does not also possess.

Rather than rely on amnesia, a far better solution is to simply present an admirable hero that players of all types and backgrounds will admire and enjoy playing. That's why video game heroes are often described in broad strokes. Lara Croft from Tomb Raider is a British archeologist. Nathan Drake from Uncharted is a charismatic yet rebellious treasure hunter. Zelda from The Princess of Zelda is a princess ruling over a kingdom. Lacking in all video game heroes are detailed descriptions of their emotional personalities, which could contradict the player's own personality.

Video games often describe heroes with appealing characteristics, which allows players of all types to embrace the hero. After all, even men can relate to the courage of Lara Croft as she explores ancient catacombs and even women can relate to Nathan Drake as he single-handedly defeats a multitude of enemies attacking him. Romance games may target young women, but both men and women can enjoy striving for love.

In video games, the player is the hero. Then the game's setting lets the player express themselves through the hero's actions and interactions with other characters and their decisions within the game world.

In general, the more detailed the hero, the more tightly bound players will be forced towards achieving a specific goal. The less detailed the hero, the more freedom players will have to do anything they want.

In Minecraft, the hero has little personality beyond their physical appearance. Thus players are free to do anything they want from killing enemies to building structures. Any stories the player experiences are created solely through the player's own actions. The game simply provides a setting for those stories to take place.

In video games like Uncharted or Tomb Raider, the hero has a more distinct personality. Thus players are more tightly bound by the story. After all, it wouldn't make sense to describe Lara Croft as an archeologist if the game let players control her in a kitchen to bake cookies and run a restaurant. Neither does it make sense to describe Nathan Drake as a treasure hunter if the game isn't going to give players various treasures to find throughout the game.

Thus the three most crucial elements in a game story are:

- The hero
- The setting
- The core game mechanics

The setting provides the world for the player to explore. The hero provides a specific type of personality that will engage players. The setting must provide the greatest possible challenge for that particular hero to perform the game's main core mechanics such as moving, fighting, solving puzzles, talking to people, or managing resources.

Games typically define the hero by their occupation and this indirectly defines the setting for the game world as well as the hero's goal. In Diner Dash, the hero is a restaurant owner named Flo. This occupation immediately defines the game world's setting as a restaurant where Flo must serve customers. The core game mechanic involves moving back and forth to take orders and serve customers in a timely manner.

Once you know who the game's hero is, you automatically know the setting and the player's goal. Then you can craft the core game mechanic to emphasize that setting. Or you can create an interesting core game mechanic first and then shape a setting and hero to match that core mechanic.

The more distinct the hero, the more defined the goal within the setting. Conversely, once you decide on a setting, you automatically know the type of hero who will fit in that setting.

Create a game world set on a remote island and your hero must be someone most challenged to be on that remote island, such as a plane crash or shipwrecked survivor. Putting a restaurant owner (from Diner Dash) on a remote island to survive among wild animals wouldn't make sense.

Thought Exercise

Pick a video game where players control a hero. What type of occupation does the hero have? How does this occupation help define the game's setting? How does the hero's occupation help define the game's goal?

How would the game experience change if the hero's occupation had nothing to do with the game's setting or goal?

Creating a Game World

The graphics of a video game can put players in any type of world from ancient Roman history to fantasy worlds with flying dragons and elves to science fiction spaceships visiting far away planets. However, creating a game world involves more than just fancy graphics. To make a game world feel real, games must also emphasize:

- Places
- Items
- Relationships

Every game world needs distinct and memorable places. When a game is based on real locations, the easiest places to highlight are actual landmarks such as the Golden Gate bridge that defines San Francisco, the Eiffel Tower in Paris, or Times Square in New York City. When players see notable landmarks in a video game, that enhances the illusion that they're actually in a real world.

If games don't use actual landmarks, they often use stereotypes to represent certain areas in the real world such as palm trees and beaches to represent Southern California, signs written in Russian to represent a Moscow subway station, or decrepit houses displaying architecture from Civil War era plantations in the deep South. By emulating known buildings, structures, or landscapes, games can suggest that players are part of those particular parts of the world.

When games need to depict worlds that don't exist such as fantasy worlds or science fiction settings, they still play on our memories of existing locations and our expectations for what that type of setting should contain.

A world of medieval fantasy will likely contain castles, primitive wooden homes, and stables for boarding horses or equivalent animals like dragons. To further ground players in the realism of the game world, the game will likely put players in familiar settings such as taverns and trading posts.

On the other hand, a world of science fiction may depict a future, but it must still be a future that players can recognize. That means futuristic settings display familiar settings such as restaurants, military command posts, and fighting vehicles such as armored mobile weapons that resemble futuristic tanks or starships that resemble technologically advanced battleships or jet fighters.

The more familiar the places in a game world, the easier players can understand and adapt to that imaginary world. The key is that every game world relies on our knowledge of common locations and expected types of locations such as a repair depot for a science fiction setting or a blacksmith shop for a fantasy or western setting.

At the simplest level, places can appear in the background, but a better solution forces players to interact with those recognizable locations as well. Put the Eiffel Tower in the background and players know they're in Paris. Now make players engage in a firefight around the base of the Eiffel Tower and then climb it to eliminate enemies, and then the realistic setting further immerses players in the game world.

Similar to familiar or expected locations are similar and expected items. A western setting feels more real when players can see cowboys sporting six-shooters in leather holsters on their hip while a fantasy setting feels more real when players can see wizards carrying magic staffs and warriors wearing armor and wielding broadswords.

Therefore games often emphasize players finding, collecting, and manipulating items that further emphasize the tone of the game world. In Fallout 3, players roam around a post-apocalyptic world where everyone uses bottle caps as currency. Bottle caps are usually a trivial item but in a futuristic world devastated by nuclear war, bottle caps represent a rarity, making them perfect as a symbol for money in that particular game world.

The more an item emphasizes the game world, the more importance players will give that item. That helps create a more engaging world.

Finally, note the relationships between different characters including the player. Non-player characters populating a game world have their own motives, history, and relationships with others. By learning how different characters relate to others and their beliefs about the game world, players can feel that the game world has more substance. If one group of elves hates another group of elves in a fantasy game, that tells players something about the dynamics of the world. Now players can use this information to make alliances to help them achieve their own goals.

Relationships characters have with others often focus on strong emotions like love, hate, revenge, or fear. The more other characters exhibit common emotions towards others, the more real the game world will feel.

Game worlds must always be grounded in reality, but that reality can be based on our imagination as well as reality. Through places, items, and relationships between characters, players can learn more about the game world they inhabit, making that game world feel more like real life.

Thought Exercise

Pick a video game with a unique setting and identify what common landmarks help make the game world feel like an actual location. Identify what items players use most often. Identify any relationships characters have with others that further defines the dynamics of the game world.

Using Story to Define the Path to the Goal

If a story defines the game setting and goal, that same story also defines everything that blocks the player from achieving that goal. Three common ways to stop players from reaching the goal include:

- Puzzles (specific physical obstacles in the game world)
- Other characters (non-player characters and other players in a multi-player game)
- Player limitations (the player's own lack of skills needed to overcome obstacles and other characters)

Once players know the goal they're trying to achieve in a game, their path to that goal should be as challenging as possible. If players can reach the goal too quickly, the game won't be fun to play. If players get frustrated from too many obstacles blocking their path, they'll stop playing. Thus games need to give players a gradual sense of progressing without being too easy or too hard.

Obstacles serve two purposes:

- They prevent players from reaching a goal too easily
- They force players to use new skills to overcome the obstacle

Puzzles represent physical obstacles that players must overcome. These can be as simple as pits or walls that players must learn to jump over, or they can be as complicated as a locked door that can only be opened if players guess the right combination.

Any physical obstacle represents a puzzle that players must analyze to determine the best way around it. By trying to get past an obstacle, players must either learn new skills or practice variations of existing skills. Only by mastering new skills can the player get past the obstacles and be ready for the next obstacle in the way.

Obstacles are generally static and predictable. Other characters (NPCs and other players) are mobile and unpredictable, especially when controlled by other humans. Characters force players to adapt to different challenges and develop new skills in the process.

Perhaps the most important reason players cannot reach their goals too easily is the player's own limitations. Think of every obstacle (physical or other characters) as a malicious teacher. They exist solely to expose the player's limitations and force the player to acknowledge those weaknesses to improve them.

Story helps give obstacles meaning. Having a wall block your way can be discouraging, but if that wall is part of a prison and you've been falsely imprisoned by an evil dictator who plans to wipe out your family, suddenly getting past that same wall has far more emotional meaning. It's the same wall, but what that wall represents is more than just a simple obstacle.

Stories provide further details on what obstacles represent and give players a purpose for overcoming them. The best obstacles are difficult precisely because they attack the player's greatest weakness at that moment. Then stories provide motivation for the player to overcome that obstacle beyond just the physical barrier to a goal.

Thus the purpose of stories in a game is to provide both a physical path and an emotional journey towards a goal.

Thought Exercise

Pick an early arcade game. Even though early arcade games could only provide simple gameplay (to make it easy for novices to learn), many of them still provide a simple story beyond the physical nature of the game. For example, strip out the animated characters in Pac-Man and you wind up with the player controlling a blob, eating dots in a maze, while trying to avoid other blobs. Even though Pac-Man lacks a story, its use of animated characters provides a simple story for players to understand.

Identify the story provided by an early arcade game. Strip out this story in this early arcade game. Would it still be as fun to play?

Pick a recent video game and identify the story. What type of obstacles must the player overcome, that's related to the story? How does each different type of obstacle (including other characters) force the player to learn and master a new skill?

The Importance of Plot in a Story

At the very least, a story defines the setting of a game and the reason for striving towards a specific goal. However, story can also define what happens, which is similar to a plot in ordinary fiction.

Plot describes what happens to the hero. Ordinary fiction offers a linear plot so no matter how many times someone watches "Star Wars" or reads "The Hunger Games," what happens to the hero never changes.

However in video games, players control the hero. That means the game's designers must decide how tightly they want to control the plot. In some games, all players go through the same major experiences and the choices they make may affect minor details (such as how NPCs react), but never affect the overall plot. Such story-driven games are most similar to ordinary fiction (books, movies, TV shows) in that all players experience the same plot no matter what they do.

On the other extreme, open world games use story to provide a setting but allow players to define their own plots based entirely on their choices. Elden Ring's story defines a fantasy world where players can raid dungeons, craft swords and arrows to sell, or cast magic spells. Grand Theft Auto's story puts players in a fictional Southern California city where they can steal cars, rob banks, and sell drugs.

The story setting defines the type of activities the game offers. Yet the story's plot creates a goal for all players to achieve. In such open worlds, players don't have to follow the plot since they can freely explore the open world, but the plot gives players a direction and hence a goal to achieve. Without such a goal, players would likely quickly tire of aimlessly exploring the game world with no purpose.

The stronger the story in defining the hero and the setting, the more defined the plot that gives players a goal. The less defined a hero and setting might be, the less of a plot players need to follow. Minecraft's story is much less defined. As a result, players can do anything they wish with no single plot to guide players toward achieving a specific goal.

In Minecraft, players create their own goals to pursue. In other games like Elden Ring or Grand Theft Auto, the story defines the setting and a loose plot that players can follow if they wish.

To prevent plot from forcing players to follow specific actions in a fixed order, many games offer side quests. The purpose of side quests is to allow players to deviate from the main plot and choose other actions they wish to take within the game world. This gives players the feeling of freedom while still being constrained by the plot of the story.

So plot in a game can vary from restrictive (everyone must follow specific events in a specific order) to loose (everyone is free to ignore the plot if they wish, but the plot creates a long-term goal to pursue).

Plot is a tradeoff between telling a linear story with only one outcome to telling a non-linear story that may have multiple outcomes. Plots can vary from linear to non-linear with side quests or player-defined quests available to vary the flow:

- Plot types

  - Linear plot - Everyone experiences the same events in a specific order
  - Non-linear plot - Following the plot is optional, but provides a long-term goal to pursue

- Quest types

  - Side quests that deviate from the main plot but offer mini-plots of their own
  - Player-defined quests

Thought Exercise

Pick a video game that you've completed and identify the type of plot the game had, a strictly linear plot or a non-linear plot. If the game offered side quests, why did you play or not play them? If the game lets players make up their own quests, how does the story affect the game setting and define the hero that the player controls?

Summary

Stories create fun by defining interesting new worlds for players to explore, identifying a goal for players to achieve, and shaping the path past obstacles towards that particular goal. Stories need a hero within a specific setting. The hero defines the type of setting and vice versa because every hero type creates certain expectations.

All stories need a hero, a setting, and a plot. The hero defines who players control, the setting defines where the game takes place, and the plot defines the order that players confront various obstacles and non-player characters.

Stories give meaning to the players actions. The more compelling the story, the more appealing the game. Stories provide motivation for players to play a game by letting them live in an alternate world of their fantasies.

Further Readings

"The Three Pillars of Game Writing – Plot, Character, Lore", Extra Credits, https://youtu.be/wNNXdoj7cCQ.

"How Level Design Can Tell a Story", Game Maker's Toolkit, https://youtu.be/RwlnCn2EB9o.

"Creating Emotion in Games: The Craft and Art of Emotioineering", David Freeman, New Riders Publishing, 2003.

"Dramatic Storytelling & Narrative Design: A Writer's Guide to Video Games and Transmedia", Ross Berger, CRC Press, 2019.

"Integrated Storytelling by Design", Klaus Paulsen, Routledge, 2021.

"Telling a Story Through Gameplay", Kaitlin Tremblay, https://www.gamesindustry.biz/telling-story-through-gameplay.

Part III
Creating a Game

Understanding the elements that make up a game can help you appreciate how games work (and how bad games fail). Knowing the different ways games create challenges that players find fun to overcome can help you better understand the mechanics of games. However, if you want to design and create games, you need to know how to make, test, and market them as well.

Designing a game requires the same types of skill as painting a picture, writing a novel, or filming a movie. First, you have to believe you can create something outside of yourself. Second, you need to visualize what you want to make. Third, you need to develop the skills and knowledge to build what you imagine. Fourth, you have to actually take action and do it.

Game design is nothing more than a skill where you can combine your talent and imagination to create something the world has never seen before. As a novice, your skill and knowledge might not equal the experts, but through time, practice, and constant learning, you can improve your skills, increase your knowledge, and gain crucial experience with each game you design. Game design is nothing more than a skill that anyone can develop.

Designing a game is just one step. Publicizing a game is an entirely different skill and making money from a game is yet another completely different, but related skillset. Some people might be happy just playing games, but others might want to try their hand at designing games.

Yet for many others, designing games can be more than a hobby; it can be an entire career. Game design is a legitimate field. This part of the book is meant to help you take your game ideas, bring them to life, and show them to the world.

Whether you make a little or a lot of money from your game designs is far less important than just the enjoyment of making a game in the first place. For many people, making games can be just as challenging and enjoyable as playing games. If you want to design a game, you can, and this part of the book will show you how.

Chapter 16
Turning a Game Idea into a Real Game

Coming up with an idea for a game essentially points you in the direction you want to go. The next step is deciding how you want to implement your idea and turn it into an actual working game. Two main ways to create a game are:

- Paper
- Digital

Paper-based games can be card games and board games, but you can also think of sports as large paper-based games where the playing pieces are actual people. Paper-based games require physical playing fields and physical playing pieces.

Digital games are games that run entirely on a computer. Digital games can completely emulate paper-based games but they commonly create interactive experiences that could not be possible with a paper-based game. One common advantage of digital games is the ability to allow a single person to play against the computer. Such solitary play is rarely possible with paper-based games that require human opponents.

Another advantage of digital games is that they test a player's eye-hand coordination and reflexes. The only type of paper-based game that also tests eye-hand coordination and reflexes are physical games like sports.

When translating your game idea into an actual working game, consider the pros and cons of each type of game.

Types of Paper-Based Games

Paper-based games are much easier to make than digital games. The three types of paper-based games are:

W. Wang, *The Structure of Game Design*, International Series on Computer, Entertainment and Media Technology, https://doi.org/10.1007/978-3-031-32202-0_16

- Card games
- Board games
- Sports

Card games emphasize randomness and relationships between information displayed on cards. Because cards can only display a limited amount of information, card games often have simple rules where the bulk of the gameplay stems from the unpredictable and wide variety of interactions that can occur when players play their cards.

Board games and sports emphasize a playing field of some kind. Unlike card games, board games may involve an element of chance or not (such as chess or checkers), but sports always involve an element of chance.

Sports emphasize a playing field, an element of chance, and more importantly, a test of physical reflexes, usually based on a handful of core movements. Baseball emphasizes hitting, running, and catching. Tennis emphasizes hitting. Skiing emphasizes downhill movement with speed and precision. Sports challenge people's movement skills. Table 16.1 lists the pros and cons of card games, board games, and sports.

When considering how to implement your game idea, focus on the core mechanic of your game idea. The four most common game mechanics are:

- Movement
- Combat
- Resource management
- Puzzle solving

Racing games emphasize movement, fighting games emphasize combat, organization simulation games emphasize resource management, and adventure games emphasize puzzle solving. Most games emphasize a single core mechanic but rely on one or more secondary mechanics as well.

Table 16.1 Comparing different types of paper-based games

Game type	Advantage	Disadvantage
Card games	Interaction between information displayed on cards. Simple rules that forces players to respond to randomness.	Always an element of luck involved in winning. Game information must fit on a card.
Board games	Can range between 100% skill-based to 100% chance-based. Can offer movement limited to a racetrack, a circular track, or an open map allowing movement in any direction. Can allow players to control one or more playing pieces.	Play limited by the size of the board or map. The greater the realism and accuracy, the more difficult the rules can be to learn.
Sports	Emphasizes physical dexterity and movement skills. Real-time interaction between multiple players.	Requires multiple people as opponents so not suited for solitary play. Requires a fixed playing field.

For example, a racing game could be implemented as a card game (Mille Bornes), a board game (Formula D), or a sport (Indy 500). In all three types of games, the core mechanic is movement.

What matters is the secondary mechanic that will define which type of game will be best. As a card game, Mille Bornes lets players practice resource management (collecting and hoarding cards) to slow down their opponents (combat).

In the board game, Formula D, players must choose different gears (puzzle solving) for their car to maximize their chance for crossing the finish line based on their current location on the track and likely numbers that will appear on die rolls.

In the actual Indy 500 race, players race cars around a track and test their dexterity skills along with managing fuel (resource management) and maneuvering around their opponents (puzzle solving).

To find the core mechanic for your game, start by defining the purpose of your game idea (such as movement for a racing game). Then define a secondary mechanic. Knowing this secondary mechanic, look for the best way to implement this secondary mechanic and that will point to the best type of paper-based game for your idea.

Thought Exercise

Think of your game idea. Identify the purpose of the game, which will define its core mechanic (movement, combat, resource management, or puzzle solving).

Now think of a secondary game mechanic you also want to emphasize. Once you know this secondary game mechanic, determine which type of game would best serve this secondary game mechanic (card game, board game, or sport).

If you want a completely skill-based game, you may want to create a board game (like chess or Go). If you want a game that emphasizes chance and resource management, choose a card game or a board game. If you want a game that emphasizes physical dexterity, choose a sport.

The core game mechanic defines the game purpose but the secondary game mechanic shapes how to implement that idea into a working paper-based game.

Types of Digital Games

Digital games require a computer, and that immediately makes them harder to create than paper-based games. Despite this barrier, digital games offer multiple advantages over paper-based games.

First, digital games can be played alone using the computer as an opponent. Second, digital games can be played with multiple players around the world, which is not possible with paper-based games. Third, digital games offer real-time action that only a sport game can match.

Perhaps the biggest advantage of digital games is that they can create visually stunning worlds for players to explore, which paper-based games cannot do except through invoking players' imaginations in paper and pencil role-playing games like Dungeons & Dragons. As technology continues to advance, graphics will get increasingly more immersive with realistic sounds and imagery (such as through virtual reality headsets).

When creating a digital game, define the purpose of your game. This purpose defines the core mechanic of your game:

- Movement
- Combat
- Resource management
- Puzzle solving

Suppose you want to make a game that explores surviving in different types of harsh climates. There might be some combat involving hunting animals or fighting off larger predators like bears, but the main action of the game could be puzzle solving such as finding and building shelter, getting food and water, and traveling across snow, rivers, or deserts without dying.

Defining your game's core mechanic indirectly defines the obstacles and challenges that players must overcome. A game emphasizing movement (such as a racing game) will include obstacles and enemies that can slow down or block movement. A game emphasizing combat will include enemies that can kill you first. A game emphasizing resource management will threaten to drain your resources faster than you can replenish them. A game emphasizing puzzle solving will try to stump you so you cannot solve the puzzle.

Once you identify the core mechanic that players will do most often, then you can define how to present your game's challenges to the player based on the purpose of your game. In other words, what will players experience through playing your game?

When creating a video game, identify the following:

- The game's purpose
- How that game's purpose shapes the core mechanic
- How that game's purpose shapes the obstacles and enemies
- What secondary mechanics help the player

Every video game needs a purpose and a tone. The purpose shapes its unique background story (genre) to appeal to certain audiences and define the entire gameplay. The tone shapes how that video game should express itself for players to experience.

For example, suppose you create a video game about ornithopter racing. (Ornithopters were early attempts to build flying machines that flapped their wings like birds.) The game purpose would be to highlight ornithopters and perhaps focus on historical ornithopters that people actually built. The tone could be comical with cartoonish graphics, or realistic in a Steampunk setting.

The combination of purpose and tone would then define the types of obstacles players would need to overcome. Perhaps players would need to constantly flap their ornithopter wings to stay in the air. Maybe cartoon birds might collide with the flying ornithopters in mid-air. Maybe rain and wind could blow ornithopters off course. Maybe balloons could get in the way.

By clearly defining the game's purpose (game setting) and tone (how that game setting is presented), defining the type of obstacles and enemies becomes easy and specific. Even though navigating a cartoon ornithopter across the screen may be similar to other types of comical flying games, the obstacles should be unique to that particular game setting, which would be obstacles from that same time period as ornithopters.

Pick another game idea such as baking pies where the goal might be to bake pies based on different customer orders that keep changing such as apple, blueberry, peach, or boysenberry pies. The goal is to bake and sell pies that people want without getting stuck with too many pies customers don't want, which will get too old and be thrown out, wasting money.

If baking pies is the game's purpose, the tone could be whimsical and light-hearted so obstacles could be getting the right ingredients mixed in the right order while mice sneak in to steal food or rival bakers or shoplifters try to steal whole pies. In this case, the challenge would be keeping pies fresh enough to sell without baking the wrong types of pies, and making the most money in the end.

Once you have the game's core mechanic defined and shaped into the player's actions, think of what secondary mechanics could help the player. For example, in the ornithopter example, the core mechanic would be movement. Thus any secondary mechanic could be combat, resource management, or puzzle solving.

Combat might be a useful secondary mechanic by letting players shoot down enemies or even other players. Combat could be particular challenging (and comical) since it would require players to keep the wings of their ornithopters flapping while trying to aim and shoot at the same time.

In the pie baking example, the core mechanic would be resource management in using limited available ingredients to bake different types of pies. A secondary game mechanic could be movement, combat, or puzzle solving. If this secondary game mechanic involves puzzle solving, players might have to figure out different ways to grab ingredients and combine them in the shortest amount of time. If this secondary game mechanic involves movement, then pies might be on a conveyor belt and players would have to keep moving to grab them before they fell off the end of the conveyor belt.

By clearly defining the game's purpose and tone, it's much easier to define the types of obstacles and enemies players will need to overcome. By identifying a secondary game mechanic, it's easy to define what could help or harm the player's chances of succeeding in the game.

Thought Exercise

Pick an idea for a game and define its purpose, which shapes the game's setting and background. Knowing this setting and background, what would be obstacles and enemies unique to this setting and background?

What is the tone of the game? How will the tone shape the appearance of the game?

The purpose of your game should identify its core game mechanic (Movement, Combat, Resource management, or Puzzle solving). Use the remaining three game mechanics to define a secondary game mechanic, which can shape ways to help or hinder the player.

Choosing a Video Game Type

Once you're clear what your game's purpose might be, its core game mechanic (to define obstacles and enemies), and its secondary game mechanic (to define ways to help or hinder the player), the next step is deciding how to present this game to players. Three ways to create an experience through digital games are:

- Text-based perspective
- 2D perspective
- 3D perspective

Text-based games are the simplest to create because they don't rely on graphics. The game presents information on the screen as text and player respond by either typing in simple commands or choosing from a menu of different text or graphic options, also known as point-and-click games. Text-based games are easiest to create but many text-based games add audio and graphics to provide visual and auditory immersion in lieu of fancy graphics as shown in Fig. 16.1.

Because text-based games lack real-time interaction, they're best for forcing players to think more strategically. Players must choose between various options throughout the game, which can trigger unexpected consequences later in the game. Players must also manage their limited resources to reach their goal. Thus text-based games are best for Resource management and Puzzle solving (not necessarily Movement or Combat except in an abstract manner).

To give players more control with real-time interaction, many video games display 2D perspectives that let players move up/down or left/right. 2D video games require graphics, but those graphics can range from simple pixelated images to stylish cartoon images as shown in Fig. 16.2. Unlike text-based games, 2D video games allow visual feedback and tactile control through a joystick, game controller, keyboard and mouse, or touch screen.

3D perspective gives players greater freedom of movement up/down, left/right, and forward/backward. Because a 3D perspective can display a more realistic world,

Fig. 16.1 Text-based narrative games often add graphics and sound to make the game more visually appealing. (Image courtesy of Inkle https://www.inklestudios.com)

Fig. 16.2 A 2D games often display simple graphics and action

graphics tend to vary from stylish and abstract to ultra-realistic. The tradeoff is that creating 3D games is much harder than creating 2D games.

Both 2D and 3D games can emphasize Movement and Combat as core game mechanics in ways that text-based games can never do. The main difference between the two is that 2D games often represent simplified worlds while 3D games tend to represent more realistic worlds.

Since 2D games display simpler graphics, they tend to focus less on exploring and more on combat, such as exploring a dungeon to steal treasure while fighting or running away from monsters. 2D games emphasize more simplified gameplay.

3D games allow greater movement along the x, y, and z-axis, which allows wider areas to explore. While 3D game settings can display graphics as simple as 2D games, 3D games tend to offer greater realism to create a more immersive game world in deeper visual detail as shown in Fig. 16.3.

A flying simulation as a 2D game might let players fly up, down, back, and forth using simple controls. A similar flying simulation as a 3D game might display detailed cockpit controls that mimics a real airplane.

Anything done in 2D can probably be done in 3D as well. In most cases, 3D games offer greater detail and realism, which provides far greater options for players to choose from than similar 2D games. Table 16.2 lists the pros and cons of different types of video games.

Card games, board games, and sports are meant to be played multiple times. Video games are different. Some video games are meant to be played once. After playing the video game once, players will know what to expect so the game often loses much of its appeal for replaying multiple times because the game never varies its challenges.

Fig. 16.3 3D games often emphasize more detailed images to create greater realism

Table 16.2 Comparing different types of video games

Game type	Advantage	Disadvantage
Text-based games	Easy to create since the game focuses on choices (puzzle solving) and resource management. Allows creating a game without the need for extensive programming or graphics skills.	Generally not a good choice for movement or Combat game mechanics. Lack of interaction and graphics appeals to a smaller niche audience.
2D games	Offers simple game rules that makes games easy for designers to create and players to learn. Graphics can range from crude drawings to stylish images.	Takes more time to create than text-based games. Requires programming, audio, and graphics skills.
3D games	Offers realistic and immersive game worlds for players to explore. Graphics can range from stylish images to realistic and detailed images.	Takes far more time to create than 2D games. Typically requires a team of people with different and unique skills.

Video games designed for single play typically focus on surprises and specific emotional experiences. Horror, romance, and mystery video games often fall in this category because the game provides specific information in a fixed order. The first time playing the game, everything is new and a mystery, but each repeated play makes the game less enjoyable since players remember the location of traps and surprises, thereby stripping the game of any further excitement and sense of exploration.

However, some video games are specifically meant to be played multiple times, much like card or board games. Such video games may play the same, but the options in each game are nearly endless, creating new challenges no matter how many times they're played.

For example, a battle royale game may always pit two teams of players to fight in the same battlefields. Since players on both teams are humans with their own unique playing styles, no two games can ever be the same, increasing the appeal for repeated play.

Thought Exercise

Pick a favorite video game and imagine it as a text-based game. As a 2D game. As a 3D game. What would be the advantages and disadvantages of each type of game?

Using your own game idea, imagine it as a text-based game. As a 2D game. As a 3D game. Which type of game seems most appealing?

Summary

When creating a game, it's important to start with your game's purpose, which can help define the core game mechanic your game emphasizes (Movement, Combat, Resource management, or Puzzle solving). Knowing the core game mechanic helps define the types of obstacles and enemies players must overcome to reach a goal.

A secondary game mechanic can provide ways to help or hinder players. By combining a core game mechanic with a story setting and a tone, you can create a unique game.

Two ways to implement any game idea is through paper-based designs or digital designs. Paper-based games include card games, board games, and even sports. Digital games include text-based video games, 2D video games, and 3D video games.

Paper-based games are the easiest to create, but can be cumbersome to simulate games in great detail. Digital games are harder to create but offer real-time interaction and greater immersion in a fictional game world.

The type of game you create depends on your game idea, your game designing skill, and the best way to implement your idea into an actual working game. The combination of background story, tone, core game mechanic, and secondary game mechanic helps define a unique game.

Further Readings

"The Many Different Types of Video Games & Their Subgenres", Vince, https://www.idtech.com/blog/different-types-of-video-game-genres.
"Board Game Types Explained: A Beginner's Guide to Tabletop Gaming Terms", Simon Castle, https://www.dicebreaker.com/categories/board-game/how-to/board-game-types-explained.

Chapter 17
Prototyping

Artists sketch ideas before committing themselves to applying actual paint. Writers jot down ideas in outlines before writing a novel, screenplay, or stage play. Filmmakers hire artists to sketch out storyboards to visually describe the major action before they shoot the final scene. In all cases, professionals start with a rough draft so they can examine whether it works or not.

Rough drafts serve several important purposes. First, rough drafts let you quickly create and test ideas. That way you can discard ideas that don't work. Often times ideas that initially sound great wind up failing when put into actual practice. Other times an idea may not quite work the way you expected, so a rough draft can identify those problems early so you can fix them.

Second, because rough drafts are meant to be created quickly, they're disposable, which means it's far easier to change ideas drastically as a rough draft early rather than trying to change it later. Disposable rough drafts help ensure designers don't get emotionally attached to any one idea just because they spent a lot of time making it.

In the world of game design, creating rough drafts is known as prototyping. Rather than go from an initial idea to a completed game (which is nearly impossible for all but the simplest of games), it's far better to start with a rough draft and create one or more prototypes first. A prototype is nothing more than a simple version of a game, or part of a game, that lets you test out your ideas to see if they work or not.

A prototype acts as an intermediate step between a jumble of ideas for a game and an actual working game. Building a prototype forces you to define how your game idea works. As a result, prototyping is an essential step in designing any game as shown in Fig. 17.1.

There are two main types of prototypes:

- Paper prototypes
- Digital prototypes

© The Author(s), under exclusive license to Springer Nature Switzerland AG 2023
W. Wang, *The Structure of Game Design*, International Series on Computer, Entertainment and Media Technology,
https://doi.org/10.1007/978-3-031-32202-0_17

Fig. 17.1 A game idea is often tested as a prototype before it can be a working game

Paper prototypes are created using nothing more than paper and pencil along with dice to create random numbers. Paper prototypes let you test your ideas quickly without any type of programming whatsoever. For example, a game designer might use a paper prototype to create a map of a game world and then move playing pieces on the map to identify areas that are too difficult or too easy to move through.

Because paper prototypes cost little to make and can be created easily and quickly, designers can try out multiple ideas in rapid succession. This increases the chance of finding the best idea to use rather than just settling for the first idea that comes to mind.

While paper prototypes can help shape a game in the early stages, they cannot accurately simulate certain types of video games such as games that rely on real-time movement. That's why game designers often test their ideas using paper proto-types and then transfer that prototype later to a digital prototype.

A digital prototype can not only let designers play the video game in a crude state, but digital prototypes let designers test out different user interface designs along with testing out any artificial intelligence (AI) code needed to move enemy units. If a video game needs to support multiple players online, a digital prototype can test this feature out as well, which a paper prototype could never do. For creat-ing video games, digital prototypes are a must.

Although digital prototypes can give immediate feedback while playing, digital prototypes take much longer to create than paper prototypes. A simple digital pro-totype might just test out different user interface designs so images can be static and clickable.

A more complicated digital prototype might need to test out movement and com-bat, which can require simple graphic elements to represent the player and any enemies. Plus a digital prototype will often require someone to write code to make the digital prototype actually work.

Although digital prototypes can give testers a much better feel for how different aspects of a video game idea might work, the time needed to create (and debug) a digital prototype can be time-consuming. Because creating digital prototypes takes time, there's a risk designers will test fewer ideas and embrace mediocre ideas just because of the time needed to create the digital prototype.

Since digital prototypes often involve writing code, there's the temptation to con-vert the prototype into the actual game. While this can be possible, it's often far better to start from scratch. The prototype exists solely to test if a particular idea works or not. Because the prototype can be created quickly, any coding will likely not be organized or designed for the future. So code in digital prototypes can help designers see what works, but then it's usually better to rewrite the code from scratch in the actual project. That way you can plan ahead and design your program properly.

For card and board games, paper prototypes are crucial to test out ideas. For a video game, a paper prototype is necessary to test out early ideas. Once those early ideas work, then designers can create digital prototypes to further refine the best of these early ideas. Ideally, a prototype should contain as little as possible except for the features the prototype needs to test.

Thought Exercise

Identify one feature in a card or board game and come up with three alternate ways that feature could work by creating paper prototypes of each alternate idea.

Identify one feature in a video game and come up with three alternate ways that feature could work by creating a paper prototype of each alternate idea.

Examine the user interface of a video game and create a simple digital prototype that displays the different user interface screens and shows how these different user interface elements work together such as showing the main screen connecting to a settings screen.

What to Prototype

The purpose of prototyping is to test out an idea, either if the idea will work or how to optimize that idea to make it better. Prototypes aren't meant to test an entire game. Instead, prototypes are meant to test parts of a game. When you're satisfied that each part of a game works on its own, then you can combine the different parts to see how they work together.

So the parts of a game you may need to prototype are:

- The movement system
- The combat system
- The user interface
- The resource management system
- The inventory system
- The economic system

Identify the purpose of the game element and design a prototype to achieve that purpose. By using prototypes of any kind (paper or digital), designers can make a game in incremental stages to increase the chances that the entire game will be fun and challenging to play. Ultimately, the purpose of creating any prototype is to test a single idea by answering a single question such as:

- Will it work?
- What's the best way to do it?
- What's fun about the prototype?

For example, if you're planning to create a unique combat system, you need to prototype the combat system to make sure it even works. Once you get the combat system to work, the next question to answer is whether the combat system could be better. Then go one step further, identify the element that's most fun, and strip away the rest.

Many times, prototypes can identify game elements that might actually be better than the original design. Rockstar Games originally designed "Race n' Chase" as a street car racing game where players could race on the streets of a city with police cars in hot pursuit. While testing the game, the developers noticed that the pursuing police cars could ram cars off the street and knock them into buildings. This proved more popular to watch and play that the company shifted the focus of the game and renamed it "Grand Theft Auto."

Game designer Gabe Cuzzillo originally tried to create a time-loop, stealth game where players had to sneak through a maze without being detected. However if guards appeared, the player could grab and throw them against the wall. That game mechanic of throwing guards against the wall proved so appealing during testing that Gabe dropped the stealth and time-loop parts of the game and renamed the game "Ape Out." Now players could control an ape and attack human guards by flinging them against the wall, which was what made the game fun to play.

The main purpose of prototypes is to convert vague, abstract game ideas into actual working systems. Instead of saying, "My game will simulate air battles between World War One German Zeppelins and British biplanes," prototypes force you to actually define rules and create algorithms for how to move units and how to resolve combat.

With a working prototype, you can test if a game idea is even fun to play or not. With a prototype, you can show others exactly what your game is and how it works.

Always have a goal or question to answer when creating any prototype. Prototypes can identify whether a game mechanic works, how to optimize that game mechanic, or whether to focus on a specific game mechanic that's more fun than anything else.

Thought Exercise

Pick an existing game and create a prototype of one system (such as its combat or movement system). What kind of game could you create based solely around this one game mechanic?

Pick a game that you don't like and identify the most annoying element. Create a prototype of this game element and improve it so you would like playing it.

The Parts of a Prototype

Every prototype must define rules for how a particular game mechanic works. Thus the purpose of the prototype is to identify if these rules work the way you expect. If not, then you'll need to modify these rules somehow by modifying a rule, deleting a rule, or adding completely new rules until the game mechanic works the way you want.

(Just remember that sometimes a flawed game mechanic can be more useful than the original design. Stay open to recognizing the benefits of any flawed rules because those flaws might actually point the way to a more interesting and better game.)

When creating paper prototypes, start with a question you want the prototype to answer. The prototype must answer the following:

- How does the prototype work in ideal circumstances?
- How does the prototype work in extreme circumstances?

Suppose a prototype tests combat. Imagine a common occurrence, such as a knight fighting an ogre, and test to make sure the game rules in the prototype work as expected. Then focus on extremes such as a knight fighting a far more powerful dragon or wizard. Do the combat rules still work?

Do the combat rules work when the player first starts the game and is relatively weak? Do the combat rules still work when the player is much stronger near the end of the game? Do the combat rules still work when the player is gradually progressing through the middle of the game? Do the combat rules still work with every possible character and weapon at all stages of the game? By testing all possible situations, a prototype can identify problems as early as possible.

Creating a prototype forces you to define the rules of the game. The rules of the game must be clear enough so they can be written down and translated into step by step instructions that players or a computer can easily follow.

Rules must translate into specific data. In a military game, tanks can move faster than infantry, who are walking, but how much faster does a tank move compared to infantry? Prototypes force you to assign numeric values to different attributes so it's clear a tank moves 4 times faster than infantry or cavalry moves half as fast as a tank. By assigning numeric values to every attribute, you can then adjust these numeric values to modify the way the rules work.

So the two most important parts of a prototype are:

- Rules (algorithms)
- Numeric values (attributes)

Rules define how part of a game works such as its movement or inventory system. Numeric values define how the rules work such as defining the movement speed of units.

If there's a problem with the way a prototype works, you can fix the problem by either adjusting the rules or adjusting the numeric values of various attributes. Changing numeric values allows for minor adjustments. Changing rules allows for major adjustments.

All numeric values only make sense relative to one another. A strength of 10 means nothing by itself, but if an armor unit has an attack strength of 10, it makes sense that an infantry unit would have a much weaker attack strength such as 4. If an infantry unity had a strength of 14 compared to an armor unit's attack strength of 10, the numeric values make it easy to see something isn't right. Either the armor attack strength is too low or the infantry attack strength is too high (or both).

When testing a prototype, the basic set of assumptions typically progress as follows:

1. Assume the rules don't work. Test and modify the rules for different situations until the prototype works as expected.
2. Assume the rules work but the numeric values are wrong. Adjust the numeric values until the prototype works as expected.
3. Assume the rules work and all numeric values are accurate. Test to make sure they work in all cases.

The purpose of a prototype isn't to prove your assumptions about the rules and numeric values are right. If you assume your rules and numeric values are right, you'll risk looking only for those cases where both the rules and numeric values work as expected. In other words, you'll try to prove you're right by ignoring and overlooking situations where your assumptions could be completely wrong.

It's far better to assume your rules and numeric values are completely wrong. Then use the prototype to test if they really are wrong or not. This subtle shift in mindset forces you to assume every rule and numeric value is wrong, so you must keep looking to prove if they are wrong. When you can no longer prove they're wrong, then you'll most likely have proven that the rules and numeric values are right.

Don't try to prove your assumptions (rules and numeric values) are right. Always try to prove your assumptions are wrong. This will help you actively look for flaws that you can fix now before they get much harder to fix later.

Thought Exercise

Think of a simple game mechanic (movement, combat, resource management, etc.) and jot down rules for how it will work and assign any numeric values to any attributes needed such as speed, attack strength, size, or whatever is most important to your chosen game mechanic.

Do your rules cover all possible situations? How did you assign numeric values to any attributes?

Study a paper wargame, which represents the most complicated types of board games because they require detailed rules to create a realistic simulation of historical events. Notice the large number of rules to define how every possible activity in the game works as shown in Fig. 17.2.

Rules must be extensive to cover all possible actions that can occur within the game. To determine the results of different actions, paper wargames often rely on extensive charts that summarize complex information in an easy to read format as shown in Fig. 17.3.

Although paper wargames may look complicated (and they are), the detailed rules, numeric values, and tables are actually hidden as code inside video games. To better understand how video games must work to cover all possibilities, study how

1.0 INTRODUCTION
2.0 HOW TO PLAY THE GAME
3.0 GAME EQUIPMENT
3.1 The Game Map
3.2 Game Charts and Tables
3.3 The Playing Pieces
3.4 Game Scale
3.5 Inventory of Game Parts
3.6 Rules Questions
3.7 Glossary of Game Terms
3.8 Use of the Percentile Die
4.0 SEQUENCE OF PLAY
5.0 MOVEMENT
5.1 Restrictions on Movement
5.2 Facing
5.3 Line Movement
5.4 Line Formations
6.0 STACKING
6.1 Stacking Limitations
6.2 How Stacking Affects Movement and Combat
7.0 TERRAIN EFFECTS ON MOVEMENT AND COMBAT
7.1 Terrain Features
7.2 How Terrain Affects Movement
7.3 Terrain Effects Chart
8.0 ARCHERY FIRE COMBAT
8.1 Restrictions on Fire Combat
8.2 Line of Sight
8.3 Effects of Fire Combat
8.4 Rate of Fire
8.5 Arrow Supply
8.6 Arrow Retrieval
8.7 Fire Combat Results Table
9.0 MELEE COMBAT
9.1 How to Calculate the Melee Combat Strength Differential
9.2 Resolving Melee Combat
9.3 Melee Combat restrictions and Prohibitions
9.4 Melee Adjustment Summary
9.5 Melee Combat Results Table
10.0 UNIT MORALE
10.1 Resolving Unit Morale Checks
10.2 Applying Unit Morale Checks
10.3 Death of King Henry V
10.4 Unity Morale Table
10.5 Morale Point Schedule
11.0 ARMY MORALE
11.1 Army Casualty Tracks
11.2 Demoralization

Fig. 17.2 Paper wargames require extensive rules to define how the game works

paper wargames work. The rules needed to create a video game are similar in complexity and completeness to the rules needed to create a paper wargame.

Paper vs. Digital Prototypes

Paper prototypes are necessary when creating card or board games. However, paper prototypes can also be useful for creating video games as well. Paper prototypes can be easy to make within seconds using nothing more than paper, pencil, and a randomizer like dice. Once a paper prototype proves it works, designers can then convert that paper prototype into a digital prototype.

Digital prototypes require a computer and coding, typically using a game engine such as Unity or GameMaker Studio. The game engine takes care of details such as collisions between two objects and detecting input from a keyboard, touch screen, or game controller. That way you can focus on defining the game element you want to test in the prototype.

TERRAIN EFFECTS				
Type of Terrain	Cost to Enter on Ground	Attack Modifier	Height	Cost to Land in
Clear	1 MP	0	0	1 MP
Soft cover	2 MP	-3	+2	2 MP
Hard cover	2 MP	-5	+3	2 MP
Bunker	2 MP	-7	+1	2 MP

Fig. 17.3 Paper wargames often rely on extensive charts and tables to summarize complex information

Fig. 17.4 Digital prototypes are necessary when creating a video game

Even better, game engines can often create games for a variety of platforms such as Windows, Linux, macOS, iOS, Android, and HTML. That means if you create a prototype on a computer, the game engine can convert that prototype to run on any computer, a smartphone, or a browser. This lets you test a digital prototype on the actual hardware you want your completed game to run on as well.

Because digital prototypes rely on game engines, they require familiarity with a particular game engine and often some basic coding skills in a programming language such as C#, C++, Lua, or a programming language specific to that particular game engine. No matter how familiar you may be with a game engine or how good you may be at coding, creating a digital prototype will always be slower than creating a paper prototype.

The advantage of a digital prototype is that it will be interactive. If you're prototyping a card or board game, you might never need to create a digital prototype. If you're creating a video game, a digital prototype is just the next step after creating a paper prototype as shown in Fig. 17.4.

Creating a digital prototype will take time. The key is to keep the graphics simple so you can focus on how the game works rather than how the game looks at this stage. Since writing code can be time-intensive (especially if you're not familiar with programming), an alternative to text-based coding is visual programming. (All game engines allow designers to program them using text-based programming languages like C# or C++. Most, but not all, game engines also let designers program a game engine using visual programming.)

Instead of writing text in traditional programming languages, visual programming lets designers create nodes and link them together. Such visual graphs clearly identify the logical flow of an algorithm and can create the logic in a video game without forcing the designer to learn a specific programming language. Instead of typing in code, designers can simply drag and drop nodes on the screen and connect them together as shown in Fig. 17.5.

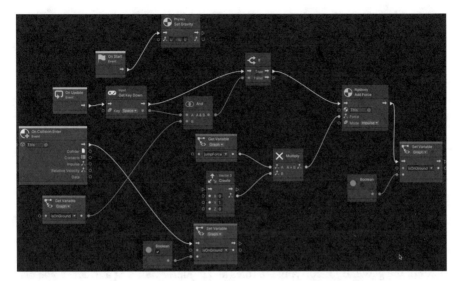

Fig. 17.5 Visual graphs consist of nodes (boxes) and connections (lines between boxes)

However, visual programming graphs have several disadvantages compared to text-based programming languages. First, visual graphs take longer to create. Second, visual graphs often require an additional layer of interpretation. That means visual graphs can run up to 100 times slower than text-based programs, especially for intensive mathematical calculations.

Third, visual graphs take up space. The more the visual graph needs to do such as calculate mathematical formulas or detect input from different types of devices, the larger and more complicated the visual graph will get. This makes visual graphs harder to modify and expand over time. Adding more code to a text-based language means adding more lines of text. Adding more code to a visual graph means drawing more nodes and connections between each node, creating a spaghetti-like jumble that gets increasingly harder to read and understand.

It's possible to program a game engine using just text-based programming languages, just visual graphs, or a combination of the two. Digital prototypes are simply another tool for prototyping video game elements, but they take longer to create and require more skill to make than paper prototypes.

Thought Exercise

Many video games, such as Portal, Doom, and Fallout, have been turned into board games. Study these video games and examine their board game versions. How could the board game versions have worked as paper prototypes to mimic gameplay in a video game?

Many board games (such as Monopoly, Battleship, and The Game of Life) have also been turned into video games. Generally the video game version of a board game simply lets the computer handle the rules, movement of pieces, and dice rolls. How could these board games have been tested using a digital prototype?

Summary

Everyone has an idea for a game, but ideas mean nothing until you're willing to do the hard work of turning that idea into a working and playable game. Nobody takes a game idea and makes a flawless game in one step. Instead, game designers create prototypes to test out different parts of their ideas until they're satisfied they might work.

Prototypes define rules and numeric values assigned to different attributes. All numeric values are arbitrary values that make sense when compared to other attributes of the game. By modifying the rules and numeric values of attributes, you can modify how a prototype works.

Prototypes should be created quickly without regard to their appearance. Because prototypes can be so easy to make, there's less attachment to keeping them. The more prototypes you create, the more ideas you can test in a short amount of time. Each prototype should be created as simple as possible to test one aspect of the game.

Paper prototypes can be created using pencil, paper, and randomizer items such as dice. Digital prototypes can be created on a computer using a game engine. Card and board games likely only need paper prototypes but video games need both paper prototypes and digital prototypes.

The whole purpose of a prototype is to force you to take an abstract idea for a game and define rules and attributes that clearly explain how that game will actually work.

Further Readings

"Game a Week: Teaching Students to Prototype", GDC, https://youtu.be/9O9Q8OVWrFA.
"Hitchhiker's Guide to Rapid Prototypes", GDC, https://youtu.be/sYWkiv1hTPM.
"Game a Week: How to Succeed, Fail, and Learn", Adriel Wallick, https://youtu.be/zsRd_0dBdAI.
"The Games That Designed Themselves", Game Maker's Toolkit, https://youtu.be/kMDe7_YwVKI.
"Lessons in Prototyping from Game Design," Amar Singh, https://medium.theuxblog.com/lessons-in-prototyping-from-game-design-8752df8daa8b.
"The Design Process: Prototyping", Plymouth State University, https://creatinggames.press.plymouth.edu/chapter/the-design-process-prototyping.
"7 Tips For Successful Video Game Prototyping", Department of Play, https://departmentofplay.net/7-tips-for-successful-video-game-prototyping.
"Introduction to Game Design, Prototyping, and Development: From Concept to Playable Game with Unity and C#", Jeremy Gibson, Addison-Wesley Professional, 2017.

"Challenges for Game Designers", Brenda Brathwaite and Ian Schreiber, CreateSpace Independent Publishing Platform, 2008.

"Tabletop Game Design for Video Game Designers", Ethan Ham, Routledge, 2015.

"Seven Steps for a Winning Hypercasual Prototype", Rotem Eldor, https://www.gamesindustry.biz/7-steps-for-a-winning-hypercasual-prototyp.

Chapter 18
Card Game Prototypes

Card games mostly involve playing with information printed directly on each card. As a result, card game prototypes must test the size and information displayed on each card. Displayed information must be consistent to make it easy for players to find the information they need at a glance, but not too overwhelming to make the game hard to understand.

In some cases, there might be a playing field of some kind where the cards must be placed and arranged, but for the most part, the main purpose of a card game prototype is to test the interaction between different cards to make sure the game is balanced, offers players multiple choices (strategies) to pursue, and constantly changes each turn to provide variety.

Card games, like all types of games, focus on three elements:

- Offense – Playing one or more cards to get closer to winning or improve the chances of winning.
- Defense – Playing one or more cards to stop other players from getting closer to winning.
- Management – Choosing the cards to keep and discard to improve your chances of winning.

In simple card games, players may not have all three options available. In blackjack, players mostly focus on offense (trying to get as close to 21 as possible without going over) and management (deciding whether to get another card, use an ace as a 1 or 11, or split cards). Blackjack players can never block other players from winning except indirectly by getting cards that other players might need.

In more complicated card games, players can choose from all three options. In poker, players try to collect the highest scoring hand (offense) and decide which cards to keep and which to discard (management). By placing large bets or bluffing, players can drive other players out of the game (defense).

When designing a card game, designers must define:

© The Author(s), under exclusive license to Springer Nature
Switzerland AG 2023
W. Wang, *The Structure of Game Design*, International Series on Computer,
Entertainment and Media Technology,
https://doi.org/10.1007/978-3-031-32202-0_18

- The different card types
- The relationships that define interactions between card types
- The game structure (number of players, fixed-length vs. no time limit goal)
- The card gameplay

Card games start by shuffling multiple cards in a deck. The game puts all players on an equal footing by giving everyone the same number of cards. However, the random nature of shuffling changes which cards each player gets, and that determines whether one player has an initial advantage over another.

Now it's up to each player to use their skill with the cards they've been dealt to create the greatest chance for winning. This combination of random chance and skill keeps card games interesting for beginners and experts alike.

Thought Exercise

Examine three different card games that can be played with an ordinary 52-card deck. How does each game handle the different values and suits (club, diamond, heart, spade) of the cards?

Examine a card game that uses its own cards. Why does this card game require its own cards? Are these cards as versatile as cards in a typical 52-card deck?

Setting Up a Card Game

Like board games and to a lesser extent with video games, card games are meant to bring people together. For that reason, card games (with the exception of solitaire) emphasize player interaction with each other.

Board games are often races where players try to reach a goal before anyone else. Video games can be played alone or with groups of people who players may never physically see or meet. Card games give people a reason to directly interact with each other, making card games more social than most other types of games. When designing a card game, keep this social aspect in mind.

Card game play revolves around three stages:

- Setting up the cards
- Playing the cards (Getting cards, discarding cards, and applying cards to help get the player closer to winning.)
- Defining a winner

Every card game requires a setup stage. Setting up the cards can be as simple as shuffling a deck of cards to randomize their position, or as complicated as creating your own deck of cards that may contain different cards from your opponent's deck, such as in Magic: The Gathering.

In most card games, players start off with an equal number of cards but the cards themselves may differ although there's still a chance players could get equivalent cards. In blackjack, both players could get 21 with an ace and a king, queen, jack, or 10. Even though only one player can hold an ace of hearts, the other player could have an ace of diamonds, clubs, or spades, which has the exact same value.

In Magic: The Gathering, players create their own decks. Not only is it extremely rare for players to build decks with identical cards, but it's even less likely that two players would deal themselves the exact same cards as well.

Card game setups almost always create unbalanced hands among players. In poker, it's possible to get dealt such a poor hand that it's nearly impossible to win. However, poker typically involves playing multiple hands. That way a single bad hand won't cause a player to lose the entire game.

Ideally, any hand players get can be a potentially winning hand with the right amount of skill in playing the cards. Even if skillful players can't turn a losing hand into a winning hand all the time, they can tilt the odds in their favor often enough to partially offset bad luck. Ultimately, skill, not luck, should determine the winner.

Thought Exercise

Card games typically start with an equal number of cards for each player. However, the contents of those cards can differ in the following ways:

- Cards usually different, but possibly equivalent (such as blackjack)
- Cards almost always different (such as Magic: The Gathering)

Can you think of a card game that begins by giving players an unequal number of cards? Can you think of a card game that begins by giving players identical cards?

The Game Sequence of a Card Game

Once a card game has been set up, the main gameplay involves evaluating, management, and application. After each player gets dealt a random set of cards, the first step is evaluating what they have.

If players have been dealt cards from the same deck, each player automatically knows which cards an opponent cannot possibly have. In poker, if one player has the three aces, there's no way any other player can have anything more than one ace. This knowledge of their own cards and the number of those type of cards in the deck can give each player an edge.

As cards get used up, players can use "card counting" where they keep track of which cards remain. In blackjack, card counting lets players make increasingly accurate predictions on which cards they could draw because they know which cards are no longer in play. To prevent this, games often have large numbers of cards to make card counting difficult, or shuffle cards after each play to eliminate card counting altogether.

In Magic: The Gathering, each player creates their own deck and draws cards from their own deck. As a result, each player has no idea what cards are in each other's deck. This makes "card counting" impossible, increasing the challenge of the game. Part of the challenge lies in creating a deck with the best combinations of cards that work together.

Once players get dealt their cards, the second step involves managing those cards. The initial hand each player gets dealt will rarely be optimal. So the challenge lies in deciding which cards to keep and use, and in some cases, which cards to discard.

At this point, another challenge comes from seeing the cards an opponent plays and deciding which cards to play in response. This third step involves playing or applying a card to improve your own chances of winning or hurting another player's chances of winning.

Ideally, players will have the perfect card to counter their opponent's last card, but in most cases, players must choose which card to play, balancing the idea between using their best card now or holding it back to deal with a potentially greater threat in the future. Based on the currently held cards and the opponent's cards, players must determine how to use their hand (known information) against their opponent's possible future moves (unknown information).

Gameplay in a card game often involves this repetitive loop of getting cards, evaluating them, and using them. The challenge is knowing which cards to use and when.

Thought Exercise

Pick a card game that uses an ordinary 52-card deck and identify the repetitive gameplay. For example, poker's repetitive loop involves getting dealt a hand, choosing which cards to discard, drawing new cards, and then placing bets. What is the repetitive loop of the card game you chose?

Pick a card game that does not use an ordinary 52-card deck. What are the major categories of cards? What is the repetitive loop of this specific card game and how could this repetitive gameplay not be possible using an ordinary 52-card deck.

Defining the Winning Conditions of a Card Game

The first step in designing a card game is deciding how players can win. This goal directly shapes the purpose of the entire deck of cards. Winning conditions can be based on the following:

- Fixed number of turns vs. no fixed time length
- One or more paths to win

When a game ends after a fixed number of turns, this creates a "ticking time bomb" effect that forces players to take increasingly risky chances to win before time runs out. Think of any timed sport such as football or basketball that forces players to get ahead before a fixed time limit ends.

Most card games do not have a fixed time limit. Instead, these games can go on as long as the players want or until one player reaches a specific goal first. Essentially, games with no time limit act like racing games where the first person to reach a goal wins no matter how long it may take.

Some card games, such as blackjack or poker, consist of short games that can be played multiple times. Other card games take longer to play. In general, the simpler the rules, the shorter the game, which allows for multiple plays. The more games played, the less players can depend on luck to help them win.

Every game needs a goal for players to reach. Thus the game becomes a race to reach that goal first. However to add variety, some card games offer two or more ways to win. This creates uncertainty since someone almost at the goal can still lose.

In Mille Bornes, players must accumulate distance cards until they reach 1000, which defines a single path to winning. On the other hand, to win the Ticket to Ride card game, players must accumulate points to win. Since players can accumulate points in a variety of ways, this creates multiple strategies players can pursue to win the game.

When creating a card game, focus on how players win, whether there's a fixed number of turns or whenever the first player reaches a goal. Also consider whether there is only one way to reach the goal or multiple ways. The goal of the game, plus the path (or paths) to that goal determine how the cards within a deck should be designed.

Thought Exercise

Pick a card game like blackjack that has no fixed time length to win. How would the game change if blackjack ended after a fixed number of hands such as ten? How would the game change if the game ended after the player has been dealt a fixed number of cards such as one hundred?

If a card game only has one way to win, how would that game change if there was another way to win? For example, the goal of blackjack is to get as close to 21 without going over, but what if you could pay extra money to allow going over 21, such as paying an extra $10 per each additional number over 21. By paying $10, you could hit 22 or less and still win the game. By paying $20, you could hit 23 or less and still win the game.

Defining Card Types

What makes card games interesting are the types of cards available and their relationships that defines how they interact. In an ordinary 52-card deck, cards have two characteristics:

- A value (2-10, Jack, Queen, King, Ace)
- A suit (hearts, diamonds, clubs, spades)

The combination of values and suits makes each card unique since there can only be one 5 of spades or one 10 of diamonds. In some games, the suits make no difference such as in blackjack where a 4 of clubs is no different than a 4 of diamonds.

In other games, the combination of values and suits can make a huge difference. In poker, a 4 of clubs can spell the difference between a straight flush (five cards in sequential order of the same suit such as a 2 of clubs, 3, of clubs, 4 of clubs, 5 of clubs, and a 6 of clubs), or a much weaker straight (five cards in sequential order of any suit such as 2 of clubs, 3, of clubs, 4 of hearts, 5 of clubs, and a 6 of clubs).

When a card game defines its own unique cards, those cards are often divided into separate types or categories that serve different purposes such as cards for:

- Getting the player closer to winning
- Protecting chances of winning (or hindering an opponent's chances of winning)
- Planning for the long-term future

Every card game must include cards that can get the player closer to achieving a specific goal to win the game. Such cards are essential such as in blackjack where the entire deck consists of cards with different numeric values ranging from 1-11.

Although adding the numeric values of cards together is the entire basis for blackjack, all games require choices. The more choices available to players, the greater the control players have over the game. If blackjack just consisted of adding cards together, the only choice would be whether to get more cards or not.

To add variety and give players additional choices, blackjack also lets players decide whether an ace should represent a 1 or an 11. An additional choice involves splitting hands if players get dealt two cards of identical values such as two aces or two 8 s. These additional rules for splitting hands or changing the value of an ace helps increase the player's chances of winning without requiring any additional cards at all.

While most card games based on a typical 52-card deck focus on cards that get players closer to winning with options for increasing (or decreasing another player's) chance of winning, card games that rely on their own cards often include additional cards for increasing (or decreasing) a player's chances of winning along with separate cards for improving a player's chance of winning in the future.

In the card game Mille Bornes, the goal is to be the first player to reach 1000 (measured in either miles or kilometers). Distance cards define the how far the player has travelled and represent the cards that get a player closer to winning.

To help or hinder winning, Mille Bornes contains additional cards called Hazards and Remedies. Hazards temporarily slow or halt another player's progress while Remedies remove these Hazards. Hazards act like attack cards to hurt other players while Remedies act like defense cards to eliminate any Hazards other players have played against you.

Finally, Mille Bornes includes additional cards to increase a player's long-term future chances of winning. These cards, called Safeties, provide permanent defense against certain Hazards as shown in Fig. 18.1.

Common card elements include:

- Card values
- Card modifiers
- Card relationships
- Wildcards

Cards typically represent a unit that the player controls, so card values define the strength of that unit. Ordinary playing cards range in value from 2 to 10 along with jack, queen, king, and ace. Because playing cards have a numeric value, they can also be used as a form randomization. Instead of rolling a die, players can draw a card to select a random number.

Cards unique to a particular game often include values as well that represent one or more characteristics of that unit such as its combat or movement ability. Such cards provide as much information as possible within the physical limitations of a card.

Card modifiers provide a way to slightly alter another card. One common modifier is a form of defense that cancels out another player's attack card. Another common modifier is a form of offense that increases a player's unit to improve its chances of success. Card modifiers create variety by giving players additional choices to consider.

Many cards have unique relationships with one another, which creates additional surprises to a game that keeps play unpredictable and challenging. One common relationship is to have one card enhance the effects of another card. This creates a doubling effect where playing one card may do something (good or bad), but adding the modifier makes that card far more powerful.

Finally, many card games include a wildcard that gives players choices for how that card can be used. In many games based on 52-card decks, adding a joker creates a wildcard that can represent any value the player wishes. Wildcards alter a game by giving players the freedom to choose what they want (within limits) rather than wait to draw a specific type of card instead.

When creating a card game, consider the main units and their values, any modifiers that can be applied to a card, any special relationships between cards, and the use of any wildcards within the game that give players choices.

Although nearly every card game has written rules, cards must display as much information as possible to let players know their options with that particular card. For consistency, cards often display information within a fixed format. That way players can easily glance at a card and look for the type of information they need without resorting to reading a rule book as shown in Fig. 18.2.

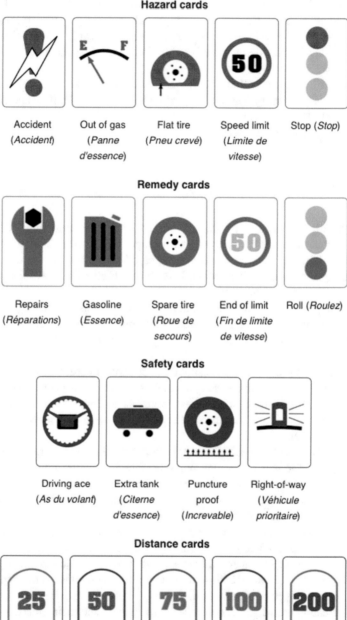

Fig. 18.1 The different categories of cards in Mille Bornes

Bug	Hacker	Crash	Virus
Prevents one program from running. Can only be remedied by applying a Patch card.	Infiltrates the computer to steal information. Can only be remedied by applying a Firewall card.	Stops a program from running. Can only be remedied by applying a Boot Up card.	Infects a program. Can only be remedied by applying an Antivirus card.

Patch	Registry Optimizer	Firewall	AntiVirus
Patches and updates a program to cancel the affects of a Bug card.	Repairs the registry to cancel the affects of a Registry Failure card.	Block unauthorized access to the computer to cancel the affects of a Hacker card.	Removes a virus to cancel the affects of a Virus card.

Fig. 18.2 Cards display information in a consistent way to make it easy to read

The main card types are those that can help the player win. Then the other card types provide ways to increase or decrease chances of winning through modifiers, relationships, or wildcards.

Thought Exercise

Pick a card game based on a regular 52-card deck and identify how the different values determine how to win the game. Are there any ways to modify the cards? Is there any special relationship between specific cards? Are there any choices a player can make due to a wildcard?

Summary

Card games can often be played on any flat surface and engage two or more players. Cards are designed to be held in groups so information printed on the card should be readily visible. Every card game needs cards that allow players to win the game, and additional cards to attack other players or defend against other players.

When playing a card game, the variety of different cards appearing keeps the gameplay interesting. The number of cards and decks can make each game unpredictable, which makes every game challenging.

Essentially, card games are puzzle and strategy games that force players to solve challenges and outwit opponents. The interaction between cards creates unique puzzles to solve and the behavior of other players helps dictate long-term strategies needed to defeat them. Combine puzzles with strategy and that's the foundation for nearly every card game in the world.

Further Readings

"Cards In War-Games With Volko Ruhnke", Georgetown University Wargaming Society, https://youtu.be/WIBpCJ09KhA.

"Designing Race for the Galaxy: Making a Strategic Card Game", GDC, https://youtu.be/JcyyeAww2wc.

Chapter 19
Understanding Game Engines

There are many ways to create a digital prototype for a video game. To prototype the user interface, use a presentation program (such as PowerPoint) where each slide represents a single screen and their order defines how one screen transitions to another. However, to prototype gameplay elements for a video game, you'll need to create a digital prototype using a game engine.

A game engine takes care of the common aspects of a video game (such as detecting collisions, dealing with gravity, and detecting input from a keyboard, mouse, touch screen, or game controller). Without a game engine, designers would have to code everything themselves. Such a process would be time-consuming and error-prone, which is why most video game developers rely on tested and proven game engines instead.

A typical game engine offers the following video game elements:

- Graphics
- Sound
- Physics
- User interface
- Input controls (keyboard, mouse, game controller, touch screen, touchpad)
- Artificial intelligence for controlling enemies
- Networking (for multiplayer play over the Internet)

Game engines provide the technical details of making a game work so designers can focus on the creative details for making their specific game. A game engine essentially provides a simple, generic video game to customize so designers don't have to create every video game element from scratch.

© The Author(s), under exclusive license to Springer Nature
Switzerland AG 2023
W. Wang, *The Structure of Game Design*, International Series on Computer,
Entertainment and Media Technology,
https://doi.org/10.1007/978-3-031-32202-0_19

How to Use a Game Engine

A game engine provides the basic foundation for creating a video game. Then it's up to the game designers to add unique assets such as player characters, instructions that define how the game works, game levels that define the location of enemies, allies, and resources, and the location of the goal that players are striving to reach.

Every game engine tends to specialize in certain features. As a result, there is no single "best" game engine to use. Instead, any choice involves finding the best game engine for your particular needs. Some game engines specialize in offering specific features for creating one type of game but lack other features for creating other types of games. A game engine might specialize in creating 2D games, but completely lack features for making 3D games. The advantage of such a game engine is that all of its features will help you make 2D games, but if you ever want to make a 3D game, you'll need to learn another game engine.

Other game engines offer multiple features, but specialize in one or two specific features. Such a game engine might offer the ability to create both 2D and 3D games, but really excel at creating 2D games over 3D games. The advantage is that if you later want to create a 3D game, you don't need to learn a new game engine. The disadvantage is that the game engine might offer features you don't need and that its features for creating a 3D game might not be as good as other game engines that make it much easier to create 3D games.

Some of the different game engine capabilities include:

- 2D games
- 3D games
- Platform support
- Programming language options
- Specialized game creation

Different Game Types

2D games restrict movement to horizontal and/or vertical scrolling, or no scrolling at all. Players may view the game from the side, top, or isometric (2.5D) perspective that simulates 3D geometry. The key is that players cannot move along the Z-axis (in and out from the screen surface).

A side perspective scrolls the background to follow the player. Side scrollers emphasize left and right horizontal movement, such as Mario Brothers. Platformer games emphasize up and down vertical movement such as Donkey Kong where players gradually ascend or descend between different platforms. The direction players must move to reach a goal determines whether the game is predominantly a side scroller (the goal must be reached by moving to the left or right) or a platformer (the goal must be reached by moving up or down).

Both a top-down and isometric (2.5D) perspective provides an overhead view of the game. Where side perspective games let you see what's to the front, back, top, and below, top-down perspective games let you see what's to the front, back, left, and right.

3D games specifically allow players to move forward and back along with side to side or up and down. First-person shooter games are one type of popular 3D game where players see through the eyes of the character that they're controlling.

Another type of perspective is an over the shoulder view where players can see the back of their character. This type of perspective allows players to see around the player character so they can spot enemies and obstacles around them easier.

If you want to create different types of 2D and 3D games, you'll want a game engine that can create all these different game types. Otherwise you may spend time learning a game engine only to find out later it won't let you create a certain type of game later.

Thought Exercise

Two popular, general purpose game engines that are nearly equal in features are Unity (unity.com) and Unreal (unrealengine.com). Visit both websites and compare their features. Based on these features, which game engine do you think would be best for your particular game idea and why?

Two less popular but rival game engines are Godot (godotengine.org) and GameMaker Studio (gamemaker.io). Godot is free and open source but GameMaker Studio is proprietary and costs money to use. By studying different game engines, you can get a better idea which features might be most important for your game idea.

Platform Support

Whether you create a 2D or 3D game, the more platforms the game runs on, the greater the potential audience. Some common gaming platforms include:

- Personal computers
- Game consoles (including handheld consoles)
- Mobile devices (smartphones and tablets)
- Web (run inside any browser)

Personal computers run on operating systems that include Windows, macOS, and Linux where Windows is the most popular PC gaming operating system. While it's still possible to sell games on discs for people to install on their computers, it's far more cost efficient to distribute games over the Internet through a gaming platform such as Steam, Epic Games Store, Itch.io, Apple Arcade, or GOG.com.

Although personal computers remain popular gaming platforms, there's an equally large market for games that run on game consoles such as Sony's PlayStation, Microsoft's Xbox, and Nintendo's Switch. In different parts of the world, game consoles are more popular than personal computers but in other parts of the world, personal computers or smart phones are used for gaming more often than game consoles. The regional market you want to target can determine what game engines you might want to use (or avoid).

Another huge gaming market are mobile computers such as smartphones and tablets that run either iOS or Android. While games for personal computers and gaming consoles are meant to be played for long periods of time (such as hours), games designed for mobile devices can be played in minutes. This means mobile games are often shorter, easier to learn, and less complicated to focus on single or dual players who are physically together.

A fourth gaming platform is the Web where games can run in any browser. Such Web games are popular with people who do not have the space or computing power to run the latest video games. As a result, Web-based games are often simple and easy to learn, much like games designed for mobile devices.

Each gaming platform appeals to different people so games need to be designed for each audience and platform. For example, a game designed for mobile devices will likely be short and easy to learn while focusing on touch screen controls. Such a game may not appeal to game console users who want more involved games that can be controlled through game controllers.

So the game engine you choose depends partly on which platforms that game engine supports. If a game engine does not support a platform you want your game to run on, you'll need to use a different game engine.

Thought Exercise

Which gaming platform would you want to reach with your game idea? Based on the gaming platform most important to you, research different game engines and identify the one you think would be best for your particular game.

Programming Language Options

To use a game engine, you need to load assets such as graphics and audio. To make your game actually work, you'll need to write code. However, game engines tend to offer one or more different programming languages. The programming language you prefer might define which game engines to consider.

Some popular programming languages used in game engines include:

- C++ (used in Unreal, CryEngine, and O3DE)
- C# (used in Unity, Stride, and Godot)
- Lua (used in Defold, Solar2D, and O3DE)
- Proprietary languages (used in GameMaker Studio and Godot)

Many game engines support only one programming language but others support multiple programming languages, letting you choose the language you like for that particular game engine. Since writing code may be too difficult for many people, many game engines also offer a visual scripting option.

With visual scripting, you create a program visually using nodes (boxes) and links (connections between the nodes). Visual scripting provides a way for non-programmers to control a game without learning programming or waiting for a programmer to write a program for them.

If a game engine offers a traditional programming language and a visual scripting option, it's possible to create a game using both, or just one or the other. Although visual scripting can be easy for non-programmers to use, they tend to get clumsy when writing large programs.

Unfortunately, visual scripts tend to run much slower than traditional programming language code. Even worse, visual scripting takes up larger amounts of space just to make the simplest program. What might take a handful of lines of text in a traditional language like C++ could take up half a screen with a visual scripting language.

The end result is that creating short, simple programs is easy with visual scripting languages, but creating large, complex programs creates a tangle of lines and boxes that become increasingly hard to understand and modify. A 100-line program in a traditional language like C++ takes up a little more space than a 50-line program. However, doubling the complexity of a visual scripting program can more than double the size of the visual script.

So the main purpose of visual scripting is to make it easy to get part of a video game working, especially for non-programmers. Then it's common to either keep the visual script program small or rewrite that visual script in a traditional programming language later.

Since traditional programming languages like C++, C#, and even Lua weren't specifically designed for games, some game engines offer proprietary languages designed specifically to make writing video games easy.

Such proprietary languages are often based on existing programming languages, such as Python, to make learning them easier. Since game engines often do not support many programming languages, you need to choose the programming language you're most familiar with first and then find a game engine that uses your favorite programming language.

If you don't mind learning a proprietary language designed specifically for writing games, consider a game engine that offers a proprietary language.

Thought Exercise

Examine O3DE (www.o3de.org) and GameMaker Studio (gamemaker.io), which both offer proprietary languages along with visual scripting. Based on what you learn about the proprietary languages used in O3DE and GameMaker Studio, would you want to use either game engine, knowing you'll need to learn a proprietary language? Why or why not?

Using Specialty Game Engines

Most game engines are designed for creating all types of video games. The advantage is that once you learn how to use that one game engine, you can apply your knowledge of that game engine to create any other types of games you wish. However the disadvantage is that general purpose game engines are not optimized for any particular type of game. That means the game engine may be unnecessarily complicated and overwhelm you with features you don't need.

As an alternative to general purpose game engines, many game designers rely on specialty game engines designed to create one specific type of game or offer a unique feature not easily found in rival game engines. By using a specialty game engine, you can create a particular type of game much easier and faster because it's focused on creating the exact type of game you want. The disadvantage is that if you want to create a different type of game, you'll need to learn and use a completely different game engine.

Table 19.1 lists specialty game engines and the types of games they focus on creating:

Unlike the more popular general purpose game engines (Unity and Unreal), specialty game engines lack a large user base, which means fewer resources for getting help in using the game engine. Specialty game engines may force you to learn a particular programming language that you may not want to use and may not be able to create games for all types of platforms such as mobile and consoles.

Ultimately, you have to decide whether it's worth learning a specialty game engine and living with that specialty game engine's limitations, or using a general purpose game engine and creating much of the game yourself that a specialty game engine could do for you instead.

Thought Exercise

Examine the specialty game engines that interest you and study its features. What features do you like? What possible limitations can you identify? For your game idea, would a specialty game engine be better than a general purpose game engine?

Table 19.1 Specialty game engines

Game engine	Specialty	Cost
Adventure Game Studio (www.adventuregamestudio.co.uk)	Adventure games	Free and open source
Aleph One (alephone.lhowon.org)	First-person shooter (FPS) games	Free and open source
Bitsy (bitsy.org)	Narrative-based, 8-pixel art games	Free and open source
Castle (castle-engine.io)	Allows game creation using the Pascal programming language	Free and open source
Construct (www.construct.net)	2D games created using visual programming	Commercial and proprietary
Ink (www.inklestudios.com/ink/)	Text-based narrative games	Free and open source
OctopusKit (invadingoctopus.io/octopuskit)	Create 2D games with the Swift programming language and SwiftUI user interface framework	Free and open source
RPG Maker (www.rpgmakerweb.com)	Role-playing games (RPG)	Commercial and proprietary
Ren'Py (www.renpy.org)	Visual novel games	Free and open source
Solar2D (solar2d.com)	2D games	Free and open source
Spring (springrts.com)	Real-time strategy (RTS) games	Free and open source
Twine (twinery.org)	Interactive non-linear, text-based story games	Free and open source
Vassal (vassalengine.org)	Building and playing adaptations of board games and card games	Free and open source
Visionaire-Studio (www.visionaire-studio.net)	2D and 2.5D point and click adventure games	Commercial and proprietary
Worldforge (www.worldforge.org)	Massively multiplayer online role-playing games (MMORPG)	Free and open source

Choosing a Game Engine

Game engines can take care of the technical details of a video game so you can focus on the unique features that make your game work. Since there are so many different game engines available, choosing one can be overwhelming. It's entirely possible that one game engine will make creating a game easy while a different game engine would make creating that same game much harder because of what features each game engine offers and your own personal preferences.

To help you decide which game engine might be right for you, consider these criteria:

- Popularity
- Ease of use
- Cost

- Programming language options
- Features
- Support

The two most popular game engines (at the time of this writing) are Unity and Unreal. Learning a popular game engine means your skills can be marketable since more companies will need people familiar with Unity or Unreal than with less popular game engines. From a job perspective, Unity or Unreal game engine experience is far more useful than learning other game engines.

Popular game engines also offer plenty of support from its millions of users. That means more books, training classes, and online resources are available for Unity and Unreal than for other game engines. In case you're not a graphic artist or can't hire one, both Unity and Unreal offer a large asset store where other people sell or give away graphic and audio assets that you can use in your own games. Other game engines rarely offer the same amount of professional quality assets.

Also consider ease of use. Unity is considered easier to learn and use than Unreal. Because of that, more independent game developers tend to start with Unity and either stay with Unity or switch to another game engine later. What one person might find easier to use, another person might find harder to use so ease of use depends entirely on your perspective.

Another factor to consider is cost. Many game engines are open source so they're free to use. Any games you create with them remain 100% under your control. In comparison, some game engines cost money just for the right to use it. Any games you create using that game engine remains 100% under your control.

Other game engines (such as Unity and Unreal) are free to use but once your game starts earning revenue above a fixed amount, you must pay a certain percentage of your profits to the game engine publisher. However, if your game never earns money past a fixed threshold, you're never obligated to pay any royalties at all.

So the three most common costs for game engines are:

- Free
- Upfront cost, but no additional costs afterwards
- Free, but must pay royalties if your game earns a certain amount

Even though there are plenty of free, open source game engines on the market, many game designers prefer Unity or Unreal because both game engines are backed by a major corporation. That means the company will continue improving the game engine on a regular schedule.

While open source game engines let you access and modify the source code, doing this yourself will take time from actually creating your game. Open source game engines have varying levels of support from a handful of volunteers to the backing of major corporations. That means open source game engines have varying levels of development where regular updates and bug fixes may occur sporadically. If you need the dependability of a reliable game engine with regular updates, your choice of potential game engines narrows considerably.

Every game engine has its strengths and weaknesses. Ultimately a game engine is a tool so it's important to choose the right tool for your particular game idea. The worst game engine in the hands of a skilled game designer will create better results than the best game engine in the hands of a novice game designer.

The more game engines you evaluate, the better you'll be able to identify the features you need so you can find the game engine that's best for you.

Thought Exercise

Make a list of the top three criteria that's most important to you (such as price, programming language used, or support). Evaluate different game engines (https://en.wikipedia.org/wiki/List_of_game_engines) and identify at least three game engines that match your criteria. Which game engine would you choose and why? Why would you not choose another game engine?

Summary

Game engines provide a foundation for creating a game so you can focus on your game details rather than on the common properties of every video game such as displaying graphics on the screen or detecting user input from a touch screen or keyboard. Because there are so many game engines available, every game engine offers strengths and weaknesses.

Game engines must be programmed, which means learning the programming language that the game engine uses. This can be a popular language such as C++ or C#, or a less popular or proprietary language. For non-programmers, many game engines offer a visual scripting option as well.

Many game engines are free and open source, but the cost of using a commercial game engine might be worth it for the support, skill marketability, third-party assets, and regular updates. When choosing a game engine, consider the long-term benefits of learning that particular game engine and its programming language.

Game engines are a crucial tool for creating video games so make sure you learn at least one game engine. The best game engine is the one that helps you create a finished game.

Further Reading

"The Complete Game Engine Overview", Perforce, https://www.perforce.com/resources/vcs/game-engine-overview.

Chapter 20
Playing Field Prototypes

Every game must be played on a playing field. For card games, that playing field can be any flat surface. For board games and sports, the playing field is a defined area that restricts where playing pieces can move and the boundaries where they must stay within. For video games, the playing field appears within the computer, but can be as simple as a single screen or as expansive as an entire open world that players can endlessly explore.

Since every game needs a playing surface, one of the first items to prototype is the playing field. Some questions a playing field prototype can answer right away are:

- What are the boundaries of the playing field?
- Where can players move in the playing field?
- What obstacles block or restrict the player's movement?
- What items help the player?
- What are players trying to do in the playing field?

Defining Playing Field Boundaries

How big is the playing field? Even in the most expansive open world video game that allows players to explore entire galaxies, players still need a specific place to do something within the game. Board games typically define a boundary based on the size of a folding board that can fit within a game box. Sports define a boundary based on an arbitrary size.

Boundaries aren't just limited to the edges. In many board games, boundaries define where players can move. Three common ways board games restrict movement include:

© The Author(s), under exclusive license to Springer Nature
Switzerland AG 2023
W. Wang, *The Structure of Game Design*, International Series on Computer,
Entertainment and Media Technology,
https://doi.org/10.1007/978-3-031-32202-0_20

- Race track
- Circular tracks
- Unlimited areas

Many children's games use a race track path that guides exactly where players can move, usually in one direction as shown in Fig. 20.1. The winner is the first player who gets to the end before anyone else.

Circular tracks allow unlimited repetition. Such games restrict movement along the circular track but players may land on the same space multiple times as shown in Fig. 20.2. Games like Monopoly use circular tracks because the game does not depend on players reaching a specific spot on the board, unlike a race track design.

Rather than restrict movement along a track, other board games may give players the freedom to move anywhere within the boundaries of the board. This gives players the freedom to choose which units to move and in which area to improve their chances of winning the game as shown in Fig. 20.3.

Video games may offer similar endless landscapes to explore, but may divide the entire game world into specific areas or levels. Each level represents mastery over a specific skill and provides a way for players to measure their progress towards winning the game.

A playing field prototype can help you define the best size for a playing field. Small playing fields force players and enemies together, which can encourage combat as often as possible. Larger playing fields allow players to avoid enemies if they wish, allowing less combat and more options such as stealth to sneak by enemies.

Fig. 20.1 A race track design defines direction, movement, and an end

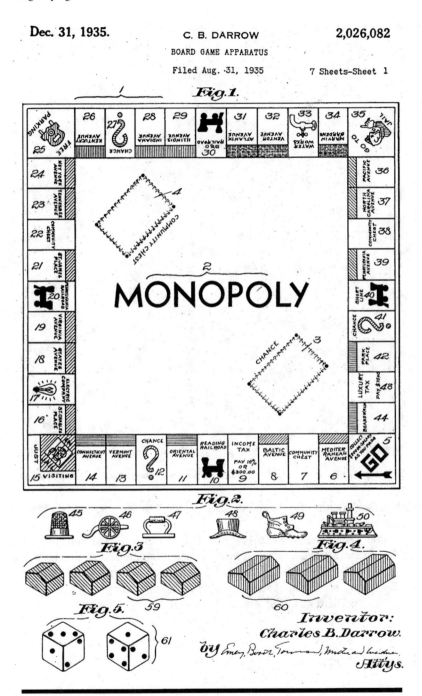

Fig. 20.2 Circular tracks allow players to land on spaces multiple times

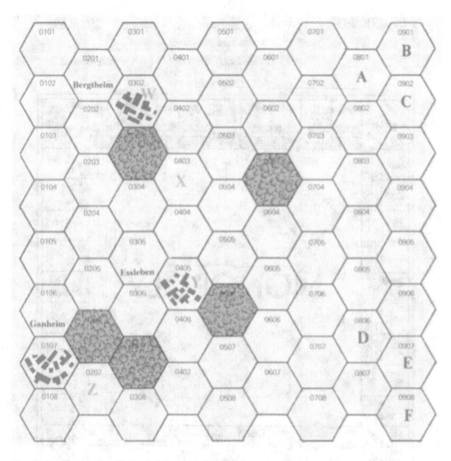

Fig. 20.3 Games may allow players to move units almost anywhere on the entire playing field

Video games often divide the entire game world into separate levels where each level can vary in size.

In battle royale games, the playing field starts out large and gradually shrinks over time to force players together, thereby increasing the chance that they'll have to fight each other. The size and shape of the playing field greatly influences gameplay. By testing out different sizes and shapes for a game's playing field, you can identify the optimum shape for your game design.

Thought Exercise

Pick a board game. How would gameplay be affected if the board were enlarged to five times its current size? How would gameplay be affected if the board size was cut in half? How does the board game ensure that all players have an equal chance of winning?

Pick a video game. How does the video game display the entire playing field? How does the video game keep players from going too far away from the main playing area?

Defining Movement Within the Playing Field

The playing field prototype must test where players can move within the game. A two-dimensional game restricts players to moving horizontally (x-axis) and vertically (y-axis), while a three-dimensional game allows players to also move along the z-axis.

The size of the playing field limits where the player can move, but within the playing field there may be additional restrictions. In baseball, the batting team's players can only run along the base paths while the fielding team's players can freely run anywhere they wish. In hockey, players on both teams may move freely anywhere they wish, but the puck must cross the blue line before any attacking players do or else they are called offsides.

In sports and many board games, the movement restrictions within the playing field are uniform, meaning that the only differences between one area and another may be its location closer or further away from a particular area. However, one area of the playing field does not contain obstacles that another area does not.

In other board games and many video games, internal obstacles are not distributed uniformly. One part of the playing field may contain a river and another part may contain a forest. Because the internal obstacles differ so drastically, there's the risk that the playing field itself will not offer players a fair chance of success depending on the location where they start.

The playing field defines the outer boundaries of the game along with the inner restrictions of movement within the game. In board and video games, movement is often confined to regularly spaces (such as squares or hexagons) where playing pieces may move. In some video games, this movement grid appears on top of any graphic terrain, but in other video games, this movement grid may exist but is invisible to the player.

Square grids, such as those found on a chess board, let players move pieces horizontally, vertically, and diagonally. The problem with diagonal movement on square grids is moving diagonally covers a greater length than moving horizontally or vertically. Thus if a playing piece can only move three squares, diagonal movement lets a piece move further than if it moved horizontally or vertically.

To fix this problem, games may use hexagons. With hexagons, playing pieces can move in six different directions. One potential problem with hexagons is the orientation of the "grain" of the hexagon grids. When a line is drawn with the "grain," the line can be perfectly straight. However when a line is drawn against the "grain," then the line must zig zag, creating an artificial path for movement in a straight line. How a game overlays hexagons on the playing field can subtly define how players can move within that game as shown in Fig. 20.4.

Most importantly, a playing field prototype can make sure that players can reach all areas of the playing field. Otherwise it's possible to design a playing field that players can never access, making it pointless to create that part of the playing field in the first place.

In some cases, there might be a good reason for why a player should not access certain parts of a playing field. In many historical simulations, the playing field represents a map of an actual area that might include part of the ocean or lakes. Such areas might be inaccessible to playing pieces to maintain historical accuracy, but any such inaccessible areas should take up as little space in the playing field as possible. Otherwise large areas of the playing field will be unusable to the player.

Essentially, a playing field prototype should test that players can move where the designer expects them to move. That means making sure there are no areas where the player cannot reach.

Just as game designers must balance the opposing forces to ensure no player has an overwhelming advantage over another, so must playing field prototypes balance the playing field so no position is more important than any other area. Otherwise players will simply crowd one particular area of the playing field and ignore the rest.

In sports and simple video games, the playing field represents a blank area. However in many video games, the playing field does not appear as a flat, blank area. Instead, the playing field may be filled with trees, buildings, bridges, or bushes.

In a wargame simulation, the terrain might contain desert, swamps, forests, mountains, and open fields. Each of these different terrain can affect movement.

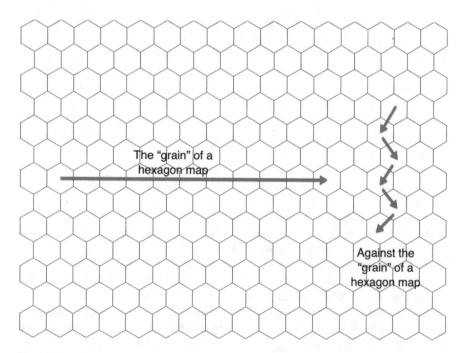

Fig. 20.4 The orientation of a hexagonal map indirectly constrains movement

Thus the playing field prototype must test to ensure all areas of the playing field are useful in some way. If part of a playing field is never useful for any reason, players will simply abandon that area over time.

In a video game, a playing field may contain walls, rivers, lava, open pits, and other obstacles that either completely block movement or slow movement down. Video game playing fields may be an open world where players can freely roam, or mazes that direct players down certain pathways.

Thought Exercise

What movement limitations define where playing pieces can be placed on the playing field? How does the playing field ensure that players have an equal chance of winning no matter what their initial starting location might be?

How do obstacles in the playing field affect where a player can move? How do obstacles in the playing field hinder the player's movement options?

Defining a Goal in the Playing Field

The most important part about a playing field is identifying a goal for players to move towards. By knowing what the goal is, a playing field prototype can test whether players can reach this goal without it being too easy or too hard.

Goals must be clear. If a goal is not obvious, then players won't have any idea what they're supposed to do. If players are confused, they won't have fun.

In many cases, goals are clearly marked so players can see them from a distance. That way even from the start, players know which direction they should go, even if they don't know exactly how they'll get there. Many video games make goals visible by making them appear as mountains or towers.

This design of goals as visible landmarks stems from the design of theme parks that use tall, distinct structures to help orient people. In Disneyland, Sleeping Beauty's castle appears in the center of the park so people in any location can easily see it from any distance. Once people can see a landmark, they can gradually make their way towards it.

That's the same principle behind designing video games. The goal should be visible so players know which direction they should go. Prominent landmarks work in video games set in the outdoors, but such prominent landmarks don't work in indoor settings such as caves or dungeons. In that case, the design of the setting should gradually funnel players in the direction they need to go.

In a dungeon, there might be multiple directions players could move, but no matter which direction players choose, it will gradually lead them towards the goal such as an exit. Such a design limits players to either moving closer towards the goal or backwards away from the goal. This makes it easy for players to know which direction they're going at all times.

Sometimes, video games might deliberately want to disorient players, such as in horror games. By trapping players in a twisting maze-like setting, the game world works against the player finding an exit. The goal of such settings is to keep players from escaping.

Any playing field should maximize its space. So the playing field prototype can identify which parts of the playing field players tend to use most. That way designers can change the output so players spend a nearly equal amount of time using all parts of the playing field.

Paths to the goal may be linear or branching. A linear path provides the greatest control over the player's experience (from a designer's perspective), but limits the player's freedom to choose. With a linear path, designers know exactly the order players will encounter obstacles, resources, enemies, and non-player characters.

A branching path provides multiple ways to reach a goal. These branching paths can be mutually exclusive, meaning if players choose one path, they may never explore any of the alternative paths. Other times, branching paths may allow players to go back and choose a different path to explore more of the map or in case they get stuck on one path and want to try a different one instead.

Paths to the goal must be clear and obvious, or else players won't know what to do and the game will feel confusing and pointless. A single path allows the game designer to control the player's experience, which is often used in games heavily dependent on stories. Multiple paths provide greater freedom for the player but less control of the order that players encounter obstacles. This creates a less defined story experience. In some open world games, players choose their own goals.

In Minecraft, players can do what they want and go anywhere they want. However, even in such open worlds, the playing field must provide clues for what players might do, such as digging for resources, building a structure, hunting animals, or exploring a specific area of the map.

Instead of creating an open world where players can do anything they want, or a single path that restricts player's choices, video games might offer multiple paths to a single goal, which gives players the option of choosing the path they like best. Multiple paths also provide players alternatives in case obstacles along one path prove too difficult to overcome. Yet just as with a single path, a playing field prototype must ensure that there are no obstacles so difficult that players cannot get past them.

Ideally, navigation through a playing area should also be fun and interesting. Players should be able to practice different skills and learn something new such as another skill or gain information about the game world that will be useful later.

Complex video games often divide the playing field into separate areas or levels. That means each level can focus on teaching players something different. One level might emphasize climbing and jumping while another level might emphasize swimming and sailing a boat.

Ultimately, a playing field prototypes need to ensure that players can find a goal and reach it.

Thought Exercise

Pick a board game. Just by looking at the board, is the player's goal clear? Even if the player's goal is not clear, how does the board show how the player can reach the goal?

Pick an open world video game. Even if there is no single goal to pursue, does the playing field provide hints at some of the different goals players can pursue?

Pick a video game that is not an open world game. How does the game show players what goal they should pursue?

Does the game offer a single path to a goal or multiple paths? How can players find the paths to the goal?

How does each playing field or level of a game surprise the player by forcing them to learn something new?

Defining Obstacles and Resources in the Playing Field

Not only must a playing field prototype define a goal for players to reach, but it must also place obstacles and resources in the player's way. Obstacles block the player's progress by stopping forward movement and/or damaging the player so they can't keep moving. In a dungeon game, a troll might block the way. To get past the troll, players must fight the troll, which gives the troll a chance to wound or kill the player.

Resources help the player reach the goal. Common resources might be food, health boosters, ammunition, weapons, treasures, or even non-player characters who can be enticed to join forces with the player.

Games often reward players with resources each time they defeat an enemy. Another option is to sprinkle a playing field with resources that players can simply find. Yet another option is to hide resources and force players to search for them.

In a fast-paced first-person shooter, resources typically appear on the ground so players can easily find and use them. In an adventure game, resources may be hidden, forcing players to solve puzzles to find them. The type of game experience a playing field creates will determine how players easily players can find resources. The combination of obstacles and resources provides different ways to affect the player's progression towards a goal.

Obstacles can be static such as walls, pits, or rivers that never change, or they can be dynamic and represent items that move around such as sliding platforms and spinning fans to avoid, or non-player characters such monsters or bandits. After players kill a monster, is the monster gone for good or will it reappear if players visit the same area at a later time?

The playing field prototype needs to test where to place obstacles and where to place resources. Too many obstacles will make the game too hard. Too many resources will make the game too easy.

The strength of each obstacle and resource can also affect the game. Obstacles may be numerous, but if they're too easy to overcome, the game will feel too repetitive. If obstacles are sparse but too hard to overcome, the game will feel frustrating. Likewise, if resources are too powerful, players won't feel challenged. If resources are too weak, the game will also feel frustrating.

The number and quality of obstacles and resources needs to be adjusted based on the purpose of the game. An adventure game promises exciting gameplay so obstacles tend to be weaker and resources tend to be more plentiful. On the other hand, horror games put players in a weak position so obstacles tend to be stronger and resources tend to be limited to further create a sense of dread and hopelessness. Whatever emotional experience the game plans to create, that's the experience a playing field prototype needs to test.

So a playing field prototype must test:

- Is there a clear goal for players to pursue?
- What are the paths to this goal?
- What are the obstacles blocking the player's path to the goal?
- What are the resources helping the player reach the goal?

Thought Exercise

In any video games, what obstacles block the player's progress? If a player cannot get past a particular obstacle, what alternatives can the player choose, if any? What resources can players find that can help them?

Summary

The purpose of a playing field prototype is to:

- Find the right size for the playing field
- Test any movement limitations within the playing field
- Test the placement and quantity of obstacles and resources within the playing field
- Make sure the goal is clear and achievable

In board games and simple video games, a playing field prototype might consist of a single large sheet of paper. For a complex video game, there might be multiple playing fields, or levels. Each level should be prototyped to determine how well it works. Then all levels should be combined to make sure they work together.

Initially, video game levels can be tested using paper prototypes. Then they can be tested using digital prototypes that provide a closer approximation of how the actual video game will work.

A game's playing field should be fun to navigate, filled with obstacles that force players to practice new skills, and designed so players know what they can do at all times to reach a specific goal. Since players will spend all of their time interacting with the playing field, it's crucial to design the playing field so it matches the design goals of your game.

Further Reading

"Basics of Game Design", Michael Moore, CRC Press, 2011.

Chapter 21
Level Design Prototypes

Board games consist of a single playing field. On the other hand, video games often consist of multiple playing fields known as levels. Levels break up a large video game into smaller, interconnected parts that represent increasingly difficult challenges for players to overcome.

Since each level acts as a separate mini-game within the overall game, it's best to prototype each level separately. Like a playing field prototype, a level prototype needs to define the size, boundaries, obstacles, and resources. However, level prototypes must also focus on additional details:

- Exploration of the game world
- Teaching players specific skills
- Advancing the story

Think of each level like an escape room where players enter and cannot leave until they solve and overcome multiple problems. Like an escape room, levels must be fun and interesting to examine until players figure out a way to get out.

Exploring the Game World

When a video game consists of multiple levels, every level must be different and surprise the player in some way. The simplest way to surprise a player is to provide another part of the game world to explore, and the best way to surprise players is to rely on contrast in several ways:

- Place
- Challenges and obstacles
- Time

© The Author(s), under exclusive license to Springer Nature Switzerland AG 2023
W. Wang, *The Structure of Game Design*, International Series on Computer, Entertainment and Media Technology,
https://doi.org/10.1007/978-3-031-32202-0_21

- Climate
- Enemies
- Difficulty

Every level occurs at a specific location. The more memorable the location, the more interesting it will be to explore. If one level involves a player exploring a cavern, that means the player must learn to navigate through tight spaces. Now for contrast, the next level should be the opposite and provide a far more open space where players can roam around an open field. This sudden change from a confined area to an open area creates greater variety while also forcing players to adapt to an entirely different part of the same gaming world.

Contrast can not only come from the environment, but also from the types of challenges the level contains. One level might force players to battle monsters in close combat using swords or clubs. Then the next level can contrast this by forcing players to battle different monsters in ranged combat using arrows or spears. One level might force players to avoid fire but the next level might force players to avoid flying objects being thrown from above.

Contrast can also come from time and climate. One level might take place in the day time of bright skies while the next level might take place at night or in the dim corridors of a castle. One level might take place in a sandy desert while another level might take place among snow drifts in the mountains.

The number and type of enemies should also change from one level to another. The simplest change is to increase the number of enemies. In the arcade game Asteroids, players control a spaceship while asteroids fly around it. The player must blow apart the asteroids while avoiding an asteroid hitting the spaceship.

The first level displayed a handful of asteroids to teach players the basic movement and shooting mechanics of the game. However, each succeeding level increased the number of asteroids flying around the player's spaceship.

Another change can be increasing the speed or capabilities of the enemies. In Asteroids, not only did each level display more asteroids, but they also started moving faster. Yet another change might be including new enemies along with enemies from the previous level, or displaying the same enemies as a previous level but with new capabilities. In Asteroids, a flying saucer pops up periodically and shoots at the player, forcing the player to dodge the flying saucer shots and the asteroids at the same time.

Finally, levels must gradually increase the difficulty whether through more enemies, faster enemies, more powerful enemies, or greater obstacles. The difficulty must be harder, but not dramatically so to ensure that players can still complete it with their current abilities.

The greater the contrast, the more variety in the game. The more variety in the game, the less likely players will get bored. Remember, the purpose of every level is to grab and hold the player's attention so they'll keep playing the game. Players must see and experience something different from each level to keep the game interesting at all times.

Thought Exercise

Pick a video game that contains multiple levels. How do the levels differ between the first level and the second? How do the levels differ between the first level and the last level?

Can you think of a game where levels do not differ in any noticeable way? Can you think of a game where later levels are easier than earlier levels with fewer obstacles and weaker enemies to defeat?

Teaching New Skills

The only way players can win in a video game is to gradually develop skills. In the beginning, players know little about the gaming world and have little idea how to play the game, let alone how to win and complete the game. That's why the first level of nearly every video game acts as a tutorial to teach players the basic moves they can make and give them confidence that they can play and master the game. Some typical lessons players learn in each level includes:

- Different ways to move
- Different ways to fight
- Different types of obstacles and enemies to overcome

In most games, the first level teaches players the basics of controlling their character whether it's a vehicle (car, airplane, spaceship) or a person. This basic level challenges players to move and dodge fixed and moving obstacles without feeling overwhelmed. Until players can master this first level, the game deliberately holds them back from succeeding levels because if they can't control their vehicle or character, they'll have no chance of succeeding in any other levels either.

Levels teach new movement skills by blatantly displaying instructions on the screen, as shown in Fig. 21.1, and by providing obstacles that players cannot overcome except by applying their new movement skills when confronted by those obstacles.

Besides learning to move, most video games need to teach players how to fight. In Angry Birds, the first level teaches players the basics of aiming a slingshot, loading different birds into the slingshot, changing the velocity by pulling back on the slingshot, and seeing how to attack enemy structures. Once players master this initial level, each succeeding level gets progressively harder with stronger structures, but also different types of birds players can shoot. This combination off additional challenges and different types of bird ammunition gradually teaches players new ways to play and win the game while overcoming increasingly difficult obstacles.

After players learn the basics to moving and fighting, levels can further challenge them by forcing them to combine existing skills or use existing skills in novel combinations. In many fighting games, players learn the basics of punching, kicking, ducking, jumping, and moving back and forth. The next step involves combining certain moves to create unique, powerful combinations that are greater than the individual parts.

Fig. 21.1 Video games can display movement control instructions when first learning the game

For example, a punch followed by a kick might cause a fixed amount of damage to an enemy, but if players learn to punch, then jump while moving forward, and then kick, this combination might create greater damage even though it still involves a punch and a kick. By forcing players to use their existing skills in novel combinations, levels can teach players how to use existing skills to win the game.

Every game level acts as a new lesson for the player to teach a new or different way to move, fight, or understand different ways to use existing skills in unique combinations. Ideally, each new level should teach multiple lessons but they should all be focused on a similar theme.

For example, if a level teaches players how to climb the side of a cliff, then the level should also teach players how to fight enemies above and below while also explaining more about the game world itself. Perhaps the cliffs will lead the player to a castle on top of a mountain or the cliffs might just lead to a flat area with forests. Learning something new, or learning new ways to use existing skills, is the key to making every level different from earlier levels.

Thought Exercise

Pick a video game and identify the lessons the first level teachers players. Pick a level in the middle and identify how the lessons learned are different from the first level. Pick the last level and identify the skills players need to complete the game. Where did players learn these necessary skills before the final level?

Telling a Story Through Levels

Many games tell a story. In linear stories, the player experiences the story much like a movie or a book except they get to make choices within the story. In non-linear stories, player actions help create their own stories that fit within the larger story world of the game.

For example, Horizon Zero Dawn takes place in a world that's been overrun by machines. Within that basic story setting, players create their own stories based on the choices and actions they make. However, every new area gives players more information about the game world background as they encounter new enemies and discover resources to help them better survive.

So whether a game is linear or non-linear, levels provide more information about the overall game story. Therefore each level must reveal more information about the story through the environment of that level along with any items the player may find or non-player characters the player may meet who can reveal more information.

When players go through levels in a specific order, information about the larger game story can be revealed in a linear fashion, much like a movie or novel. When players can choose which levels to explore in any order, the story information from each level cannot depend on information revealed in another level. Thus story information can play a lesser role in shaping the player's experience in the level.

Every level adds information to the overall game story, but every level should also tell a story of its own. This level story must define the player's goal within that level. In Donkey Kong, each level story was simple. A gorilla has captured a princess and it's up to the player to rescue her.

In Fallout 3, the overall story is about the player finding what their father plans to do with a secret project, but each level has specific goals for the player to achieve as well. The goal of an early level is simply for the player to find a way out of an underground vault to go searching for their father in the open wilderness. The goal of another level is to rescue their father from a scientist. Each level goal supports the larger goal of the overall story.

When designing levels, start by identifying the game's overall story setting. Then make sure every level tells a different part of the story. Now within each level, define the starting point for players and the exit point from that level. It's entirely possible there could be two or more ways players can exit a level such as two different doors in a dungeon that lead to the outside.

The structure of each level must tell story that fits within the overall game world story setting, but provides a unique challenge to the player from start to finish:

- What's the player's goal?
- What's stopping the player from reaching the goal?
- What skills and resources does the player need to overcome the obstacles and enemies in the way?
- How can the player achieve that goal?

A level goal might consist of a single task such as finding an exit to a dungeon. However, sometimes a level goal might consist of several tasks, such as collecting multiple treasures scattered throughout the level. The order that players collect the treasures doesn't matter, just as long as they collect all of them. When a level provides multiple paths to a goal, the player has greater freedom to choose the order they pursue each objective.

Not only must the goal be clear, but the path to that goal must be clear as well. A game can explicitly define the goal, such as in a cut scene where a non-player character tells you what you're supposed to do next.

A second approach are implicit goals. These types of goals occur when players figure out their goal based on what they see in that level. A player finding themselves in a cavern would quickly figure out they need to find an exit. In the game Journey, there's a mountain that appears in the distance, which clearly signals that players should constantly move towards that mountain.

Explicit goals occur when the game tells the player what to do. The goal is clear but learning about the goal can feel clumsy. Implicit goals occur when the player figures out what they should do. The goal may not be as clear but it can hold more meaning since the player themselves feel they have chosen this goal (even though the game environment gives players no other choice).

Once players know their goal within a level, the next step is how can they achieve that goal? One simple way to create obstacles is to take existing obstacles from a previous level and modify it by either changing how it behaves or increasing its number or size.

In Super Mario Brothers, players must jump on top of pillars. However, later levels display man-eating plants that pop up out the tops of these pillars periodically, giving pillars a new and added threat.

Obstacles and enemies can block a player's progress, but another obstacle can be a fixed time limit. This forces players to reach a goal by a specific time, so every obstacle and enemy that gets in the way may not threaten to stop the player completely, but can slow the player down enough to keep them from reaching the goal.

If a level does not have a time limit, players can freely explore the entire level at a more leisurely pace. This can encourage exploration that a time limit actively discourages. Time limits represent another type of obstacle a level can offer to make achieving the level goal harder.

When players get past all the obstacles and enemies in a level, they need to know they've succeeded. Since completing a level represents a major milestone, this event must be larger and more emotional than anything that had gone on before in the level. The end of a level is where the player must defeat the final level enemy, often called the boss level.

This final enemy isn't just bigger and tougher than anything else in the level. This final enemy must also test the player's skill that they developed throughout the level. So if the level emphasized vertical movement and fighting, then players can only defeat the boss enemy by demonstrating mastery of vertical movement and fighting.

Think of all obstacles and enemies in a level as different lessons for the player to learn, and the final boss as the ultimate test that can demonstrate the player has achieved a certain level of skill. Failure to defeat the boss means the player must practice the level skills some more. Defeating the boss means the player has mastered the level's lessons and is ready to move to the next level.

When players encounter levels in a specific order, each level can build on the skills of the next. When players have greater freedom to choose which levels to access at different times, then each level must teach a separate skill that's still challenging whether it's the first level a player explores or the last. By defeating the boss, players know without a doubt that they've mastered a particular level.

Stories are nothing more than the gradual progression of enemies and obstacles that culminate in forcing the player to defeat the biggest enemy of all at the end. The emotional state of the player gradually changes over time.

Initially, the player starts each level from an emotional state of uncertainty facing the unknown. Then as the player gradually explores the level, they're forced to learn new skills to overcome stronger and different obstacles and enemies. This gradually builds up the player's confidence. Just when players feel they've mastered the skills necessary to overcome every obstacle and enemy in the level, they must face the biggest, strongest, and scariest enemy of all that throws everything in doubt once more. Only by defeating this final enemy can players feel a sense of accomplishment that validates all their hard work getting to that final point.

Each level needs to provide its own climactic emotional conclusion. Then the last level must be the biggest, toughest, and most emotional battle of all. Levels don't just put obstacles and enemies in the player's path. Instead, levels use obstacles and enemies to create a gradually increasing emotional experience from start to finish.

Thought Exercise

Watch a favorite movie and notice the four main parts of a story:

- A hero has a goal but enters an unfamiliar world
- The hero can't reach a goal because obstacles and enemies get in the way
- The hero must learn new skills
- The hero can finally overcome multiple enemies, including the biggest threat of all, by mastering new skills

Pick a video game with multiple levels and examine one or more levels. Do they start by putting players in an unfamiliar environment with a goal to pursue? Do obstacles and enemies force players to learn new skills? Can the player defeat the final enemy using the skills learned and mastered throughout the level?

The Mechanics of Level Design

Once you understand that levels must teach players new skills while creating gradually increasing emotional experiences, you must also understand the mechanics of level design. Levels must keep surprising the player.

If a level consists of a dungeon, there must be corridors and rooms for players to explore, so players must constantly see something different. Exploring an area once should be different from any other area, but returning to that same area could also be different to avoid repetition.

Suppose a player is exploring a dungeon and finds a dead body. Returning to that same area later might show that body stripped of flesh from rats. This creates greater realism within the game world and keeps previously visited areas different in subtle ways because something is always changing.

In many games, players can choose a difficulty level such as easy, medium, or hard. That means each level must be designed for all three types levels of difficulty. An easy difficulty level might omit certain obstacles and enemies while a medium difficulty level might add additional obstacles and enemies. A hard difficulty level might modify obstacles and enemies to be even harder to overcome. With each difficulty level, the level must be tested to ensure it offers the right amount of challenge for players.

One final consideration for designing a level is speed running. Many players enjoy timing how fast they can get through a level so levels can be tested to make them fun to navigate. To encourage constant forward movement, levels should not contain any dead ends, which will force players to backtrack over previously visited areas.

Instead, levels should allow players to always move forward without retracing their steps. Movement alone should be fun, allowing players to express themselves through different types of movement such as running, jumping, climbing, or flying. The more ways players can move through a level, the greater their freedom and the more likely movement will feel fun.

Spacing between various obstacles can also be important. Too much space between obstacles and the level will create dread space where nothing important seems to occur. Too little spacing means players may feel overwhelmed. Spacing out obstacles and enemies is important to make sure all parts of a level are enjoyable to visit.

When designing a level, don't forget to consider height. Can players jump up or down, or climb up or down? Vertical movement allows a level to contain two or more floors within a level, allowing more room for exploration. By forcing players to consider vertical as well as horizontal movement, levels create greater variety.

Ultimately, level design is more than just placing objects on a map. It's more like designing a theme park ride that tells an engaging story from start to finish that gradually builds to a climax at the end.

Thought Exercise

Pick a video game with multiple levels and examine one level to look for the following:

- Surprises
- Variable difficulty levels
- Movement

As players move through the level, what kind of surprises does the level offer? If players backtrack through a previously explored level, does anything change?

If the game lets you choose a difficulty level, how does the game level change between difficulty levels such as between Easy and Hard? How does the level make movement fun?

Does the level offer vertical movement? If not, how could vertical movement change a level? If a level does offer vertical movement, how would that level change if vertical movement were taken away?

Summary

Levels are more than just maps within a video game. Instead, levels represent ministories that must teach players new skills and reveal additional information about the gaming world. Levels are meant to be fun to explore and move through.

Right from the start, players should have an idea of what goal they're supposed to pursue. Then every obstacle and enemy blocks the player while gradual lying teaching the player how to develop new skills and knowledge. The final test occurs at the end when players must overcome the biggest enemy of all, applying all the skills they learned throughout the level.

Levels tell emotional stories that start with an unfamiliar setting, then gradually introduces the player to new skills and knowledge. Think of levels as a tutorial designed to make players feel mastery. Only when they can demonstrate this mastery by defeating the boss can they move on to another level in the game.

Further Reading

"Game Development Essentials: Game Design", Travis Castillo and Jeannie Novak, Cengage Learning, 2008.

Chapter 22
Movement Prototypes

Movement lets players improve their chances of winning. In board games, movement might involve moving one or more playing pieces a fixed or random distance determined by a spinner or dice. In a video game, movement involves controlling one or more playing pieces around a playing field using a keyboard, mouse, touch screen, or game controller.

Movement prototypes need to test one or more of the following:

- Movement types
- Distances
- Movement for other purposes

Testing movement usually requires a playing field prototype of some kind. This playing field prototype doesn't have to be complete, just representative of the playing field that players will move on.

Types of Movement

Two main ways games regulate movement are turn-based vs. real-time and predictable vs. random movement. Most board games offer turn-based movement since it's easier to implement. The problem with turn-based movement is that if there are multiple players, players have to wait their turn, giving them nothing to do until it's their turn.

One solution, especially for children's games, is to make each turn short. That way nobody has to wait long for their turn. Another solution is to give other players a chance to respond to the current player's turn. In Monopoly, players can make deals with other players, forcing those other players to make decisions separate from their own turn. In Pandemic, players are cooperating to win the game so every

© The Author(s), under exclusive license to Springer Nature
Switzerland AG 2023
W. Wang, *The Structure of Game Design*, International Series on Computer,
Entertainment and Media Technology,
https://doi.org/10.1007/978-3-031-32202-0_22

action one player takes indirectly affects the choices other players will have in their own turn. Giving other players something to do during another player's turn can be crucial to keep everyone actively involved.

In video games, movement can be turn-based or real-time. Turn-based video games act like digital board games except that the computer takes care of the rules and tracking each player's resources.

With turn-based movement, players must rely on their brains to determine the best action to take. With real-time movement, players must rely on their brains and their reflexes. Choosing the best move won't matter if your reflexes can't support your decision. Likewise, having the fastest reflexes won't matter if you're constantly making the wrong choices.

Thus real-time movement offers a greater challenge to analyze conditions and choose the best option within a limited period of time. Turn-based movement can be like chess where players can take their time analyzing a situation. Real-time movement is more like speed chess where players must make moves within a limited time. Thus time itself becomes an obstacle that players must overcome.

Besides making the best split-second decisions, consider how many ways there are to move in a video game. Video games may offer a handful of different ways to move (walk, run, jump) but within the game, players can often combine multiple movements to create unique results. The more movement options available and the more ways they can be combined, the greater the freedom of movement players can experience and enjoy.

In turn-based movement, the emphasis lies in analysis. In real-time movement, the emphasis lies in analysis while moving or while your opponents are moving. Such an ever-changing, dynamic situation makes real-time movement feel more realistic and challenging.

A second consideration for movement lies in predictable or random movement. To create uncertainty, many board games rely on random movement using a spinner, cards, or dice to determine how far a player can move. With random movement, players can only react.

Random movement has two meanings. First, it could mean all possible movement values are equally likely to occur. Rolling a single die means the numbers 1 through 6 all have an equal chance of occurring.

Second, it could mean that some numbers have a greater chance of occurring than others, even though all numbers are random. Rolling two dice means the only possible numbers are 2 through 12. Yet, 2 and 12 can only occur 1 out of 36 times, which means both of those numbers are far less likely to occur than a 7, which can be formed by a 4 and a 3, a 5 and a 2, or a 6 and a 1. With so many different ways two dice can add up to 7, 7 will occur far more often than either 2 or 12.

In some cases, you may want all possible values to have an equal chance of occurring, but in other situations, you may want some values to occur more often than others. So even though a random value will occur, some values are more likely than others.

In many strategic board games, players can choose their movement. They may move all, some, or none of their units. They also have a choice of moving units up to their maximum movement value or anything less including not moving at all.

In addition, terrain can affect movement such as increasing movement on roads or slowing movement when crossing swamps or rivers. Such variation of movement options gives players greater control over the positioning of their units so they can pursue long-term strategies that would be impossible to do if movement were random.

In video games, movement is often completely under the player's control where they can move in different directions, distances, and speeds. However, such movement has limits, forcing players to decide the advantages of moving quickly or slowly in any particular direction.

Video games typically give players complete control over their movement because part of the challenge lies in mastering movement within the game. Random movement may occur in limited situations, such as determining the success of a player making a risky move such as leaping for a moving train or jumping from one skyscraper rooftop to another.

In such risky moves, video games may introduce an element of chance where the player might fail and either die or suffer damage. Such randomization forces players to choose between safer movements that may not move them closer to the goal, or riskier movements that could move them faster towards the goal at the risk of possibly failing altogether.

In general, random movement appears more often in board games while predictable movement appears more often in video games. Predictable movement gives players added control and responsibility for their choices, which encourages players to develop their movement skills until they can master their actions.

Thought Exercise

Examine a board game that uses random movement such as a children's game. How would the game change if players could choose their movement? Examine a board game that uses predictable movement such as a military simulation game. How would the game change if movement were completely random?

In a video game, how many basic ways can players move? How many ways can they combine movement options to create unique results? Compare two similar video games. Which one offers the best ways to move and why?

Testing Distances of Movement

When moving playing pieces, the first question is balancing between moving too much or moving too little. In a board game like Monopoly, players roll two dice to determine how far they move. Thus the minimum amount is 2 and the maximum amount is 12.

Rolling one die would limit movement from 1 to 6 spaces, which might feel too little as players would take too long to get around the board. Rolling three dice would limit movement from 3 to 18, which could be too fast, allowing them to skip over too many properties . To test movement in board games, start by finding the balance between minimum and maximum movement.

To find this proper balance, examine how movement affects the outcome of the game. Suppose a racing game let players throw three dice to determine movement. Since getting 18 (a 6 on three separate die) is such a rare occurrence (1 in 216), any player that gets an 18 would move so far ahead that the odds of other players catching up would be much less. That means one lucky throw of the dice could essentially win the game for that lucky player.

By identifying this problem, you can determine that the maximum movement should be much less. Then examine the minimum movement. In Monopoly, the minimum movement is 2 (two 1 s on two separate die), which has a 1 in 36 chance of occurring. One unique feature of this minimum movement of 2 is that it makes it impossible for players to land on the next adjacent square.

Although Monopoly players could move at 2 squares a turn, this minimum movement distance is rare and unlikely to occur too often. Now suppose Monopoly players moved by throwing a single die. That means movement from 1 to 6 squares would be equally likely to occur. If a player moved too slowly around the Monopoly board, there's a chance they could run out of money before passing Go. Because of this, the minimum movement cannot be too low or occur too often so players can get around the board to pass Go and collect money.

By identifying how extremely low and extremely high movement values affect the game, designers can find the proper range.

In games with different types of units, such as tanks and infantry, unit movements are based on their relationships. Suppose a tank can move twice as fast as infantry. It's relatively easy to assign a movement value to a tank that's twice the value of an infantry unit's movement value. However, now designers must test both movements to make sure the game works.

If tank movement seems too fast, then its value must be lowered, which will directly affect the infantry unit's movement. Now infantry might appear to move too slowly, which means increasing the infantry unit movement, which also increases the tank's movement.

Adjusting movement values of different units can be one way to find the optimal values for both types of units. Another option is to adjust the scale of the map. By increasing or decreasing the scale of the playing field, designers can adjust the movement of units without altering any actual movement values. (Or they can do both.)

In video games, movement must match the player's expectations where the game's setting shapes the player's expectations. A game where players control different types of World War I biplanes would create a completely different set of expectations compared to a science fiction game where players control futuristic starship fighters dodging asteroids while firing missiles.

Ultimately, movement is the way players can get closer to winning the game. Test movement until it feels too slow, then test until movement feels too fast. Movement should feel fun, engaging, and interesting. Since the bulk of the game will involve movement, it's crucial to make sure all forms of movement create the emotional effect that you want players to experience.

Thought Exercise

Pick a board game and cut the way players move in half. Then double or triple its movement. How does each type of movement alter gameplay?

Pick a video game and identify its game setting. How does its game setting define a player's expectations for how to move within the game? Imagine if movement were halved or doubled, would the movement still match the expectations from the game setting?

Movement for Other Purposes

Movement typically changes the location of one or more units so the main purpose of movement is to put your units in the best possible position so you can win the game. However, movement has several other purposes beyond just changing a physical location:

• Movement for puzzle solving
• Movement for resource management
• Movement for combat

Many video games offer puzzles for players to solve before they can advance or gain the resources needed to deal with upcoming obstacles and enemies. Such puzzles often force players to move items to press down on switches, reflect light beams, or push items into jumping platforms so the player can reach previously inaccessible areas.

This type of movement is meant to solve a puzzle and does not move the player physically closer to the game's goal. However, it may force the player to use existing movement skills or learn new movement skills to help solve the puzzle.

Movement can also be used for resource management. In the board game Monopoly, moving past Go gives players $200 dollars that they can use to pay bills or buy properties. In video games, players often need to find a store or trading post so they can convert their money or treasures into useful resources such as weapons, armor, or tools such as shovels and ropes. In this case, players must move to a store or trading post but this movement does not directly get them closer to the overall game goal in the same way that ordinary movement does.

One common use for movement involves movement as combat where moving represents a way to defeat enemies. In Super Mario Brothers, players have a choice of either avoiding enemies (by jumping over them) or attacking enemies (by jumping on top of them). When movement becomes a form of combat, it can be predictable (such as Mario jumping on enemies that works every time) or unpredictable (such as fighting games where a player can rush an enemy to knock them down, but which may not always succeed if players time their movement wrong).

Movement for puzzles, resource management, or combat should be identical or similar to movement used to get players from one location to another. That way players don't have to learn any new type of movement skills.

Thought Exercise

Pick a board game where movement involves resource management or combat. How would the game change if this resource management or combat were taken away from movement? If a board game does not use movement for resource management or combat, how would the game change if either of these were added?

Pick a video game that uses movement to solve a puzzle. How is this movement necessary to solving the puzzle? If the game were to eliminate movement, how would this affect trying to solve the puzzle?

Prototyping Real-Time Movement

Turn-based video games are easy to prototype on paper since such prototypes act like board games. However, video games that rely on real-time movement require difficult considerations when creating a prototype.

Many video game designers create digital prototypes to test real-time movement, but it's possible to test real-time movement on paper. Real-time movement involves a strict time deadline and hidden decisions that only become apparent to other players or enemies after players have committed to a specific action.

One way paper prototypes can emulate real-time movement is to give players a time limit to make decisions (such as 15 seconds), which can be enforced by a human referee or a timer. Before this time limit expires, players must choose an action and reveal it. This can capture the hectic rush to make decisions in a hurry.

To choose an action, players could write down their choices, but this could be tedious. A better solution might be to create options as cards that players can select. Now players just need to select an option defined by a card that shows which action they chose.

A second option is to let players make decisions simultaneously without a time limit. Then players reveal their choices at the same time. By eliminating a time limit, a game emphasizes analysis over reaction, which creates a different feel for the game. Such simultaneous movement forces players to anticipate their opponent's moves and outthink them. By applying a time limit to this same action, the paper prototype suddenly forces players to react faster and more intelligently than their opponents.

Note that any paper prototype that emulates real-time movement is just meant to capture the feel of gameplay that forces players to make split-second decisions over and over again. In first-person shooter games, split-second decisions form the heart of the game. The paper prototype can test whether the variety of options available to the player is too low or too high, and whether making rapid decisions would be fun as the main action in the game.

Thought Exercise

In real-time movement video games, the computer takes care of tracking simultaneous movement. In a paper prototype, players need to choose and reveal their actions at the same time, with or without a time limit. Pick a video game that uses real-time movement and create a paper prototype that mimics the game's choices and gameplay feeling.

Summary

The two main ways to regulate movement are turn-based and real-time. Turn-based movement typically occurs in board games but also many strategy video games as well. The idea behind turns is that each player can analyze the current situation, make a decision, and then see the results of that decision before another player takes their turn.

Turn-based movement emphasizes strategy. On the other hand, real-time movement emphasizes reflexes and quick decision-making along with choosing the best strategy within a limited time frame. Real-time movement is commonly found in video games but some board games offer a limited form of real-time movement.

To give players greater control, most video games make movement predictable, but occasionally video games offer unpredictable movement options that offer greater rewards in return for greater risks. Many board games use random movement where players cannot predict how far they may move on each given turn. Many simulation board games do offer predictable movement to model movement of actual vehicles or military units.

Every movement involves traveling a certain distance. Prototypes must test that movement distance so it's neither too slow or too fast. Adjusting movement can involve changing the movement values of various playing pieces or adjusting the scale of the playing field map.

Finally, movement can be more than just traveling from one location to another. Movement can involve puzzle solving, resource management, or combat. Movement should give players multiple options so they can freely express themselves through movement within a game.

Further Reading

"Good Game Design – Movement", Snoman Gaming, https://youtu.be/tAE2H5qJ8A8

Chapter 23
Combat Prototypes

Combat prototypes test whether fighting another player or non-player character feels fair and realistic for that particular game setting. In a realistic military simulation, weapons would need to look and act like their real world counterparts. However, in a fantasy or science fiction setting, weapons would need to look and act like what most people believe about those game settings.

For example, people expect a laser to be powerful in a science fiction world, so if it barely causes any damage to an ordinary person, players would feel the weapon is unrealistic. On the other hand, a bow and arrow in a fantasy game setting would likely kill a human if a single arrow hits in the right area, but won't likely kill a much larger animal with one shot such as a dragon.

Combat involves choosing between different types of attacks and different weapons against different enemies and their unique defenses that might minimize or negate an attack altogether. Essentially, combat prototypes must test whether a game offers enough variety to make every possible type of attack viable under different situations.

Choosing Weapons

In strategy games, playing units might represent entire military divisions such as infantry, armor, or artillery. When playing units represent large groups, their attack and defense strength is abstracted as an arbitrary number, based on their relationship to other playing units.

In tactical games where players control individual units such as swordsmen, soldiers, tanks, airplanes, or even ships, combat can get more detailed. Instead of assigning an abstract attack/defense strength, games often give players a choice of weapons to use where each weapon offers various advantages and disadvantages.

© The Author(s), under exclusive license to Springer Nature
Switzerland AG 2023
W. Wang, *The Structure of Game Design*, International Series on Computer,
Entertainment and Media Technology,
https://doi.org/10.1007/978-3-031-32202-0_23

A sword might offer the advantage of causing a decent amount of damage while letting players hold a shield in the other hand. A halberd is much longer and can attack from a further distance while requiring two hands to hold. That means players cannot hold a shield. A crossbow offers attacking from a distance, but becomes nearly useless in close combat. By offering a variety of weapons for players to choose, a game forces players to pick the best weapons for their playing strategy as shown in Table 23.1.

Giving players a choice of weapons creates a greater sense of freedom in choosing how to arm themselves. Sometimes weapons have various costs so players must balance how much they're willing to spend in return for the weapons they want (or can afford).

Once players choose one or more weapons, they need to master those weapons in different settings and against different enemies. The challenge for the game designer lies in making sure no weapon is too over-powered (so players use it all the time) or under-powered (so players never choose it at all). Every weapon must excel against certain enemies and falter (or be completely ineffective) against other enemies.

Thought Exercise

Pick a game where players can choose from multiple weapons and notice the different characteristics of each weapon such as weight, cost, attack strength, ammunition load, etc. Which weapon offers the most power? What is the disadvantage of this powerful weapon? Which weapon is the weakest? What is the advantage of this weakest weapon?

Table 23.1 Different weapons offer various attack values and weights

Weapon table		
Weapon	Dice	Strength
Dagger	1−1	–
Rapier	1	9
Club	1	9
Hammer	1+1	10
Cutlass	2−2	10
Short sword	2−1	11
Mace	2−1	11
Small ax	1+2	11
Broadsword	2	12
Morningstar	2+1	13
2-handed sword	3−1	14
Battleaxe	3	15

Are there any two weapons that would make sense to use together? Are there any two weapons that have no reason to use together? Is there any weapon optimized for specific situations or enemies? If so, what is the weakest weapon for specific situations and enemies and how can players still use that weakest weapon to still triumph in the end?

Determining If an Attack with a Weapon Hits

Just having a weapon is no guarantee that players will hit anything with it. This forces players to balance the tradeoff between weapons that cause lots of damage (if they hit) vs. weapons that have a high chance of hitting (but cause much less damage).

For example, a two-handed broadsword will cause massive damage but it's clumsy to wield, which makes it less likely to hit anything. On the other hand, a club is easy for anyone to swing around but it may not cause much damage unless it happens to hit a vital area like a person's head.

For greater realism, many games define odds for hitting with a particular weapon and additional odds for hitting specific areas of an enemy. This makes it possible to hit an enemy but hit a non-vital area (such as armor), causing little or no damage. Players also have the chance of getting a lucky hit on a vital area, causing far more damage than normal. Adding in chance for hitting and additional chance for hitting vital areas creates greater variety that can create surprising and unexpected results.

Hitting an enemy can be a combination of that weapon type, the range between the attacker and the defender, the terrain of the defender, and the condition of the defender (stunned, demoralized, etc.) as shown in Table 23.2.

Once players determine they hit an enemy, the next step may be determining where the damage occurred. This means a player could repeatedly hit an enemy but get unlucky enough to hit armored, non-vital areas, or that a player could hit an enemy once and get a lucky hit that cripples the target as shown in Table 23.3.

The To Hit table determines the odds of hitting an enemy based on various factors such as range to target (the further away, the less likelihood of hitting), terrain of the defender (towns will provide better protection than open fields), and the type

Table 23.2 Players may first need to determine if they even hit a target

To hit table		
Range	Die roll needed to hit	Effect on attack factor
Adjacent	Automatic	Doubled
2–5	1–9	Doubled
6–10	1–4	Normal
11–20	1–3	Normal
21 or more	1–2	Halved

Table 23.3 An effects table
determines where the
damage occurs

Effects table	
Roll	Area hit
2	Port wing
3–5	Superficial damage
6	Port wing
7	Nose
8	Starboard wing
9	Pilot compartment
10–11	Superficial damage
12	Starboard wing

of weapon attacking (pistols are much weaker with less chance to hit than a flame-thrower or a rocket launcher).

A To Hit table outlines the odds that an attacker actually hits an enemy. Another type of table might be an Effects table that determines where an attacker hit. In man to man combat, hitting an enemy in the arm can create a different effect than hitting an enemy in the leg. In vehicle combat involving tanks or planes, hitting an engine creates a different effect than hitting an exposed gunner or pilot.

Thought Exercise

Pick a board game (such as a wargame, military simulation) and examine the numerous tables needed to create realistic combat results. Wargames require numerous tables to add uncertainty to combat. By studying how these multiple tables work and interact with one another, you can see how paper wargames simulate combat in a particular battle. Such transparency makes playing a paper wargame tedious, but clearly shows you how the game works, making it easy to alter the tables to modify the gameplay.

In comparison, pick a video game that simulates combat. Because the video game calculates results in the background, the way it works remains hidden from players, making it difficult to modify or even understand why certain weapons behave the way they do.

Dissect a video game and convert it to a paper wargame. Notice how many charts and tables you may need to simulate greater realism in the game.

Understanding Combat Results Tables (CRTs)

In some games, combat is 100% certain such as in chess, checkers, or backgammon. In games with guaranteed combat results, the best defense is to avoid giving an enemy a chance to attack in the first place. Failing that, the second best defense is to defend vulnerable units. In backgammon, this occurs by covering units so no playing piece is left alone and vulnerable to attack. In chess, players can position other playing pieces so an enemy attacking a specific playing piece will lose more than they gain, which discourages an attack.

In many other types of games, combat represents a calculated risk. The basic dilemma revolves around whether a player should attack an enemy or not and how much force to use. The more force applied to a single target, the greater the chance of success. The less force applied, the lower the chance of success. Thus players must decide, at all times, not only what target they should attack but how much force to allocate against this single target.

Since players don't have unlimited units to attack, the choice becomes whether to attack a small number of units that have a greater chance of success or attack a larger number of units that have a lower chance of success.

To calculate the various risks in combat, games need an algorithm that specifies the odds of success based on the attacker's strength and the defender's strength. Rather than write these combat algorithms out, it's far easier to summarize them in a table called a Combat Results Table (CRT). The purpose of such a table is to show the likely odds between different types of attacks as shown in Table 23.4.

By studying the Combat Results Table in a board game, players can estimate their odds of success and better understand how the game works. Generally, attackers need a 2–1 advantage before attacking. However in video games, the CRT is buried as code that's hidden from view. This means players cannot understand how combat works except through trial and error.

Even then, they won't truly understand how the game's combat system actually works. For this reason, board games can often be more educational in understanding game mechanics because all possible details are clearly outlined in plain view.

In strategic games, a Combat Results Table assumes that an attacker can successfully hit a defender. In many games, especially those that simulate individual combat, the game must determine if the attacker hit, and then determine where the attacker hit as shown in Table 23.5.

So during an attack, players may need to consult three different tables:

Table 23.4 A combat results table shows various results that can occur depending on the attacker and defender strength

Combat results table								
Odds	1–4	1–3	1–2	1–1	3–2	2–1	3–1	4–1
Die Roll								
1	AK	AK	AK	AW	AW	AW	DR	DR
2	AK	AK	AW	AR	AR	AR	DR	DW
3	AK	AW	AR	AR	AR	AR	DR	DW
4	AW	AR	BW	BW	DR	DR	DW	DK
5	AR	NE	DR	DR	DW	DW	DW	DK
6	AR	DR	DW	DW	DW	DK	DK	DK

AK Attacker killed, *AW* Attacker wounded, *AR* Attacker retreat, *BW* Both wounded, *NE* No effect, *DR* Defender retreat, *DW* Defender wounded, *DK* Defender killed

Table 23.5 A damage
location table determines
where an attack hit a defender

Damage location table	
Die roll	Area hit
1–2	Left leg
3–4	Right leg
5–6	Left arm
7–8	Right arm
9	Left shoulder
10	Right shoulder
11–14	Abdomen
15–18	Chest
19–20	Head

- To Hit – Checks if the attacker even hit the enemy. If so, check the Effects table.
- Effects – Checks to see where the attack hit the enemy.
- Damage – Checks to see how much damage the attack caused in the area defined by the Effects table.

The combination of a To Hit, Effects, and Combat Results Table combines to create greater realism, especially when simulating combat between individual units such as soldiers, planes, tanks, or ships. When consulting each type of table, certain conditions may give a modifying advantage to the attacker, the defender, or both.

If the defender is dug into a trench or inside a city, the attacker is at a disadvantage. If the defender is caught in the open at the bottom of a hill, the defender is at a disadvantage. To simulate these advantages and disadvantages, games may include modifiers for one or more combat tables.

By understanding modifiers that increase or decrease the attacker and defender's strength along with the odds of hitting, board games can give players a deeper understanding of the tradeoffs they need to make when deciding when to attack, who to attack, and whether the odds of success are worth taking or not.

The advantage of a board game listing game mechanics in various tables is that players can develop a better understanding of the game mechanics. The disadvantage is that consulting so many tables can get tedious and time-consuming, making it harder to play the game.

With video games, the opposite is true. By hiding the game mechanic details, video games are much easier to play, but mask the deeper understanding of its game mechanics that a board game can offer.

Since video games cannot force players to consult and understand various tables listing the odds of successful combat, video games must rely on the game experience to teach players odds and choices. For example, a medieval combat game might give players a choice of using a dagger (that's easy to use but causes minimal damage) or a battle axe (that's unwieldy to use but causes extreme damage if it hits).

A board game might represent these weapon differences as tables listing numeric values that clearly show how a dagger has a greater chance of hitting but with small amounts of damage while a battle axe has a lower chance of hitting but with massive amounts of damage.

A video game must convey this information to the player through play. Whipping a dagger around should feel fast and fluid, but players should also see that stabbing with a dagger causes minimal damage, especially against large enemies such as trolls, minotaurs, or dragons.

When players wield a battle axe, their movements should be slower and clumsier, making hitting enemies harder. However when the battle axe hits, players should see that it causes massive damage. Thus through gameplay can players gradually understand the tradeoffs in weapons and attack strategies in a video game that they could easily spot by examining a table in a board game.

Thought Exercise

Pick a video game that allows players to attack enemies, and try to determine a Combat Results Table that can predict the odds of attacking. If the video game depicts attacks on individual people or vehicles, is there a chance that players will attack an enemy but miss? When players attack enemies, can they aim for specific areas of the target or is this determined randomly?

Pick a board game and study the Combat Results Table (CRT) to get a better understanding how combat works. What type of modifiers can increase or decrease the attacker or defender's strength? How could you translate a board game's Combat Results Table into a video game and make it clear the different odds of success when attacking?

Summary

Combat may be the prime purpose of a game (such as in first-person shooter or military simulation), or just a minor part of the game (such as in trading or puzzle games). If combat is the prime purpose of the game, determining the results of combat can get more detailed because that's the experience players want. If combat occurs on a strategic scale or is not the prime purpose of the game, combat can be abstracted by just determining combat results.

Combat can vary between 100% certain (backgammon, chess, checkers, etc.) or uncertain. Both types of combat styles shape the way players attack and defend. If combat is certain, play becomes more strategic in defeating an opponent. If combat is uncertain, play may take calculated risks that can turn the tide of a game.

At the simplest level, combat can involve determining whether an attacker's strength is enough to overcome a defender's strength. When combat involves a comparison between an attacker's strength compared to the defender's strength, players must decide how much force to apply against a defender. This risk involves attacking a few units with a fairly certain outcome or attacking many units with much less certainty in the outcome.

More detailed combat may require a To Hits table first to determine if an attack even hits a defender. The defender may increase their defensive strength through terrain such as defending in a forest or a town that provides additional protection. In man to man combat, armor may also prevent an attacker from hitting any vital area of the defender.

A game might create even greater realism by including an Effects table that determine if an attacker does successfully hit, where the attack actually hits on the defender. For individuals, hits might occur on an arm or leg. For vehicles such as tanks or planes, hits might occur on the engine, wing, tread, or on the people inside the vehicle.

If a player hits (To Hit table) and hits a specific area (Effects table), the final result can be determined by a Combat Results Table (CRT) that determines how much damage actually occurred. Adding an element of chance makes combat unpredictable and thus more realistic.

There's always a tradeoff between chance and realism. Too much chance makes combat feel unrealistic. Too little chance can make combat too certain and actually less enjoyable within the context of a particular game.

Combat represents the way players can overcome enemies, whether as the primary goal of the game or a secondary means of achieving the main goal. For many games, combat is what makes games fun and challenging to play so it's important to test out combat in prototypes as often as possible.

Further Readings

"Simulating War: Studying Conflict through Simulation Games", Philip Sabin, Bloomsbury Academic, 2014.
"Wargame Design: The History, Production, and Use of Conflict Simulation Games", Strategy & Tactics Staff, 1977.

Chapter 24
Resource Management Prototypes

In many games, resource management acts as a way to increase your chances of winning the game. In role-playing games, players must manage their money and inventory so they can buy items such as weapons, armor, healing potions, or food. In other games, resource management is the whole purpose of the game. In a stock market simulation game, players need to buy and sell stocks. In a city management simulation, players must run a city by allocating money for services such as road repairs and police protection while taxing citizens.

Resource management is about choosing the following:

- Resources
- Results
- Time

Testing Resources

In any game, players will have a choice of different resources they can choose. In a game that lets players control the actions of an individual soldier in modern day combat, those resources could be a pistol, rifle, hand grenade, or mortar. In a game that lets players control entire armies, those resources might be tanks, machine guns, or artillery.

The two types of resources are:

- Currency
- Game items

Currency represents money that players earn and spend. In Monopoly, currency represents actual cash that players earn by passing Go, through luck when drawing

© The Author(s), under exclusive license to Springer Nature Switzerland AG 2023
W. Wang, *The Structure of Game Design*, International Series on Computer, Entertainment and Media Technology,
https://doi.org/10.1007/978-3-031-32202-0_24

cards, or by collecting rent from properties. In a game like Democracy, which puts players in charge of a country as president or prime minister, the game's currency is measured in "political capital" that players can spend to make changes.

Players typically collect or earn currency on a regular basis, either in a fixed amount (Collect $200 by passing Go) or in varying amounts, depending on the player's current situation in the game. A fixed amount ensures that players will always receive something. A varying amount risks players falling into a deepening financial hole that they can never recover from, making it impossible to win the game past a certain point.

In Monopoly, one player tends to dominate to the point where there's no way other players can possibly win as they're forced to sell properties with no hope of ever getting them back. This means their chances of earning any money keeps going down while their chances of paying the dominant player their remaining money keeps going up. In every game, this inevitable downward spiral occurs where there's no chance players can possibly win. To mitigate this as much as possible, designers may want to keep players in the game as long as possible.

In poker, players can stay in the game as long as they have money. It's possible for players to lose all their money in the first hand, but since players have a choice of how much to bet, they have more control over their fate (unlike Monopoly). Since poker gives players new hands each game (increasing the chance that they'll get luckier than their opponents), players have a better chance of playing longer and staying in the game.

While the object in some games (like poker) is to collect the most currency, other games are different. Instead, currency is only useful so players can purchase game items and those game items will help players win the game.

Game items provide advantages. In a financial game like Monopoly or a stock market simulation, game items represent investments that can earn more currency. By investing well, players can increase their currency hoard so they can buy even more game items.

In other video games, game items may increase a player's attack or defense capabilities. This indirectly helps players defeat enemies so they can collect more treasures that represents another form of currency. The fun comes from deciding which game items to buy based on their cost and advantages.

To test resources, a prototype should define how players earn currency. Experiment with giving players no currency and then unlimited currency to see how that affects the gameplay. Then test various currency levels for how much players start with and how much players earn periodically. Test also for how often players should receive currency.

Create multiple game items at different prices: inexpensive, medium, and expensive. Each game item should provide different ways to generate additional currency either directly (such as properties in Monopoly) or indirectly (such as armor and weapons in a role-playing game that increase a player's chances of surviving a battle so they can loot a dungeon). The trick lies in balancing the cost of a game item compared to its advantages.

No game item should be better or worse than any other game item. What will determine which game item is better or worse will be the circumstances of the game, which will be different in every game. If one game item were inherently superior to the others, there would be no reason for players to choose any other game item. Thus the superiority (or inferiority) of a game item occurs only through the current events in the game.

Thought Exercise

Pick a board game that involves resource management (typically money) and identify how much each player starts with and how much they earn periodically. What happens if you change the starting currency amount? What happens if you change how much players earn periodically? What happens if you change how often players receive additional currency?

Game items typically range in price from inexpensive, medium, and expensive. Think of the different prices for properties in Monopoly such as the cost of Park Place (expensive) to Baltic Avenue (inexpensive).

Pick the cheapest game item. What is the advantage of buying this game item? What is the disadvantage? Pick the most expensive game item. What is the advantage of buying this game item? What is the disadvantage?

In your game prototype, define the following:

- The currency used in your game
- The amount of currency players start with
- The amount of currency players receive periodically (and how often players receive this currency)

Knowing the currency in your game prototype, define the following:

- How many different game items (choices) are available
- The pros and cons of each game item to ensure none are overwhelmingly dominant or completely useless
- The cost of each game item

Testing the Results of Game Items

Players buy game items to increase their chances of winning. The challenge lies in choosing which game items to buy and use. That means all game items must be as equal as possible. Otherwise players may just choose one game item all the time or ignore other game items all the time.

What makes each game item superior (or inferior) to another lies with its relationship to the current game condition. So for every game item, there must be a moment when that game item is superior to every other game item, completely inferior to every other game item, and neither good nor bad compared to every other game item.

Although every game item must be equal, they offer varying ratios of risk vs. reward such as:

• High risk, high reward
• Medium risk, medium reward
• Low risk, low reward

In many first-person shooter games, players can choose from a variety of weapons. A pistol might cost the least but causes minimal damage. A rifle costs more but causes more damage. A gatling gun costs (and weighs) much more, but causes a large amount of damage.

Which weapon players choose can vary depending on cost, weight, and ammunition requirements. To test out these costs, risks, and rewards, start with just three game items that represent the High, Medium, and Low risk/reward.

Make sure the High risk/reward item is the highest/strongest/most expensive item. Based on these characteristics, make sure the Low risk/reward item is the lowest/weakest/least expensive item. Then choose an item that falls in the exact middle as a Middle risk/reward item.

The purpose of just prototyping with three game items is to test the high and low extremes. By experimenting with the extreme high and low game items, you can adjust their values until they work within the game where working depends more on the feel of the game rather than any specific types of metrics. Defining the high and low values sets the boundaries for all other game items.

In Monopoly, the extreme low values are represented by Baltic Avenue and Mediterranean Avenue while the extreme high values are represented by Boardwalk and Park Place. Every other property falls within the range of these two extremes.

In Doom, the extreme weakest weapon is the player's own fists that can punch an enemy. The extreme strongest weapon is the BFG 9000.

In stock market simulation games, the High, Medium, and Low risk items are often stocks (High risk/reward), mutual funds (Medium risk/reward), and bonds (Low risk/reward).

By simply starting with these High, Medium, and Low game items, you can test these values and once they work, it's easy to add additional items that fit within these extreme high and low boundaries.

Thought Exercise

Pick a game that has a resource management system and identify the High, Medium, and Low risk/reward game values. How would the game change if the High value game item doubled in cost? How would the game change if the Low value game item cost were cut in half?

To create a fair resource management system in your own game prototype, focus on:

- Making sure players never have too much or too little currency to purchase game items
- Making sure that all game items can be superior (and inferior) depending on the current game conditions

Testing Short and Long-Term Time Limits

In most games, players have currency that they can use to buy game items that have an effect on the game right away, such as choosing a more powerful weapon. However, some games introduce a time element where players can invest in a game item that will not produce any benefits until sometime in the future.

This forces players to decide whether to buy game items that can make an immediate impact now, or invest in game items that can't be used until later. Just as with game items with High, Medium, and Low risk/reward, so should there be game items with High, Medium, and Low time limits.

A Low time limit means the game item can be useful right away. A Medium time limit means the game item can't be used right away but can be used relatively soon. A High time limit means the game item won't be useful until a long period of time passes.

The longer the time restriction, the greater the benefit. The shorter the time restriction, the lower the benefit.

In the military simulation, Hearts of Iron, players control entire countries during World War Two. A Low time limit allows players to buy equipment (planes, tanks, ships) that can fight battles right away. A Medium time limit allows players to invest in more advanced equipment that won't be available depending on how much players invest in research and development.

The challenge is that if players focus solely on buying equipment with Low time limits, eventually their equipment will become obsolete. This forces them to spend currency buying equipment they can use right away (Low time limit) as well as investing in more advanced equipment (Medium time limit) that will be ready in the future.

If players fail to invest in more advanced technology, they risk having their armies wiped out by opponents with more advanced technology. If players invest in too much advanced technology, they risk getting wiped out in the present.

High time limit items represent the greatest risk with the greater reward. In Hearts of Iron, players might invest in jet fighter planes, rockets, or atom bombs. The time needed to fully research these most advanced weapons take the longest, but their impact could be devastating if players can introduce them before their opponents can.

By having game items that offer benefits with different time limits, games create additional challenges for players to consider. If players buy inexpensive (Low risk) items now, they'll risk not having better items in the future. If they invest in better (High risk) items for the future, they'll risk not surviving long enough to reap the benefits of their long-term investments.

Resource management involves making choices that often involve:

- Cost
- Combat strength
- Weight
- Size
- Time to receive any benefits

Resource management with time limits forces players to think tactically (the present) and strategically (the future).

Thought Exercise

Game items often return benefits that increase the chance of winning. This can mean more:

- Currency
- Additional game items
- Greater combat strength

The sole purpose of buying any game items is to increase the odds of winning. Players must choose game items that match their strategy while also choosing game items that will help them defeat any other player's strategies.

Test to make sure any game items with time limits don't take too long so players can actually use them. Test to make sure players have an incentive to invest in game items with Medium risk/reward/time limits in addition to buying game items with Low risk/reward/time limits. Test to make sure it's possible for players to get any High risk/reward/time limit game items.

Time limits force players to plan ahead and devote precious currency to balance between immediate benefits, medium-term benefits, and long-term benefits. This balancing act makes resource management challenging and fun.

Summary

Resource management may be the core mechanic of a game or just one part of the game. In either case, resource management should be fun, interesting, and challenging. Players should have a variety of options to choose but no single option should ever be dominant (and no single option should ever be completely useless). By making every single option equal but different in some way, players have the freedom to choose the game items they want.

To purchase game items, players need to earn currency. This currency can be money, experience points, or any other measurement unit that fits your particular game. Currency can buy game items, which can then create more currency directly or indirectly.

When deciding which game items to buy, players must balance the pros and cons of each since in a balanced game, all game items should be equal. One of the biggest choices players may make is choosing game items based on time.

Short-term time limits mean players can buy and use a game item right away. Long-term time limits mean players must invest in a game item and can only receive the benefits sometime in the future. This can mean gaining a huge advantage but players must last long enough to gain this advantage.

Resource management is all about testing different values for currency and game items. Start with the extreme high and low values to define the boundaries of acceptable values. Then it will be easy to fill in additional game items within these two extreme boundaries.

Ultimately, resource management is all about increasing the chances a player can win the game based on the short-term and long-term decisions they make.

Further Reading

"The Fundamentals of Game Economy Design", Tom Hammond, https://content.userwise.io/the-fundamentals-of-game-economy-design

Chapter 25
Puzzle Prototypes

Puzzles act like locked doors. Players encounter a puzzle (locked door) and then must figure out how to solve this puzzle (unlock the door). Once they do this, they can continue the game beyond the puzzle.

Some games are nothing but puzzles such as Candy Crush or Tetris, which constantly challenges players to match or align objects on the screen. Other games include puzzles as obstacles for players to overcome. Sometimes players can still play the game without solving the puzzle but other times they must solve the puzzle to continue playing.

When designing puzzles, follow these guidelines:

- The puzzle must have one (or more solutions) so it can be solved
- The puzzle cannot be too easy
- All clues needed to solve the puzzle are in plain sight

To make sure a puzzle can be solved, start with the solution and then work backwards to where the player begins. For example, imagine a Rubik's cube with all colors properly aligned on each side, which clearly shows that the puzzle can be solved. Now if you scramble the Rubik's cube, it's obvious there's a way to get from the scrambled state back to the solution as shown in Fig. 25.1.

Solving a puzzle requires the following:

- One or more steps
- A core mechanic (spatial manipulation, word play, number play, matching, speed, logic)

The simplest puzzle requires one step to solve, such as a locked door with a key on the floor. Players simply need to pick up the key to unlock the door. However, if the key is hidden, that adds an additional step. If players need to find a chest that contains the key, that adds another step. Each additional step makes the puzzle progressively harder to solve because each step must be completed in the right order.

© The Author(s), under exclusive license to Springer Nature
Switzerland AG 2023
W. Wang, *The Structure of Game Design*, International Series on Computer,
Entertainment and Media Technology,
https://doi.org/10.1007/978-3-031-32202-0_25

Fig. 25.1 Seeing a
solution first clearly shows
that a puzzle, such as a
Rubik's cube, can be
solved

When creating puzzles, decide from the start if there will be just one solution or multiple solutions. With crossword puzzles, there's only one possible word that can solve each part of the puzzle. With a Rubik's cube, there are multiple ways to solve the puzzle.

Once players solve a single solution puzzle, there's little enjoyment to solving it again. Puzzles that offer multiple solutions can be played over and over again, but their very nature means they tend to be less detailed and more abstract (think Tetris or a Rubik's cube).

To test puzzle prototypes, make sure players know the following:

- What goal they're trying to achieve
- The core mechanic for solving the puzzle
- How to interpret positive and negative feedback

Defining Puzzle Solutions

Puzzles are only interesting if players know what they're supposed to achieve and how they're supposed to achieve it. Therefore the first step in testing a puzzle prototype is to determine if people understand what the puzzle is and how to go about solving it.

That means the rules for solving puzzles tend to be simple. The challenge doesn't lie in the restrictions of the rules but in the nature of the puzzle itself. For example, the rules for solving a crossword puzzle are simple:

- Read the clues for each vertical or horizontal line of a puzzle

- Fill in that line of boxes where only one letter appears in each box

Although the rules for a puzzle may be simple, finding the right solution is not and that's where the challenge lies. In many video games, players must solve a puzzle that involves a locked door. The rule is simple: find the key that unlocks that door. The challenge lies in finding where that key might be, which requires deciphering clues sprinkled around the game.

Finding the key is the solution (and opening the door with the key is trivial). The challenge is figuring out where the key might be. A poor puzzle might force players to exhaustively search an area for the key. A much better puzzle might require the player to decipher clues they found earlier in the game. Once players correctly decipher these clues, these clues lead the player to the key.

So the puzzle solution must be clear. Then the rules must be simple. Finally, there must be clues to help players follow the rules to find the solution. This combination of a clear solution, simple rules, and clues must exist in a puzzle so a puzzle prototype can verify that all of these features exist in your puzzle design.

Think how a Rubik's cube meets these criteria:

- Puzzle solution – Displays one color on each side of the cube.
- Puzzle rules – Turn, rotate, and manipulate rows of cubes.
- Puzzle clues – The colors visually show how close (or far away) you are from the solution.

Thought Exercise

Pick a physical puzzle. Can you understand the goal you must achieve to solve the puzzle? Are the rules simple to understand? What clues does the puzzle offer to help you find the solution?

Pick a puzzle in a video game that you like. Can you understand the goal you must achieve to solve the puzzle? Are the rules simple to understand? What clues does the puzzle offer to help you find the solution?

Pick a puzzle (in a video game) that you think is unfair or poorly designed. Do you dislike it because the solution is unclear? The rules aren't simple and easy to understand? The clues are too confusing to help you solve the puzzle?

If you have a puzzle prototype, show it to others and ask them to identify the following:

- Does the puzzle make it clear what the solution is that players need to achieve?
- Are the rules of the puzzle simple and easy to understand?
- Does the puzzle provide clues to help players find a solution (and are those clues too easy or too hard)?

When testing a puzzle prototype, the key are the clues. If the clues are too hard to understand, the puzzle will be too frustrating. If the clues are too easy, the puzzle won't be challenging enough. When testing a puzzle prototype, focus on making the clues easy to understand but challenging to use.

The different colors of a Rubik's cube makes these clues easy to understand while still challenging players how to manipulate the cube next. The clues in a crossword puzzle describes the right word so players must decipher the deliberately vague clue based on the number of letters of the word along with occasional letters intersecting from other known words of the crossword puzzle.

Testing Core Mechanics

The solution to a puzzle should be clear to both players and the puzzle designer. What makes a game fun is the core mechanic or rules that players must repeat over and over again. With a Rubik's cube, the core mechanic involves manipulating rows in different directions. With a crossword puzzle, the core mechanic involves filling in boxes with letters that form a single word. With Tetris, the core mechanic involves manipulating different geometric shapes as they fall.

The puzzle's core mechanic is where the challenge and fun lies. In a poor puzzle, this repetitive core mechanic is simply not fun to do because it's tedious and boring. Think of a combination lock where players must exhaustively try different three-digit combinations until they open it. The constant and likely failure of each attempt is simply not fun because there's no choice.

Manipulating differently shaped and colored geometric objects can be fun because players have a choice to determine which orientation to manipulate the object and which horizontal direction to place the object as shown in Fig. 25.2. In general, the more choices, the better.

Crossword puzzles can be frustrating because some clues are simply too hard to understand. However, players can choose which clues to solve first, and each time they solve one clue, the letters intersect to provide clues for letters that make up the missing words.

Puzzles are fun because the core mechanics keep getting players closer to the solution. Because of this positive feedback, even the most challenging puzzles can be hard to put down when players feel that they're on the verge of solving the puzzle.

If puzzles are used throughout a video game, those puzzles often get progressively harder and more complicated. The goal is to teach players new skills and ways to solve similar puzzle, which will later help them win the game.

Thought Exercise

Pick a puzzle and identify the core mechanic players must repeat. What makes this core mechanic interesting? How does this core mechanic help players get one step closer to the solution?

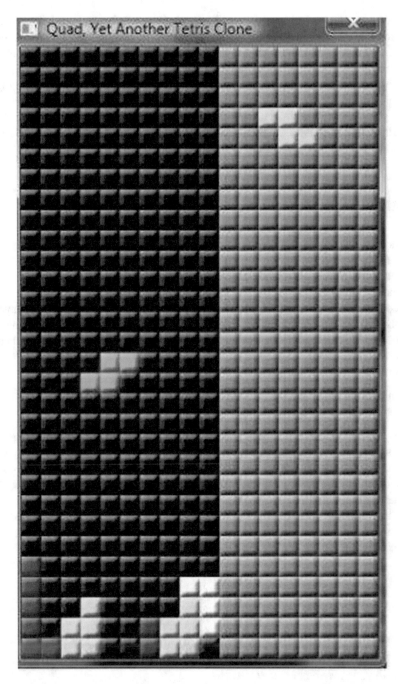

Fig. 25.2 Different colors and shapes challenges players to rotate and position geometric objects in place

In Tetris, the random appearance of geometric shapes keeps surprising players and forcing them to make split-second decisions on how best to manipulate and place it. On the other hand, trying to find the three-digit combination to a lock is not fun because each failed combination does nothing but eliminate one possible combination out of thousands. Because progress is so slow, trying different three-digit combinations is not fun.

In your puzzle prototype, what is the core mechanic players must repeat? Is this repetitive core mechanic fun by offering players choices? Does this core mechanic get players closer to the solution?

Testing Puzzle Clues

Clues serve two purposes in a puzzle. First, clues give players a direction and guidance for how to solve the puzzle. Second, clues should provide feedback letting players know how close (or far) they're getting to the solution of the puzzle.

Sudoku involves filling boxes with numbers where each row and column does not contain duplicate numbers. Sudoku puzzles appear partially filled in so players can use the process of elimination to fill in different boxes. Once they fill in some of the boxes, it's easier to deduce which numbers should go into other rows and columns as shown in Fig. 25.3.

So clues serve two purposes in a puzzle:

- Clues point players in the right direction to solving the puzzle.
- Each time players solve one clue, it's easier to solve other clues

Clues provide positive feedback that keeps giving players a sense of progress. Solving one row or column in a Sudoku puzzle gives players confidence they can solve another row or column. On the other hand, exhaustively trying three-digit combinations on a lock offers no clues for how to get started or how close the player's guesses might be.

When creating a puzzle prototype, make sure that clues give players a direction and create a positive feedback loop that make the puzzle's solution increasingly easier to solve.

Thought Exercise

Pick a puzzle and notice what clues the puzzle offers to get you started in the right direction. Are these initial clues helpful and clear? When you solve one clue, does this help you solve other clues?

Show your puzzle prototype to others and ask them to identify the initial clues your puzzle offers. Then ask them to identify whether solving one clue helps them solve another clue.

Fig. 25.3 Sudoku provides
clues to help players solve
the puzzle

5	3			7				
6			1	9	5			
	9	8					6	
8				6				3
4			8		3			1
7				2				6
	6					2	8	
			4	1	9			5
				8			7	9
5	3	4	6	7	8	9	1	2
6	7	2	1	9	5	3	4	8
1	9	8	3	4	2	5	6	7
8	5	9	7	6	1	4	2	3
4	2	6	8	5	3	7	9	1
7	1	3	9	2	4	8	5	6
9	6	1	5	3	7	2	8	4
2	8	7	4	1	9	6	3	5
3	4	5	2	8	6	1	7	9

Adding a Theme to a Puzzle

Since puzzles often involve manipulating objects (of different shapes, colors, or sizes), words, or numbers, puzzles often add a theme that provides a larger game world. Candy Crush uses the idea of colorful candy pieces for players to manipulate. Jigsaw puzzles display images such as landscapes, famous landmarks, or animals in the wild. Even crossword puzzles may contain clues where the words are related to a specific topic such as sports, movies, or popular songs.

Themes make puzzles more relatable. A puzzle that challenges players to match different colors and shapes isn't as exciting as a puzzle that challenges players to match different colored objects as shown in Fig. 25.4. This added theme simply provides context for the puzzle so it's easier for players to understand and more fun to play than simply manipulating abstract color objects.

Puzzles that are obstacles in a video game often reflect the theme of the overall game. A video game set in the future might contain puzzles involving computer hacking. Yet a similar video game set in medieval times might contain the exact same puzzle but with a historical theme to match the game's setting. Themes are optional but colorful ways to make puzzles more enjoyable.

Fig. 25.4 Displaying unique shapes and colors makes match 3 puzzle games easy to understand

Thought Exercise

Pick a puzzle and identify whether it has or does not have a theme. If the puzzle has a theme, how does this theme make the puzzle more enjoyable? If the puzzle lacks a theme, does this omission make the puzzle less enjoyable?

In your own puzzle prototype, ask if a theme would make the puzzle easier to understand and fun to play.

Making Puzzles Solvable

No matter how difficult a puzzle may appear on the surface, every puzzle must be solvable. When puzzles are the sole purpose of play, such as crossword puzzles or Rubik's cubes, players know they can find a solution eventually. When puzzles appear in video games, sometimes puzzles may seem unsolvable.

If players can't solve a video game puzzle, there are several choices:

- Allow players to skip the puzzle.
- Provide hints that players can receive, often at a cost.
- Provide multiple ways to solve a puzzle to increase the odds that players will find at least one solution.
- Provide various difficulty levels that players can choose (Easy, Medium, or Hard).

Puzzles in video games should never completely halt a player's progress because that can create a frustrating experience where players risk just quitting the game altogether. Ideally, every puzzle should be solvable, but because people of different skill levels, experience, and knowledge may attempt the puzzle, puzzles designers should plan for alternates.

Puzzles should be obstacles that players feel provide a challenge that they can overcome. Thus creating a puzzle will always involve a tradeoff between being too easy and being too hard.

Thought Exercise

Pick a physical puzzle. How can players get help if they get stuck? Pick a puzzle in a video game. What happens if players get stuck?

In your own puzzle prototype, what happens if players get stuck? What alternatives will your puzzle offer in case players can't find the solution?

Summary

Puzzles can either be the sole purpose of a game or an obstacle within a game. Resource management challenges are often puzzles in disguise that force players to make tradeoffs between which resources to cultivate and how long to nurture them.

Puzzles need a clear solution that's obvious for players to solve. Clues provide players with a direction to take for solving the puzzle. Clues must get players started and help them solve additional clues in an increasingly positive feedback loop. The more clues players solve, the easier it will be to solve all remaining clues.

Rules represent simple mechanics that players must do repetitively to solve the puzzle. This combination of a clear goal, simple rules, and clues provide the basis for creating a challenging and enjoyable puzzle.

Above all, make sure every puzzle can be solved. Since not every person will be able to solve a puzzle, plan for alternatives that can help players solve your puzzle eventually. The goal of every puzzle is not to frustrate or block players, but to provide them with a fun challenge that forces them to think and experiment until they find the right answer, even if they need a hint now and then.

Further Reading

"Designing Video Game Puzzles", Damien Allan, https://www.gamedeveloper.com/design/designing-video-game-puzzles.

Chapter 26
Selling a Game to the Market

Game ideas are meant to be completed. Whether the game makes millions of dollars or nothing at all, the main goal is to complete the game idea you started because that experience of completing a game will give you the confidence that you can tackle a larger, more ambitious project in the future. If you start a game but never complete it, you'll never have that confidence that you can finish a project.

Completing a game is crucial, but you may have multiple goals for completing a game such as:

- Testing a game concept
- Learning a particular game engine
- Learning a particular programming language
- Making a social statement
- Learning a new skill (such as graphics design, level design, programming, sound design, etc.)
- Creating a game to give away for others to enjoy
- Creating a game to add to your portfolio
- Creating a game to learn about submitting games to an app store
- Creating a game as a hobby
- Creating a game to improve upon an existing game to show you can do it better
- Creating a game to make money

In other words, there are many reasons why you might want to complete a game beyond just making money. Whether that game is super primitive and ugly or visually stunning and exciting, what matters is that you finish your project. Before you start any new project, identify the outcome you want to achieve.

Then outline the steps you plan to take so you can achieve that outcome. These steps may actually be wrong or misleading, but you need a plan to follow so you make steady progress towards your goal.

© The Author(s), under exclusive license to Springer Nature
Switzerland AG 2023
W. Wang, *The Structure of Game Design*, International Series on Computer,
Entertainment and Media Technology,
https://doi.org/10.1007/978-3-031-32202-0_26

Even if your planned steps don't work, you'll be forced to find a new step that will get you closer to your desired outcome. It's not important that your plan be flawless. In fact, it's far more likely that your plan will be flawed either by missing steps or including steps that may not be useful. The process of following your plan will identify which steps are right or wrong, and that will give you valuable experience for the next game project you tackle.

Ultimately, the goal of completing a game is to give you experience, knowledge, and confidence to create another game. The more games you create, the easier it will get and the more challenging ideas you can pursue. Game design most likely won't be a get rich quick scheme but a long marathon of constant learning, failure, and frustration. In the end, the rewards can be immensely satisfying.

Thought Exercise

Identify the main reason why you want to create a game. Even if you plan for a game to make money, it's not a failure if it doesn't make you a millionaire overnight. Most games earn a little money but not enough to provide a full-time income for the developer.

Think of each game you make as another step towards stretching your capabilities, giving you more experience in game design and creation, and forcing you to better understand the marketing and business aspect of game development.

Over time, all of these skills and experiences will simply give you more opportunities to create more, bigger, and better games in the future.

Create a plan for turning a rough idea into a complete game that someone else can play. Having a deadline will force you to keep working on your game even if it's just an hour or less a day.

Becoming a Professional Game Developer

Many people dream about becoming a game developer, but far too many people fail to pursue their dreams. Even those who pursue their dreams often give up too soon at the first sign of discouragement.

Whatever you want to do, you can do it. The quickest route to disappointment is to wait for someone else to give you permission to do what you want. The surest route to success is to give yourself permission to do what you want regardless of your circumstances, education, resources, or what others around you might say.

If you want to design games, you may think you need to get a job with a large game studio. The truth is that you can start designing games right now whether anyone recognizes your talent and skills or not.

Never wait for permission to pursue your dream or you risk waiting forever.

Some common paths people take to becoming a game designer includes:

- Getting a job in the gaming industry, preferably with a large game studio
- Working with an independent (indie) game developer in a team
- Working as a solo game developer

Most people aspiring to become game designers and developers pursue the obvious route of getting a job in the gaming industry. The advantage is that you get to work in the gaming industry so you can get paid to learn from other professionals and spend your time working on games.

The disadvantage is that not every job in the gaming industry will be interesting. You may get stuck in a niche performing necessary tasks but limiting your exposure to other parts of game design. If you're stuck in a job where you're not learning other aspects of game development and you're working long hours to make games that other people have designed, you may not have time to nurture your own skills in designing and developing games.

This trap can also apply to anyone who fails to get a job in the gaming industry but gets a job in another industry. That job may not give you time or experience designing games. Instead, the job may give you a steady income and the illusion of security, but it's still up to you to take what little free time you have to continue studying and designing games because nobody else will care about your dream of designing games more than you.

That means even if you're stuck in a boring job, no matter how well paid it might be, you must still learn in your spare time as much as you can about game design and development so you can achieve your ultimate dream of making a game of your own.

Rather than work for a large company where you risk getting stuck in a limited role, you might also work for an indie game developer that consists of a small team. Working for an indie game developer most likely means less money, but because there are fewer people on the team, it does mean more experience doing two or more jobs.

Since there are more indie game developers than large game studios, it can be easier to find a job with one of them. In addition, you'll likely gain far more experience working for an indie game developer since teams will be smaller, forcing everyone to do multiple tasks. The drawback may be that the pay and job could be less secure and you may work hard and get less security, benefits, and money.

No matter what happens, you can always pursue the solo game developer route. This will force you to learn all aspects of game development including marketing, graphics design, sound design, programming, and advertising. Best of all, anyone can become a solo game developer.

The drawback is that solo game developers must do everything themselves (or with a small team) and being a solo game developer means performing tasks that may have little to do with game design (such as marketing, accounting, and advertising).

No matter which route you take, there will always be a way for you to become a game developer either on your own, with an indie team, or with a large game studio. All options have their pros and cons but they all give you an opportunity to become part of the gaming industry in one form or another. If you want to make games, the only thing stopping you is your own fear, reluctance, and uncertainty, and that's something only you can overcome.

Thought Exercise

Make plans for how you could get a job at a large gaming studio, at an indie gaming studio, or just become a solo game developer. Which option looks most appealing to you and why? Which option looks easiest to you and why? Which option looks hardest to you and what can you do to make it easier?

If you have to take a job just to pay your bills, how can you structure your free time to continue pursuing your dream of game designing? If you lack certain skills, such as graphics design or programming, what plan can you create to help you overcome those deficiencies (take a class, read a book, hire someone to do this task for you, etc.)?

Making Money with Games

You can make money designing games. You can also make money selling toilet paper, paperclips, ball bearings, and rubber gloves. If your sole goal is to make money, there are easier ways to do this than by making games.

You should only pursue game design if that's what you want to do. Then find a way to make money doing it. If you want to make money from a game, the best time to start planning how you'll make money from a game is before you start making that game.

Once you've created a plan for making money from your game, you can then design your game to optimize your chances of making money. If you make a game first and then try to figure out how to make money from it later, your game won't be optimized to make money so the entire process will be much harder.

There are multiple ways to make money from a game. Some common ways include:

- Selling a game to another company and collecting royalties
- Selling a game direct to consumers
- Making money from in-app purchases
- Making money from advertising
- Making money from a crowd funding site
- Working on a game for a gaming studio
- Selling your source code
- Applying your game design skills in non-gaming industries

In the old days before the Internet, game designers could make a game by either working for a larger company or selling their completed game to a larger company. This larger company then spent money to duplicate the game, package the game, ship the game to distributors, and then take a percentage of the profit while paying a royalty for each game sold.

With royalties, the game designer can focus on making games and let a game company take care of printing, production, packaging, marketing, distribution, and advertising. This process is still available, but the high cost of packaging and shipping increasingly makes this path only viable for a limited number of games. While card and board games still need to be sold through a distributor, video games can now avoid distributors and go straight to consumers.

The most direct way to make money is to sell a game straight to consumers through an online gaming store platform like Steam (store.steampowered.com/games), BattleNet (us.shop.battle.net), GOG (www.gog.com), Epic Games Store (store.epicgames.com), or GamersGate (www.gamersgate.com).

The advantage of selling directly to consumers is that you don't need permission from any game company and you keep the bulk of the game sales with a percentage of each sale going to the online gaming store platform.

The disadvantage of selling through an online gaming store platform is that each platform already offers hundreds, if not thousands, of games so the odds of consumers finding your particular game is low.

Although online gaming stores can reach thousands of people, most of those people will never know your game exists. That means you must spend time marketing and promoting your game separate from any time spent designing more games.

To promote games, game developers often rely on periodic sales to attract attention. That way some people will buy the game and those people will likely tell others about it. In the mobile game market, game developers initially tried selling their games, but many people were reluctant to buy anything without a chance to try the game out first.

The next strategy mobile game developers used was to offer two versions of their game. A free version gave people a taste of how the game worked. If people liked the game, they could buy the paid version that offered more challenges and longer gameplay.

Finally, mobile game developers found the most success with free games that completely lowered the barrier to trying out the game. If people liked the game, they could buy in-app purchases that added new features to the game. Another variation was free games that included advertising that paid the developers. Free to play games quickly dominated the market because they made finding new games risk-free.

Since making a new game from scratch takes time and money, the biggest risk is funding a game long enough to bring it to market, and keeping it on the market long enough for it to start making money. To eliminate this problem, many game developers post their projects on crowd funding sites to raise money. Once they have the money to make the game, it's simply a race to make that game before the crowd-funded money runs out.

Because making a game and trying to sell it on your own can be so time-consuming, difficult, and costly, many game developers prefer to make a game under contract with a larger gaming studio. That way the gaming studio takes all the financial risk, but they also take the bulk of the profits as well.

Every year, hundreds, if not thousands, of games appear on the market where most of them will barely break even or actually lose money. To recoup the cost of making a game, many game developers recycle their source code. One way to do this is to create a similar game but with different graphics, story background, and setting. So if you make a first-person shooter game based on a science fiction world, you might recycle the source code to create a similar first-person shooter game based on a historical world filled with gunslingers, bounty hunters, and sheriffs. Each time you recycle the source code, you can improve it and thus create a new game in much less time and expense.

A final way to recycle source code is to sell it. Many sites let developers sell their source code so that others can modify it and create their own games. Selling source code can be a way to profit from a failed game.

Although many people want to make games, many game designers and developers learn unique skills that can be applied to non-gaming industries. Since video games increasingly display realistic images, the television and movie industry often relies on game engines to create special effects faster and cheaper than before.

Architects, automotive designers, and aircraft manufacturers use game engines to model buildings, cars, and planes completely within a computer before they spend time making physical prototypes. Even though you may want to make games, any skills you develop as a game designer can be useful in so many industries outside of the traditional gaming world.

With so many ways to make money from a game, start by shaping your game around one or more money-making techniques. Making a game takes time and money with no guarantee of success, much like making a movie, writing a novel, or painting a picture.

Don't make games because you think you'll get rich. Make games because you want to make games, but make sure you look at how to profit from your hard work as well. Here are some guidelines for increasing your odds of making money making games:

- Make games that you find interesting. (Don't chase trends and create copy-cat games.)
- Make games with a distinctive visual and narrative style. (Don't make games that look and feel like other games.)
- Target a niche. (Don't try to make games that appeal to everyone because they'll wind up appealing to no one.)
- Make the best game you can. (Don't think you can slap a game together quickly just to make money.)

Summary

Whether you make a full-time income, a part-time income, or just occasional money from a game, the important goal is to make games because you enjoy doing so and find the process fun and challenging. Ideally, you want to get paid as much as possible for your work, but that likely won't happen from your first game or even your tenth game.

However, the more games you make, the more experience and knowledgeable you'll get, and the better and more sophisticated games you can create. As long as you enjoy making games and keep moving forward, you'll find success in one form or another.

The profit from making games involves more than just money. There's also the satisfaction that comes from setting a goal for yourself and achieving it. That type of emotional satisfaction that comes from facing the unknown, overcoming challenges, trusting yourself, and creating something tangible out of your imagination is something that's too often absent from ordinary jobs.

Making games can be nearly as fun as playing them, so keep making games and keep having fun. You can make people happy through games, but you'll never know how many people's lives you might affect until you make a game of your own.

So what are you waiting for? Start making a game today. There's a whole world out there just waiting to see what you might create.

Further Reading

"GAMEDEV: 10 Steps to Making Your First Game Successful", Wlad Marhulets, Unfold Publishing, 2020.

Appendices

Appendix A: Gaming Supplies and Open Source Video Games

If you're interested in making a paper-based game such as a board game or a card game, it's easy to make pieces from ordinary office supplies. You can use index cards, cardboard, colored paper, and pieces from existing games like dice or playing pieces to make quick paper prototypes. If you need to create more polished paper prototypes, consider buying game supplies from online sources such as:

- BoardGamesMaker.com
- Gameparts.net
- 99centgameparts.com.

If you're interested in creating video games, nearly every game engine offers tutorials and sample games you can study. That way you can modify the source code and add graphic assets to change the game.

However, you can also learn the intricacies of video games by studying open source video games. Such open source video games allow you to examine the complete working source code and multimedia assets (graphics and audio) so you can not only see how they work together, but also make your own changes to the game mechanics, user interface, or graphic appearance.

Open source video games typically mimic popular video games or video game genres such as first-person shooters or strategy games with a 2.5D perspective. Some popular open source video games include:

- 0 A.D. (play0ad.com), an empire building strategy game like Age of Empires.
- Armagetron Advanced (www.armagetronad.org), a 3D version of Tron.
- Cataclysm: Dark Days Ahead (cataclysmdda.org), a turn-based survival game set in a post-apocalyptic world.

W. Wang, *The Structure of Game Design*, International Series on Computer,
Entertainment and Media Technology,
https://doi.org/10.1007/978-3-031-32202-0

- Cube 2: Sauerbraten (sauerbraten.org), a first-person shooter similar to Cube.
- FlightGear Flight Simulator (www.flightgear.org), a real-time airplane simulator that mimics Microsoft's Flight Simulator.
- FreeCiv (www.freecivweb.org), an empire-building strategy game similar to Civilization.
- Freedoom (freedoom.github.io), a clone of Doom.
- FreeOrion (www.freeorion.org), a turn-based space empire and galactic conquest similar to Master of Orion.
- MegaGlest (megaglest.org), a real-time strategy game that emphasizes big battles and epic adventures similar to Glest.
- Minetest (www.minetest.net), an open world game similar to Minecraft.
- OpenTTD (www.openttd.org), a simulation game similar to Transport Tycoon Deluxe.
- Pioneer (pioneerspacesim.net), a single player space adventure game similar to Frontier: Elite II.
- SuperTuxCart (supertuxkart.net), a cartoonish racing game similar to Mario Kart.
- The Battle for Wesnoth (www.wesnoth.org), a turn-based strategy game set in a fantasy world.
- Xonotic (xonotic.org), a first-person, arena shooter similar to Unreal.

If you're interested in working in the gaming industry but don't yet have experience, contributing to an open source video game can give you that valuable experience.

Keep track of what you contribute, what you learned, and what skills you developed. That experience will prove you can work on a video game development team as a paid professional one day.

Appendix B: PC Bootup Game Rules

PC Boot Up is a card game for two or more players where players attempt to be the first one to boot up their computer. Players use cards that represent different programs, problems, and solutions to boot up a PC and hinder other players from booting up their PCs. The game is meant to teach people the common types of problems that could prevent a computer from booting up along with the specific solution to solve each problem.

Game Components

PC Boot Up is a card game that consists of four types of cards:

- Problems
- Solutions
- Safeties
- Programs

Problem Cards

Problems cards are used to prevent another player's PC from booting up. A player must eliminate all Problem cards (by using a Solution or Safety card) in order to play a Program card. It is possible to play one or more Problem cards against another player.

The seven types of Problem cards are labeled Bug, Disk Fragmentation, Registry Failure, Virus, Hacker, Crash, and Trojan Horse. Players cannot finish booting up their PC until they eliminate all Problem cards from their PC.

Bug – represents a common error that can suddenly cause any program, such as an operating system or word processor, to act erratically or stop working altogether. All software contains bugs, which means that all programs can suffer problems caused by a bug.

Disk Fragmentation – represents a problem with the way some operating systems store files on a hard disk. When an operating system stores files as closely as possible, changing or deleting a file can leave empty gaps between existing files. When you add a new file, the operating system stores part of a new file in one gap and part of that same file in another gap, causing fragmentation even if your hard disk is largely empty.

Registry Failure – represents a common problem with some operating systems that use a special database called a registry, which every program uses to store data. Because every program needs to use the registry and multiple programs modify the registry contents all the time, it's common for certain data, called registry entries, to get deleted by mistake or placed in the wrong area. This can cause the computer to slow down or even cease working altogether.

Virus – represents a malicious program known as a computer virus, which spreads between computers and can delete files, causing a computer to act erratically or cease working.

Hacker – represents an unauthorized intruder, known as a hacker, who can sneak into your computer and cause havoc such as deleting files or causing your computer to stop working.

Crash – represents a failure that causes a program to act erratically or fail completely. Although crashes can often be linked to software bugs, computers sometimes crash simply because of unpredictable circumstances that cannot always be duplicated.

Trojan Horse – represents a malicious program that tricks you into running and installing it on your computer, where it can then delete files or adversely affect the performance of a computer.

Solution Cards

Solution cards are used to eliminate a Problem card that another player places on your PC to keep you from successfully booting up. The seven types of Solution cards are labeled Patch, Defragmenter, Registry Optimizer, AntiVirus, Firewall, Boot Up, and Anti-Spyware.

Each type of Solution card can eliminate one specific Problem card as follows:

Problem card	Solution card	Safety card
Bug	Patch	Cloud Computing
Disk Fragmentation	Defragmenter	UNIX
Registry Failure	Registry Optimizer	UNIX
Virus	AntiVirus	Virtual Machine
Hacker	Firewall	Honeypot
Crash	Boot Up	Cloud Computing
Trojan Horse	Anti-Spyware	Virtual Machine

Patch – represents a software patch or update designed to fix and remove bugs from a program.

Defragmenter – represents a special utility program that reorganizes all the files on a hard disk so that every file is complete and not broken up into multiple pieces within empty gaps between other files.

Registry Optimizer – represents a special utility program designed to fix and repair problems with the registry by removing incorrect registry data and either deleting it or placing it in its correct location.

AntiVirus – represents a special utility program designed to identify and remove viruses from a computer.

Firewall – represents a special utility program designed to block unauthorized access to a computer through the Internet or over a local area network.

Boot Up – represents the process of either turning on a computer for the first time or restarting a computer that is already turned on. Booting up can often clear up problems caused by unpredictable program crashes.

Anti-spyware – represents a special utility program that can identify and remove malicious programs that can sneak into your computer without your knowledge, such as a Trojan Horse.

Safety Cards

Safety cards are used to permanently protect your computer against specific Problem cards. The four types of Safety cards are labeled Cloud Computing, UNIX, Virtual Machine, and Honeypot.

Cloud Computing – represents the ability to store software on a single computer, which allows multiple users to run that single program over the Internet. As a result, individuals no longer need to worry about constantly installing patches or dealing with program crashes. The Cloud Computing card protects your computer from the Bug and Crash cards.

UNIX – represents the UNIX operating system, which does not suffer from disk fragmentation or registry failures like other operating systems. UNIX deliberately stores files as far apart as possible on a hard disk, which greatly reduces the problem of disk fragmentation except when a hard disk is nearly full. UNIX also does not rely on a registry, which completely eliminates any possibility of registry problems. The UNIX card protects against the Disk Fragmentation and Registry Failure cards.

Virtual Machine – represents the ability to run one operating system (known as a guest) within another operating system (known as a host). A virtual machine cannot stop viruses, but they can isolate an operating system to make it difficult for viruses to find and infect. In addition, a virtual machine can "clone" an operating system so if a virus or Trojan Horse does wreck it, the virtual machine makes it easy to delete the file representing the infected operating system and replace it with a previous, clean and uninfected version of that same operating system. As a result, a virus attack on a virtual machine can be quickly negated within seconds. The Virtual Machine card protects against the Virus and Trojan Horse cards.

Honeypot – represents a special program designed to lure a hacker into a harmless, isolated part of a computer that displays fake, but seemingly important data. The goal is to trick a hacker away from a legitimate computer that contains important data, and trap the hacker into a fake computer where the hacker can do all the damage he wants, but the files are fake so nothing will cause problems. The Honeypot card protects against the Hacker card.

Program Cards

Program cards are used to boot up your PC. The five types of Program cards are labeled Word Processor, Spreadsheet, Presentation, Web Browser, and E-Mail.

Word Processor – represents a program for creating, editing, and formatting text for creating letters or reports.

Spreadsheet – represents a program for performing numeric calculations.

Presentation – represents a program for organizing and presenting information using text and graphics.

Web Browser – represents a program for accessing the Internet.

E-Mail – represents a program for sending and receiving e-mail messages.

How to Win

Players need to play one of each type of Program cards to win. Players cannot play a Program card if they have an unsolved Problem card. Before a player can play a Program card, that player must first play a Boot Up card.

The first player to successfully play a Boot Up card and all five Program cards while eliminating all Problem cards using a Solution or Safety card is the winner. To successfully boot up your computer, you must play all of the following cards:

Boot Up (or Cloud Computing)
Word Processor
Spreadsheet
Presentation
Web Browser
E-Mail

Until you play a Boot Up card for the first time, you cannot play any Program cards. The one exception is that you can play a Cloud Computing card instead of a Boot Up card.

In addition, you cannot have any unresolved Problem cards such as a Bug or Virus card. To eliminate a Problem card, you must either use a Solution card or a Safety card. You can only play a Program card as long as you do not have any Problem cards played against you.

How to Play

Shuffle the cards and deal six (6) cards to each player. Players may never look at another player's cards. Place the remaining cards face down. This represents the Draw Pile.

Determine which player will go first, second, third, etc.

During each player's turn, a player can do one of the following:

- Play a Boot Up (or Cloud Computing) card to start the boot up process of your own PC. (You only need to do this once.) Lay the Boot Up card face up in front of you to show that your PC is booting up.
- Play a Program card to complete the process of booting up your own PC. Lay the Program card face up to show which programs your PC has managed to load. When you are the first player to have all five different Program cards (Word Processor, Spreadsheet, Presentation, E-Mail, and Web Browser) face up in front of you, you are the winner.
- Play a Problem card to attack another player. (A player who has not played a Boot Up card cannot be attacked with a Problem card by other players.) Lay the Problem card face up in front of the player you are attacking. That player cannot play any Program cards until removing the Problem card with a Solution or Safety card.

- Play a Solution or Safety card to eliminate any Problem cards against you. Place both the Solution and Problem card face up next to the Draw Pile. These face up cards represent the Discard Pile. Once you play a Safety card, you only return the Problem card to the Discard Pile but you never return a Safety card to the Discard Pile.
- Discard one card.

Each player concludes a turn by drawing a new card from the Draw Pile. Once the Draw Pile runs out of cards, reshuffle the Discard Pile and flip it face down to turn it into the Draw Pile.

Play continues with each player taking a turn until one player successfully boots up a PC by playing a Boot Up, Word Processor, Spreadsheet, Presentation, Web Browser, and E-Mail card.

Sample Game Play

Sam and Julie want to play PC Boot Up so they first shuffle the cards, deal each player six (6) cards, and place all remaining cards face down to represent the Draw Pile.

Turn #1

Same goes first and does not have a Boot Up card. Since Julie has not yet played a Boot Up card, Sam cannot play any Problem cards in his hand against her. Sam also cannot play any Solution or Safety cards (because there are no Problem cards against him).

Sam also cannot play any Program cards until he plays a Boot Up (or Cloud Computing) card first. Since there is nothing Sam can do, his only option is to discard a card and draw a new one.

Julie has a Boot Up card so she plays it by placing the Boot Up card face down in front of her. Now she draws a new card. At this point, Julie can now be attacked by a Problem card and she can also play any Program card.

Turn #2

Because Julie has played a Boot Up card, Sam can now attack her with a Problem card, so he places a Virus card in front of Julie. Sam now draws a new card.

Julie does not have an AntiVirus or Virtual Machine card to eliminate the Virus card. Julie also cannot attack Sam because he has not played a Boot Up card yet. Furthermore, Julie cannot play any Program cards in her hand because a single Problem card (the Virus card) has stopped her PC from booting up. Julie's only option is to discard a card and draw a new one.

Turn #3

Sam plays a Boot Up card and draws a new card. Because he has played a Boot Up card for the first time, he can now play Program cards in later turns. Julie can now play Problem cards against him.

Julie plays an AntiVirus card to eliminate the Virus card that Sam played against her. Both the Virus and AntiVirus cards are placed on the discard pile.

At this point, both Sam and Julie have played a Boot Up card so their PCs have started the process of booting up and they can now play Program cards.

Turn #4

Sam plays a Word Processor card and draws a new card. All he needs now is to play a Spreadsheet, Presentation, Web Browser, and E-Mail card and he will win.

Julie plays a Hacker card against Sam and draws a new card. At this point, Sam cannot play any further Program cards until he can remove the Hacker card by playing a Firewall card (or a Honeypot card). However, Sam can still play any Problem cards against Julie.

Turn #5

Sam does not have a Firewall card to eliminate the Hacker card preventing his PC from booting up. However, Sam does play a Trojan Horse card against Julie and draws a new card.

Julie does not have an Anti-Spyware card to eliminate the Trojan Horse card. However, Julie chooses to play a Crash card against Sam and then draws a new card. Sam now has a Hacker and a Crash card preventing his PC from booting up. Before Sam can play any Program cards, he must remove both the Hacker and Crash card using a Firewall and a Boot Up card respectively. There is no limit to the number of Problem cards you can play against another player.

Eventually when the Draw Pile runs out of cards, Sam and Julie will shuffle the cards, place them face down as the new Draw Pile, and continue playing until one of them has finished playing a Word Processor, Spreadsheet, Presentation, Web Browser, and E-Mail card without a single Problem card still played against them.

Campaign Game

Normally you can play PC Boot Up as a single game where the first person to successfully boot up is the winner. However, you can also play PC Boot Up as an extended campaign game where each player earns points and the first player to reach 1,000 points is the winner.

When playing multiple games, award points to all players as follows:

- 100 points to the winner
- 25 points for each Program card played
- 10 points for each Safety card played in response to an opponent playing a Problem card against you. (You do not get any points for holding an unplayed Safety card, nor do you get points for playing a Safety card before an opponent has played a Problem card against you.)
- 50 extra points if you boot up your computer and win before your opponent has even played one Program card

If a player wins, that player will always earn a minimum of 100 points for winning plus an additional 125 points for each Program card (5 Program cards * 25 points) played for a total of 225 points.

Game Components

The PC Boot Up game consists of 144 cards divided into the following categories:
    Problem cards

- Bug (3)
- Crash (5)
- Disk Fragmentation (3)
- Hacker (3)
- Registry Failure (3)
- Trojan Horse (3)
- Virus (3)

Solution cards

- Anti-Spyware (8)
- AntiVirus (8)
- Boot Up (19)
- Defragmenter (8)
- Firewall (8)
- Patch (8)
- Registry Optimizer (8)

Safety cards

- Cloud Computing (1)
- Honeypot (1)
- UNIX (1)
- Virtual Machine (1)

Program cards

- E-Mail (10)
- Presentation (10)

- Spreadsheet (10)
- Web Browser (10)
- Word Processor (10)

About PC Boot Up – The Game

PC Boot Up is copyrighted (c) 2023 by Wallace Wang. You are hereby granted the right to make copies for personal and not-for-profit use, but you are forbidden to make copies of this game, in any form (electronic or physical) for resale of any kind without express written permission.

You may freely distribute and modify this game as long as you do not charge for access to this game.

Game Designer Notes

PC Boot Up is based on the popular Mille Bornes card game. The purpose is to teach novices the basics of using a computer along with common problems they are likely to encounter. Once players understand the common types of computer problems that can stop them from using a computer, they can also learn the common ways to resolve each type of problem.

Appendix C: PC Bootup Game Playing Cards

To play the PC Bootup game, use the following game card template to print, or simply make up your own variation.

Bug

Prevents one program from running. Can only be remedied by applying a Patch card.

Bug

Prevents one program from running. Can only be remedied by applying a Patch card.

Bug

Prevents one program from running. Can only be remedied by applying a Patch card.

Patch

Patches and updates a program to cancel the affects of a Bug card.

Patch

Patches and updates a program to cancel the affects of a Bug card.

Patch

Patches and updates a program to cancel the affects of a Bug card.

Patch

Patches and updates a program to cancel the affects of a Bug card.

Patch

Patches and updates a program to cancel the affects of a Bug card.

Disk Fragmentation

Slows operating system to a crawl. Can only be remedied by applying a Defragmenter card.

Disk Fragmentation

Slows operating system to a crawl. Can only be remedied by applying a Defragmenter card.

Disk Fragmentation

Slows operating system to a crawl. Can only be remedied by applying a Defragmenter card.

Patch

Patches and updates a program to cancel the affects of a Bug card.

Defragmenter

Reorganizes the files on a hard disk to cancel the affects of a Disk Fragmentation card.

Defragmenter

Reorganizes the files on a hard disk to cancel the affects of a Disk Fragmentation card.

Defragmenter

Reorganizes the files on a hard disk to cancel the affects of a Disk Fragmentation card.

Defragmenter

Reorganizes the files on a hard disk to cancel the affects of a Disk Fragmentation card.

Virus

Infects a program. Can
only be remedied by
applying an Antivirus
card.

Virus

Infects a program. Can
only be remedied by
applying an Antivirus
card.

Virus

Infects a program. Can
only be remedied by
applying an Antivirus
card.

AntiVirus

Removes a virus to
cancel the affects of a
Virus card.

Defragmenter

Reorganizes the files on
a hard disk to cancel the
affects of a Disk
Fragmentation card.

Defragmenter

Reorganizes the files on
a hard disk to cancel the
affects of a Disk
Fragmentation card.

AntiVirus

Removes a virus to
cancel the affects of a
Virus card.

AntiVirus

Removes a virus to
cancel the affects of a
Virus card.

Registry Failure

Kills the operating
system. Can only be
remedied by applying a
Registry Optimizer card.

Registry Failure

Kills the operating
system. Can only be
remedied by applying a
Registry Optimizer card.

Registry Failure

Kills the operating
system. Can only be
remedied by applying a
Registry Optimizer card.

AntiVirus

Removes a virus to
cancel the affects of a
Virus card.

Registry Optimizer

Repairs the registry to
cancel the affects of a
Registry Failure card.

Registry Optimizer

Repairs the registry to
cancel the affects of a
Registry Failure card.

AntiVirus

Removes a virus to
cancel the affects of a
Virus card.

AntiVirus

Removes a virus to
cancel the affects of a
Virus card.

Hacker

Infiltrates the computer to steal information. Can only be remedied by applying a Firewall card.

Hacker

Infiltrates the computer to steal information. Can only be remedied by applying a Firewall card.

Hacker

Infiltrates the computer to steal information. Can only be remedied by applying a Firewall card.

Firewall

Block unauthorized access to the computer to cancel the affects of a Hacker card.

Registry Optimizer

Repairs the registry to cancel the affects of a Registry Failure card.

Registry Optimizer

Repairs the registry to cancel the affects of a Registry Failure card.

Registry Optimizer

Repairs the registry to cancel the affects of a Registry Failure card.

Registry Optimizer

Repairs the registry to cancel the affects of a Registry Failure card.

Crash

Stops a program from running. Can only be remedied by applying a Boot Up card.

Crash

Stops a program from running. Can only be remedied by applying a Boot Up card.

Crash

Stops a program from running. Can only be remedied by applying a Boot Up card.

Firewall

Block unauthorized access to the computer to cancel the affects of a Hacker card.

Firewall

Block unauthorized access to the computer to cancel the affects of a Hacker card.

Firewall

Block unauthorized access to the computer to cancel the affects of a Hacker card.

Firewall

Block unauthorized access to the computer to cancel the affects of a Hacker card.

Firewall

Block unauthorized access to the computer to cancel the affects of a Hacker card.

Boot Up

Starts up the computer to load the operating system or cancel the affects of a Crash card.

Boot Up

Starts up the computer to load the operating system or cancel the affects of a Crash card.

Boot Up

Starts up the computer to load the operating system or cancel the affects of a Crash card.

Boot Up

Starts up the computer to load the operating system or cancel the affects of a Crash card.

Boot Up

Starts up the computer to load the operating system or cancel the affects of a Crash card.

Boot Up

Starts up the computer to load the operating system or cancel the affects of a Crash card.

Boot Up

Starts up the computer to load the operating system or cancel the affects of a Crash card.

Boot Up

Starts up the computer to load the operating system or cancel the affects of a Crash card.

AntiVirus

Removes a virus to cancel the affects of a Virus card.

AntiVirus

Removes a virus to cancel the affects of a Virus card.

Registry Optimizer

Repairs the registry to cancel the affects of a Registry Failure card.

Boot Up

Starts up the computer to load the operating system or cancel the affects of a Crash card.

Boot Up

Starts up the computer to load the operating system or cancel the affects of a Crash card.

Boot Up

Starts up the computer to load the operating system or cancel the affects of a Crash card.

Boot Up

Starts up the computer to load the operating system or cancel the affects of a Crash card.

Boot Up

Starts up the computer to load the operating system or cancel the affects of a Crash card.

Trojan Horse

Sneaks into a computer to sabotage it. Can only be remedied by an Anti-Spyware card.

Trojan Horse

Sneaks into a computer to sabotage it. Can only be remedied by an Anti-Spyware card.

Trojan Horse

Sneaks into a computer to sabotage it. Can only be remedied by an Anti-Spyware card.

Defragmenter

Reorganizes the files on a hard disk to cancel the affects of a Disk Fragmentation card.

Boot Up

Starts up the computer to load the operating system or cancel the affects of a Crash card.

Boot Up

Starts up the computer to load the operating system or cancel the affects of a Crash card.

Boot Up

Starts up the computer to load the operating system or cancel the affects of a Crash card.

Boot Up

Starts up the computer to load the operating system or cancel the affects of a Crash card.

Crash

Stops a program from running. Can only be remedied by applying a Boot Up card.

Crash

Stops a program from running. Can only be remedied by applying a Boot Up card.

Boot Up

Starts up the computer to load the operating system or cancel the affects of a Crash card.

Boot Up

Starts up the computer to load the operating system or cancel the affects of a Crash card.

Defragmenter

Reorganizes the files on a hard disk to cancel the affects of a Disk Fragmentation card.

Registry Optimizer

Repairs the registry to cancel the affects of a Registry Failure card.

Firewall

Block unauthorized access to the computer to cancel the affects of a Hacker card.

Firewall

Block unauthorized access to the computer to cancel the affects of a Hacker card.

Patch

Patches and updates a program to cancel the affects of a Bug card.

Anti-Spyware

Removes a malware infection to cancel the affects of a Trojan Horse card.

Anti-Spyware

Removes a malware infection to cancel the affects of a Trojan Horse card.

Anti-Spyware

Removes a malware infection to cancel the affects of a Trojan Horse card.

Anti-Spyware

Removes a malware infection to cancel the affects of a Trojan Horse card.

Anti-Spyware

Removes a malware infection to cancel the affects of a Trojan Horse card.

Anti-Spyware

Removes a malware infection to cancel the affects of a Trojan Horse card.

Patch

Patches and updates a program to cancel the affects of a Bug card.

Cloud Computing

Eliminates the need for constant software patches by permanently protecting against the Bug and Crash cards.

Word Processor

Allows the creation of documents such as letters, reports, articles, or books.

Honeypot

Lures unauthorized users to a harmless part of the computer by permanently protecting against the Hacker card.

Virtual Machine

Eliminates the problem of virus infections by permanently protecting against the Virus and Trojan Horse cards.

Word Processor

Allows the creation of documents such as letters, reports, articles, or books.

Word Processor

Allows the creation of documents such as letters, reports, articles, or books.

Word Processor

Allows the creation of documents such as letters, reports, articles, or books.

UNIX

Eliminates disk fragmentation and registry errors by permanently protecting against the Disk Fragmentation and Registry Failure cards.

Word Processor

Allows the creation of documents such as letters, reports, articles, or books.

Word Processor

Allows the creation of documents such as letters, reports, articles, or books.

Word Processor

Allows the creation of documents such as letters, reports, articles, or books.

Spreadsheet

Simplifies the ability to create financial, scientific, or mathematic calculations.

Word Processor

Allows the creation of documents such as letters, reports, articles, or books.

Word Processor

Allows the creation of documents such as letters, reports, articles, or books.

Word Processor

Allows the creation of documents such as letters, reports, articles, or books.

Spreadsheet

Simplifies the ability to create financial, scientific, or mathematic calculations.

Spreadsheet

Simplifies the ability to create financial, scientific, or mathematic calculations.

Spreadsheet

Simplifies the ability to create financial, scientific, or mathematic calculations.

Spreadsheet

Simplifies the ability to create financial, scientific, or mathematic calculations.

Spreadsheet

Simplifies the ability to create financial, scientific, or mathematic calculations.

Spreadsheet

Simplifies the ability to create financial, scientific, or mathematic calculations.

Spreadsheet

Simplifies the ability to create financial, scientific, or mathematic calculations.

Spreadsheet

Simplifies the ability to create financial, scientific, or mathematic calculations.

Spreadsheet

Simplifies the ability to create financial, scientific, or mathematic calculations.

Presentation

Allows the creation of slideshow presentations to summarize different information.

Presentation

Allows the creation of slideshow presentations to summarize different information.

Presentation

Allows the creation of slideshow presentations to summarize different information.

Presentation

Allows the creation of slideshow presentations to summarize different information.

Presentation

Allows the creation of slideshow presentations to summarize different information.

Presentation

Allows the creation of slideshow presentations to summarize different information.

Presentation

Allows the creation of slideshow presentations to summarize different information.

Presentation

Allows the creation of slideshow presentations to summarize different information.

Web Browser

Connects to the Internet to view text, graphics as well as playing audio and video.

Web Browser

Connects to the Internet to view text, graphics as well as playing audio and video.

Web Browser

Connects to the Internet to view text, graphics as well as playing audio and video.

Presentation

Allows the creation of slideshow presentations to summarize different information.

Web Browser

Connects to the Internet to view text, graphics as well as playing audio and video.

Web Browser

Connects to the Internet to view text, graphics as well as playing audio and video.

Web Browser

Connects to the Internet to view text, graphics as well as playing audio and video.

Presentation

Allows the creation of slideshow presentations to summarize different information.

Web Browser

Connects to the Internet to view text, graphics as well as playing audio and video.

Web Browser

Connects to the Internet to view text, graphics as well as playing audio and video.

E-Mail

Connects to the Internet to send and receive messages including files such as audio or video.

E-Mail

Connects to the Internet to send and receive messages including files such as audio or video.

Web Browser

Connects to the Internet to view text, graphics as well as playing audio and video.

Web Browser

Connects to the Internet to view text, graphics as well as playing audio and video.

E-Mail

Connects to the Internet to send and receive messages including files such as audio or video.

E-Mail

Connects to the Internet to send and receive messages including files such as audio or video.

Anti-Spyware

Removes a malware infection to cancel the affects of a Trojan Horse card.

E-Mail

Connects to the Internet to send and receive messages including files such as audio or video.

E-Mail

Connects to the Internet to send and receive messages including files such as audio or video.

E-Mail

Connects to the Internet to send and receive messages including files such as audio or video.

Anti-Spyware

Removes a malware infection to cancel the affects of a Trojan Horse card.

E-Mail

Connects to the Internet to send and receive messages including files such as audio or video.

E-Mail

Connects to the Internet to send and receive messages including files such as audio or video.

E-Mail

Connects to the Internet to send and receive messages including files such as audio or video.

PC Boot Up

The card game where you try to become the first player to boot up your computer to load a word processor, spreadsheet, presentation program, web browser, and e-mail program. Players can slow down your computer with bugs, crashes, and viruses.

The purpose of the game is to teach the basic problems of starting up a computer and the common tools needed to fix those problems.

You are free to make copies for individual use only, but not for resale in any form.

Copyright (c) 2023 by Wallace Wang

Index

© The Editor(s) (if applicable) and The Author(s), under exclusive license to   277
Springer Nature Switzerland AG 2023
W. Wang, *The Structure of Game Design*, International Series on Computer,
Entertainment and Media Technology,
https://doi.org/10.1007/978-3-031-32202-0

Printed in the United States
by Baker & Taylor Publisher Services